ALEXANDER'S REVENGE

ALEXANDER'S REVENGE
Hellenistic Culture through the Centuries

EDITED

BY

JON MA. ASGEIRSSON

AND

NANCY VAN DEUSEN

THE UNIVERSITY OF ICELAND PRESS

2002

Cover design. Alda Lóa Leifsdóttir

Layout: University of Iceland Press

Printing: Gutenberg

PRINTED IN ICELAND

ISNB 9979-54-513-5

TABLE OF CONTENTS

CONTRIBUTORS

JON MA. ASGEIRSSON,
University of Iceland

NANCY VAN DEUSEN,
Claremont Graduate University

VINCENT CORRIGAN,
Bowling Green State University

JAMES D. HESTER,
University of Redlands (retr.)

RONALD F. HOCK,
University of Southern California

CHRISTOPHER KLEINHENZ,
University of Wisconsin, Madison

BARIŠA KREKIĆ,
University of California, Los Angeles (retr.)

JAMES OTTÉ,
University of San Diego

CLAUDIA RAPP,
University of California, Los Angeles

BRENDA DEEN SCHILDGEN,
University of California, Davies

ERNST F. TONSING,
California Lutheran Unversity, Thousand Oaks

RICHARD A. ZIONTS,
Pennsylvania State University

PREFACE

During the second half of the last decade of the twentieth century, Jon Ma. Asgeirsson, then Associate Director of the Institute for Antiquity and Christianity at Claremont Graduate University, and Nancy van Deusen, Professor of Music at Claremont Graduate University, organized in collaboration with the Claremont Consortium for Medieval and Early Modern Studies various lectures and symposia on the Claremont Campus in Claremont, California.

At the encouragement of Mr. Rafael Chodos, Esq., Chairman of the Advisory Board of the Institute for Antiquity and Christianity and a Fellow of the Board of Visitors of the Center for Humanities at Claremont Graduate University, a selection of various presentations from this collaborative effort was made for the purpose of introducing in a publication an example of the range of topics and interests dealt with in the various symposia organized by the editors of this volume.

For several years the collaboration between the Institute for Antiquity and Christianity and the Claremont Consortium for Medieval and Early Modern Studies has resulted in many visiting lectureships and semi-annual conferences held at Claremont. The combined effort has brought together specialists in very different fields including Ancient Near Eastern Studies, the Classical worlds of Greece and Rome, as well as biblical studies and archaeology on the one hand and Early Medieval through Early Modern studies, as well as music in particular on the other hand.

With this in mind, the present volume consists of twelve articles ranging in scope from approximately the third century BCE through the period of the Early Modern Age. It takes its origin in the period immediately following the death of Alexander the Great to trace the impact of his unsurpassed legacy in terms of cultural impact for subsequent centuries — that may still be claimed in many respects to be in place. With regard to his influence on education, art, music, literature, the biblical world, philosophy, and demography, Alexander the Great may well be said to have revenged his untimely death in his mid thirties!

By offering a selection of studies into the many fields of culture affected by the "Alexandrian Age" it is the hope of the editors that his continued influence may be revisited from the broad perspective reflected in the studies offered in this volume. At the same time all the contributions of this volume together point forward to the present world situation whether with regard to ethnic conflicts, the revival of rhetorical understanding, or intertextual realities so indisputably triggered by the genius mind of Alexander the Great.

The editors would like to express their most sincere gratitude to Rafael Chodos for his enthusiasm to see this selection published and to the University Press of the University of Iceland for agreeing to publish the volume. Thanks are also due to Dr. Robb Dennis and Rubén Dupertuis, a doctoral student at Claremont Graduate University, for their computer assistant and initial editorial work. Finally, but not least, Mr. Asgeir Magnusson and Mr. Jon Jonsson read the proofs in the last stage of the work and for their help the editors are most grateful.

Jon Ma. Asgeirsson, Professor of New Testament Studies and Early Christianity at the University of Iceland
Nancy van Deusen, Professor of Music at Claremont Graduate University and Chair the Claremont Consortium for Medieval and Early Modern Studies

ABBREVIATIONS

abr.:	abridged
Ad fam.:	*Epistulae ad familiares*
Augustus:	*Divus Augustus*
BCE:	Before Common Era
CE:	Common Era
comm.:	commentator/commentary
Conf.:	*Confessions*
Comp.:	*De Compositione verborum*
De avar.:	*De avaritia*
Dem.:	*De Demosthene*
De eloc.:	*De elocutione*
ed./eds.:	1. editor; 2. edited by/editors
Fam.:	*Rerum familiarium libri*
fig./figs.:	figure/figures
f./ff.:	folio/1. folios; 2. following
fr.:	fragment
Geogr.:	*Geographia*
Inf.:	*Inferno*
Inst. or.:	*Institutio oratoria*
Lives:	*Lives of Eminent Philosophers*
Par.:	*Paradiso*
PG:	Patrologia graeca
PL:	Patrologia latina
Purg.:	*Purgatorio*
repr.:	reprint
retr.:	retired
rev.:	revised
RSV:	Revised Standard Version
SBL:	Society of Biblical Literature
tr./trans.:	translator/translated by
v.:	verso

INTRODUCTION

The influence of Alexander the Great and the definition of Hellenistic Culture (especially with regard to a given period in history) are a focus of a continuous debate. Yet, the legacy of Alexander the Great will not be demarcated by specific pointers in history. As the studies to follow exemplify in different ways, his revenge is, indeed, the perpetuation of classical ideals made possible through his intervention in the course of history some twenty-three centuries ago. Viewing the achievements of Alexander the Great from the perspective of meta-history, in which the present is ever new with respect to the past and the future, eliminates the many attempts at watering down Hellenic and other classical sources during the reign of Alexander and his successors on the one hand as well as endeavors of subsequent centuries following their reign to replacing them with modern conceptions of social and cultural intimidation on the other. The roots of the epistemic imitations of tomorrow may be blurred in the fragmentary knowledge of the past but they have survived in a way perhaps without parallel in human history exactly because of Alexander the Great. In view of his untimely death, would there be a sweater revenge than that[1] —that of making Hellenistic Culture the channel of past and future realities in what came to shape the course of civilization half around the globe?

The Chria (from the Latin, plural: chriae; Greek *chreia*, plural: *chreiai*) and the literary genre of the epistle constitute the basic themes of the first part of the present book. A prominent element in classical Greek and Hellenistic rhetorical education, the chria (an action or a saying attributed to a certain person) had almost come to oblivion from the eighteenth century on except as a lexical entry. During the renewed interest in classical and medieval rhetoric during the twentieth century, the chria emerges again as one of the most curious components in rhetorical instruction and composition. Its importance has been noted above all within the field of biblical studies particularly over the past twenty-five years as well as in the field of Hellenistic philosophical tradition. The literary genre of the epistle is one of the most common forms of rhetorical literary composition. As with other literary genres, it may contain chriae and many other rhetorical and literary components but being addressed to a person or an audience it stands in close connection with speeches (judicial, deliberative, and epideictic) or some of the most basic forms of rhetorical argumentation.

Research in the field of rhetorical composition and hermeneutics has revolutionized the insights and understanding of ancient and medieval texts in the Western world as well as given new insights into the way modern textual creation takes place. Even though traditional rhetorical instruction survived from the ancient world into the eighteenth century university education its disappearance from that scene has made the endeavor of scholars today even harder in their reconstructive efforts of analyzing the impact of classical rhetoric and its later developments for the reading of ancient and medieval texts. Elementary (preliminary) manuals (*progymnasmata*) for the instruction of rhetoric as well as technical handbooks (*technai*) having to deal with the more theoretical part of rhetoric have survived from the ancient world along with various medieval texts on later instruction and theory in the field of rhetoric. Analyzing the methods and theories has proven a complicated task, Aristotle's groundbreaking work on rhetoric being a case in point. However, the larger task has hardly seen the day of light, namely, of assessing the relation between the rhetorical paradigms and their application in the composition of speeches and texts on the one hand and education on the other. What is the imitative function of rhetoric? How has the curious and handy element of chria been developed? How does rhetoric join speech and text?[2] The three essays in this first part contribute exactly to these problematic issues of rhetoric in education, argumentation, and the building of a literary genre.

Ronald F. Hock directs attention to the impact Alexander the Great and his successors had on education in the expanding Hellenistic cultural environment. He notes that most scholars of late have paid attention to the use of chriae at the level of rhetorical education (the last stage in the curriculum) where their use not only constitute a certain compendium of sayings attributed to individuals of distinction but also perpetuates their influence on the present ethos. Hock turns his investigation to the primary and secondary levels of education in each of which he discovers a prominent role of the chria. At the first level the chria functions both as an exercise for writing skills and for reading (assuming writing was taught before reading) exemplified by Hock with reference to ostraca and papyri from Egypt. At the second level Hock shows how students would deepen their skills in writing and reading using exercises of declension and taking on metric definitions and the reading of passages from classical literature. The chria, thus, becomes a companion all through the Hellenistic educational system.

Jon Ma. Asgeirsson shows how the tension between rhetoric and philosophy all through the classical world to the period of Late Antiquity is materialized in the skilful and artistic application of rhetorical argumentation. Again, here, the chria comes to play a fundamental role in its Hellenistic philosophical context. Asgeirsson questions the late age of the established pattern of elaboration of the chria as exemplified in the works of Hermogenes from the second century CE. Viewing the critical stand on rhetoric in the thinking of Philodemus of Gadara (first century BCE), he establishes a pattern of elaboration of a chria in Philodemus' refutation of a certain philosopher. Indeed, Asgeirsson demonstrates how the application of a chria elaboration becomes a fundamental principle in the transformation of the idea of rhetoric as an artistic embellishment or merely ancillary to philosophy to the making of rhetoric as the source of persuasion and literary composition.

James D. Hester summarizes the history of research in the field of rhetorical studies and the New Testament and St. Paul's letters in particular. Noting that handbooks on rhetoric do not dedicate much room for discussion on letter writing, Hester observes that this sort of literary composition has been considered part or closely linked to epideictic speech writing. However, Hester finds it most problematic to identify the letters of St. Paul to both the forms of letters listed in the handbooks and the characteristics of traditional speech writing. Hester argues that considerations about a writer's inventions must precede any formal analyses of a given text (letter). He concludes that inventional aspects are those that mold the formal matters of St. Paul's letter writing and, indeed, those that make them not fit into any particular genre listed in the handbooks.

The Character and characterization are the basic motives of the second section of essays in this volume. The making of a character (Greek: *prosopopoiia*) is as a matter of fact yet another basic category in the traditional manuals of rhetoric. Modern theories on the role of the readers in texts or the interaction of real and implied readers as well as narrators and authors is not an invention of modern literary criticism. Characterization is, indeed, one of the most important elements in the learning process of literary composition along with argumentative elaboration. Characters are often used to convey different or opposite arguments in a discourse and they are an indispensable part of a narrative plot. Authors may at the same time use (a) specific character(s) to present their own ideals or the cultural values they assume or prefer to emphasize in their message to the real reader whom they have in mind at the time of their composition.

The characters presented in the three essays of this section are the hero, the sage, and the teacher. All are most prominent in the emerging cultural interchange following the death of Alexander the Great. Indeed, the role of all three come to interact in a way unparalleled before. Already in the classical period of Greece the perception of the hero had undergone a transformation. The victorious hero could now appear in the act of personal conviction such as in the person of Socrates as a prisoner and victim of conscience. The philosopher turns into a hero for the sake of the sword of his mouth and reasoning. The fate of Socrates, thus, becomes the paradigm par excellence among Cynic philosophers closer to the turn of the calendar. The ultimate goal of philosophical reasoning, the search for virtue, had been made equal to the death of a martyr. Within Second Temple Judaism the ideal of the hero as a persona who sacrifices himself for the betterment of his country had been known for centuries. At the time of the battle of the Jews with Alexander's successors in the second century BCE the idea emerges in which the slain hero is believed to have not only died a heroic death but to have made an impact exceeding its death for subsequent generations. This idea is most prominently conveyed in the stories of the tortured sage. The Joseph story may be the best known of this genre. The story revolves around two moments: the one of which is the unjustified treatment against the persona and the other the utter faithfulness of the sage towards his evil doers. But if the Joseph story came to a gratified conclusion while Joseph and his brothers were still alive, the same is not the case with regard to the fate of the Jewish royals against the forces of the Seleucid Empire and the Romans. Indeed, the social circumstances had to project this happy ending into the future beyond death and grave in the untold eschaton![3]

Ernst F. Tonsing illustrates the very diverse roles the character of Alexander the Great has assumed from Late Antiquity to the Modern Period in artistic creations of his very portrait within the Graeco-Roman cultural environment. From his native Macedonia where Alexander appears as a royal prince to the presentation of him as a mythological figure of semi divine and human origin, the young ruler has become timeless through the centuries. His becomes a story of ever increasing attributes depicting him as hero and a sage on the one hand and a divine being on the other embellished with passion and the contemporary stimulus of the artist.

Richard A. Zionts explores the influence of Nicander of Colophon upon Epiphanius of Salamis—a leading apologist against many minority groups within the early Christian development. Placed in the lineage of sages the apologists revelas a transformation of the idea of a sage. From being more or less passive or to the point of being asked to do something if not making a comment (an important revelation) more or less by chance, the apologist (and the rabbi) step forward in a role of an authoritative interpreter. Whether by appointment or self-authentification, the apologist speaks or writes as a person of ultimate authority. Zionts traces the ongoing important influence of classical ideals in the Hellenistic world. Present already in the New Testament literature this phenomenon continues through the second to the fifth centuries to reach a crucial link between the periods of Late Antiquity and the Medieval Age.

Nancy van Deusen exemplifies how three intellectuals of the University of Paris and the University of Oxford envisioned Alexander the Great in the thirteenth century. At the heart of their discussion are the issues of longing and options with regard to '*ductus, tractus,* and *conductus*'. The voice of Aristotle the teacher echoes in the background when she pays attention to the very problematic issues related to translation from one language to another as demonstrated in the translation of Aristotle's *Physics* into Latin. Not only do Latin translations of the thirteenth to the fifteenth centuries manifest how difficult a task it proved to be but the need for endless commentaries on the work prove its challenge beyond reasonable doubt. Indeed, the words of the *Physics* are too abstract to be grasped except with the aid of applicable examples according to context. Thus, translation is always also an act of interpretation. Van Deusen shows how the three teachers of the thirteenth century carefully treat the many important concepts of such a thinker as Aristotle without ever falling into the trap of generalizing such a work as the *Physics* on the basis of but a single category such as the much misunderstood concept of *primus motor*. Indeed, *primus motor* is not about the source of motion but motion as *ductus* exemplified in the character of Alexander the Great.

The Cosmos and cosmopolitanism constitute the basic motives of the third section of essays in this volume. If words are difficult to comprehend in the *Physics* of Aristotle, the atom remains at the core of cosmology in the Hellenistic thinking: a constant over against the diversity of the cosmopolitan reality and confusion over power along the Mediterranean rim. The Hellenistic view on the atom stands against the findings of Aristotle about the physical world in which earthly phenomena are subject to change (corruption) unlike their transcendent origin. A tractate, entitled *De mundo*, dedicated to Alexander the Great and considered attributed to Aristotle (since the fifth century) offers an important contribution to the question of Aristotelian and Christian ideology against the issue of atomism as presented by such authorities as Democritus, Epicurus, and Lucretius in spite of its uncertain date. The tractate contains statements about the universe very much like those of Aristotle in *De caelo* (1.10) but also statements contrary to the Aristotelian idea about the transcendence of God. Thus, the tractate maintains the entire universe is subject to divine providence (397b 13-16). These arguments make the tractate less in harmony both with regard to genuine works by Aristotle and for instance Christian doctrine on a demarcated divine providence such as the Patristic tradition attributed to Aristotle. As such *De mundo* may explain a link in the development away from atomism in favor of the Aristotelian and Christian triumph against those theories throughout the Medieval period.

Ethnic diversity of the cosmopolitan environment of the medieval period falls along the tracks of rhetorical characterization. Characters, imaginary or real, constitute as such the colorful disparity of the cosmos and its mirror in the individual polis. It has been noted how the issue of diversity becomes a prominent concept in the thinking of early Christian theologians and philosophers all through the climax of the scholastic period in the late thirteenth century. The discussion evolves from defining characters in their very context to the application of diversity to sounds. A further development of this thinking includes the disputation on the very reality of diversity as well as the identification of varied characters (*characterae variarae*) to sound. The basis of this process is seen in the works of the Cappadocian fathers of the third Christian century. Thus, the being of God himself consists of a diverse set of attributes; God is thus the origin of diversity and reveals himself in various manners and consequently may be known in different ways: finally, diversity becomes, in the thinking of these fathers, the source for understanding human beings themselves. If human diversity, thus, has one origin (substance), human diversity is fundamental for the understanding of what humanity means.[4]

James Otté challenges the criticism of the atom by Aristotle. In so doing he traces the opinions of both predecessors and successors of Aristotle in the field of natural philosophy. Yet, the atomism of Epicurus in the fourth/third century BCE and Lucretius in the first century BCE shared the same fate of being ousted throughout the period of the Early Middle Ages. The reasons for this rejection, Otté maintains, are basically due to Christian perceptions of nature in terms of beauty and the expectation of a new world under a new heaven— at the expense of Epicurean materialism.

Claudia Rapp traces the origins of cosmopolitanism to the present date in order to establish its connotation as a global city as well as for comparing this meaning with the sense of the residents of Constantinople during the Byzantine period. Constantinople, she claims, was, as part of Byzantine culture, a city consisting of people of various ethnicity. While foreign visitors would be kept at a certain distance, immigrants were readily granted civil rights and considerable freedom with regard to practicing their religion and native habits. Religion and ethnic origins were indeed the fundamental factors of anyone's personality. At the same time citizenship was constituted on the basis of homage to the emperor, taxation, and acknowledgment of the Christian faith while religious freedom was granted to a certain degree. Constantinople becomes a locus in which the government creates its own image to the inhabitants and the entire world—as a center of a wide range of cultural fascinations, business transactions and political dealings for over one thousand years.

Bariša Krekić investigates the development of Byzantium in the Late Middle Ages or at the point when Venice emerges as an influential city in the

Byzantine Empire during the eleventh century. She shows how this change in power structure takes place as a consequence of the great schism in 1054 at which juncture the conflicts of the church caused an ever increasing rupture between the East and West. The status Venice gained further gave it control over colonies in the Balkan area charged with religious and ethnic conflicts and indistinctness. Krekić focuses on the Serbian situation in particular for showing just how the Serbs were made subject to cultural and political forces of the outside world as well as to what she calls 'symbiotic relationships'.

The Cartography or matters of mapping the world constitute the common topic of the fourth and last section of this book. Contemporary accounts of the conquests of Alexander the Great over new territory and non-Macedonian civilizations are viewed with little favor for instance by the Hellenistic Jewish Sibyl behind the Third Book of the *Sibylline Oracles*. While the main part of the oracles is considered composed during the middle of the second century BCE in Egypt, other parts of the oracles may reach back to the actual conquests of Alexander whereas the latest addition to the collections in book three date to the first century CE. The verses 381-400 of Book Three are *vaticinia ex eventu* in which the first part predicts the decline of the Macedonian ruler after the fall of Babylon. The second part predicts an evil fate upon all of Macedonia following Alexander's victories in the East. This sentiment against Alexander and Macedonia forms part of the polemics against Hellenistic influence in general among the Jews of the Second Temple Judaism culminating in the Maccabean revolt of the second century BCE. In the first Christian century, Plutarch offers a very different opinion about the expansion politics of Alexander the Great. Indeed, he claims that the diffusion of Greek culture towards the East will have been of greater value to the world than the theories of any philosopher before or after the first century CE of Plutarch. Yet, it is exactly due to Alexander's philosophical training that Plutarch is able to explain his success or on the basis of 'knowledge, self-mastery, and courage' that together display his nobility.

Long before copperplate printing of maps was launched in the sixteenth century England, mapping the world had been an object of the imagination, social realities, and music—together with actual geographical cartography. The victorious lead of Alexander the Great had further long been replaced with the Roman and Byzantine empires permeated with the global sign of the cross. Whether at the level of intertextuality as in Dante's *Divina commedia* or Boccaccio's critique in the *Decameron* of the social and political realities of the fourteenth century Italy, the biblical world of the Old and New Testaments provided the plates for mapping the world and/or creating new borders within its world. Even within the liturgical tradition of Christianity, this globalization takes form in the various parts of the mass as well as in the international language of musical scores. Thus the poet, the narrator, and the instrumentalist (vocalist) all play the part of medieval propaganda for globalization. All through this process the conflicts of economics, politics, and religion mirror the twenty-first century cultural situation in a world which has become a mere global village–the magma chamber of cross-cultural encounters.[5]

Christopher Kleinhenz pays attention to the viewpoint from which a phenomenon is put in perspective: How does the planet earth look from space? A spot of colors compared to the narrow viewpoint from within the Mediterranean rim. In the age of space technology games of virtual reality are but at best a match to the force of imagination of the medieval mind. Yet, each mode is revealing of the kind of soul-searching he maintains are fundamental for comprehending exactly the person's point of view, its very stand, within the world, the universe. With regard to Dante (1265-1321 CE), the Mediterranean makes up the borders of reference when it comes to the voyage of his pilgrimage. Only in a divine vision its limitation become crystal clear revealing at the same time the true model of the imperfect material world. Thus, reality and imagination (metaphor) compensate each other—a fact of truth just as much in the Medieval period as at the present date.

Brenda Deen Schildgen makes a comparison of Boccaccio's (1313-1375 CE) and Chaucer's (1340-1400 CE) reception of Islam in the fourteenth century. The encounter of the west with Islam during the Late Middle Ages is yet another forerunner to the process of globalization culminating in the present date conflict between Islamic civilization and Western multi-cultural society. Schildgen shows how both authors express respect for Islamic learning, indeed, at a time when it had become classical for the influence of such authorities as Avicenna (980-1037 CE) and Averroes (1126-1198 CE). However, while Boccaccio argues for a favorable embracement of Islam, Chaucer denounces contact with Islam beyond philosophical learning and commercial contacts. Behind this difference she notes the authors' geographical locations: the Mediterranean versus Northern Europe. This is, finally, a factor in the shaping of the aesthetic direction of their writings as well as a testimony to Christian authors' attitude towards Islam.

Vincent Corrigan investigates the Codex Calixtinus as the best attestation to the cult of St. James the Great (called son of thunder along with his brother St. John in Mark 3.17) in the city of Santiago de Compostela in Spain. The two brothers along with St. Peter belonged to the closer group of apostles and St. James is the first of the apostles to suffer death as a martyr according to Acts. Corrigan observes that due to a legend the Saint's body was to have been moved to the site of Compostela and buried there, thus, making the city equal in attraction to Jerusalem and Rome during the medieval period. While the cult of St. James is known to have been used against Islamic influences in Spain, Corrigan pays attention to the international elements in the Book of Liturgies in the Codex Calixtinus. This First Book of the codex contains all the texts and musical scores for the celebration of the Saint's feasts. It is in these texts, like sermons, that Corrigan finds a curious attestation to the international climate of Compostela. Because of its appeal to pilgrims, the city had become an attraction for the then known world. Likewise, the musical part of the First Book of the codex demonstrates an equal attraction of internationality—best exemplified in the 'group of Alleluias'. Thus, a new text may be added to a known melody of Alleluias. A text is presented in the biblical languages with no hint at verses in Arabic. Once again, an international flavor within the limits of the Christian image of the world.

The interdisciplinary focus of the essays offered in this book comprise to the haunting realities of the post Alexander world of Greatness and Global uncertainty—a globalization of multiplicity or the colonization of the globe by a winner far removed from the agenda of cultural amalgamation of Alexander the Great.

Notes:

[1] Cf. Robin Lane Fox, *Pagans and Christians* (New York, NY, 1987); Averil Cameron, ed., *History as Text: The Writing of Ancient History* (Chapel Hill, NC & London, 1989); G. W. Bowersock, *Hellenism in Late Antiquity*, Jerome Lectures 18 (Ann Arbor, MI, 1990); Dennis R. MacDonald ed., *Mimesis and Intertextuality in Antiquity and Christianity,* Studies in Antiquity and Christianity (Harrisburg, PA, 2001).

[2] Cf. Hans Dieter Betz, *Galatians: A Commentary on Paul's Letter to the Churches in Galatia*, Hermeneia: A Critical and Historical Commentary on the Bible (Philadelphia, PA, 1979); Ronald F. Hock & Edward N. O'Neil, *The Chreia in Ancient Rhetoric*, Vol. 1, *The Progymnasmata*, SBL Texts and Translations 27, Graeco-Roman Religion Series 9 (Atlanta, GA, 1986); Burton L. Mack & Vernon K. Robbins, *Patterns of Persuasion in the Gospels*, Foundations and Facets: Literary Facets (Sonoma, CA, 1989); Vernon K. Robbins, ed., *The Rhetoric of Pronouncement*, Semeia 64 (Atlanta, GA, 1993); George A. Kennedy, *A New History of Classical Rhetoric* (Princeton, NJ, 1994); Steven Mailloux, *Rhetoric, Sophistry, Pragmatism*, Literature, Culture, Theory 15 (Cambridge, MA, 1995).

[3] Cf. Donald R. Dudley, *A History of Cynicism: From Diogenes to the 6th Century A.D.* (1937; repr. Chicago, IL, 1980); Jane P. Tompkins, ed., *Reader-Response Criticism: From Formalism to Post-Structuralism* (Baltimore, MD & London, 1980); Mark Allan Powell, *What is Narrative Criticism?*, Guides to Biblical Scholarship: New Testament Series (Minneapolis, MN, 1990); Burton L. Mack, *Who Wrote the New Testament? The Making of the Christian Myth* (San Francisco, CA, 1995).

[4] Richard McKeon, ed., *The Basic Works of Aristotle* (New York, NY, 1941); Jill Kraye, "Aristotle's God and the Authenticity of De mundo: An Early Modern Controversy," *Journal of the History of Philosophy* 28/3 (July 1990), 339-58; Giovanni Reale & Abraham P. Bos, *Il trattato sul cosmo per Alessandro attribuito ad Aristotele*, Monografia introduttiva, testo greco con traduzione a fronte commentario, bibliografia ragionata e indici, Pubblicazioni del Centro di ricerche di metafisica, Collana temi metafisici e problemi del pensiero antico. Studi e testi 42, 2nd ed. (Milan, 1995); Nancy van Deusen, *Medieval Diversity and the Charivari*, Occasional Papers of the Institute for Antiquity and Christianity 36 (Claremont, CA, 1996).

[5] Cf. James H. Charlesworth, ed., *The Old Testament Pseudepigrapha*, Vol. 1, *Apocalyptic Literature and Testaments*, New Translations from Authoritative Texts with Introductions and Critical Notes by an International Team of Scholars (Garden City, NY, 1983); D. Brendan Nagle & Stanley M. Burstein, eds., *The Ancient World: Readings in Social and Cultural History* (Englewood Cliffs, NJ, 1995); John Thorley, *Documents in Medieval Latin* (London, 1998); Peter S. Hawkins, *Dante's Testaments: Essays in Scriptural Imagination* (Stanford, CA, 1999).

Ronald F. Hock

THE CHREIA IN PRIMARY
AND SECONDARY EDUCATION

Introduction

One of the most enduring, if little known, legacies of Alexander or, more accurately, of the Hellenistic age that his conquests inaugurated is the educational curriculum which received its definitive structure and sequence shortly after Alexander, spread throughout the Hellenistic world, and continued, little changed, for the rest of antiquity and on into the middle ages. This curriculum involved three stages: during the primary stage an elementary teacher (γραμματιστῆς) taught students, roughly seven to eleven years of age, to read, write, and compute; during the secondary stage a literary teacher (γραμματικός taught students, now eleven to fifteen years old, the subjects of grammar, literature, and elementary composition; and, finally, during the tertiary stage a sophist (σοφιστής) trained students, fifteen and up, to write ever more complex essays and finally to compose and deliver advisory, judicial, and celebratory speeches, although some students might also go on to study philosophy.[1]

This brief summary of the three stages of education is, of course, a generalization, and as such we must allow for variations in the conventions of instruction, given the many centuries and societies that this generalization is meant to cover. Indeed, the most recent scholarship on education is qualifying this generalization by emphasizing the fluidity, variation, and social factors that must be taken into account when applying this generalization to any one place, time, or social group.[2] Nevertheless, for our purposes here this generalization is adequate, and any necessary modifications to specific aspects of it will be identified at the appropriate place in the analysis. I merely rehearse this generalization at the outset in order to place my discussion of the role of the chreia in primary and secondary education within the broad outlines of these first two stages of education.

The chreia (Gr. χρεία, Lat. *chria*) is a literary form that has been much in vogue in Claremont, California, and elsewhere of late.[3] Special emphasis has been directed, however, toward investigating the role of the chreia in the early stages of tertiary or rhetorical education, specifically in its use as the subject for students' first attempts at argumentative composition, that is, in the so-called elaboration (ἐργασια) where the point of the saying or action in the chreia is confirmed through a series of eight modes of analysis and argument.[4]

The elaboration of the chreia did not develop, however, until perhaps the first century CE and certainly by the second, as is clear from the *Progymnasmata* of Hermogenes of Tarsus.[5] In contrast, the chreia itself goes back to the early Hellenistic period, when it began to be used as a literary form for preserving the wit and wisdom of philosophers as well as many others, ranging from kings to courtesans.[6] Indeed, our earliest evidence for books of chreiai derives from around the time of Alexander,[7] and Alexander himself became a favorite figure in chreiai.[8]

At any rate, the popularity of the chreia that began about the time of Alexander helps to explain why this form was taken up by educators and introduced into the educational curriculum. Indeed, the chreia came to play a role in all three stages of education, but, since others have shown interest in the chreia at the rhetorical stage, the focus here will be on the primary and secondary stages. Accordingly, the attempt here will be to identify more precisely the ways in which the chreia functioned in the curricula of the early stages of ancient education.

The Uses of the Chreia in the Primary Curriculum

We begin with the primary curriculum, and in particular with the methods used to teach students to read and write. Teaching students to read, for example, involved a lengthy process which began simply with students learning the letters of the alphabet and then progressing to ever more complex tasks: learning syllables in all combinations; words of one, two, three, four, or even five syllables; simple sentences like maxims; and short passages. Such is the progression as reflected in the few and brief discussions in ancient literature[9] as well as in the standard modern treatments of ancient education of Henri I. Marrou and Stanley F. Bonner.[10]

Recently, however, this sequence has come under sophisticated and sustained scrutiny. Raffaella Cribiore, in particular, has made a comprehensive study of both the literary evidence and the papyri, ostraca, and tablets that document the methods by which students learned to read and write. She finds that the curricular sequence summarized above is in need of two important qualifications, one regarding how students learned to read and the other how they learned to write.[11]

First, as far as learning to read is concerned, Cribiore identifies one important exception to the graded series of progressing from letters to short passages. Scholars, depending largely on the literary evidence, have missed the importance that teachers attached to having students learn to write and read their own names. Cribiore, citing considerable documentary evidence, however, shows that students practiced their names as soon as they learned the letters of the alphabet and continued to do so alongside the later stages in the series and indeed well into the secondary or grammatical curriculum. Being able to read and write one's name was essential for many students who received only limited schooling and hence could later participate in their literate society, if only to the extent of signing a letter or contract.[12]

Cribiore's second qualification has to do with how students learned to write with confidence and skill. Learning to write, she argues, did not follow the same sequence that reading did, as scholars have tended to assume.[13] She challenges this assumption after an analysis of student hands. Previously, scholars were content to describe student hands rather vaguely—as, say, uneven, irregular, and clumsy.[14] Cribiore, however, constructs a typology of student hands which takes into account the increasing skill students attained as they practiced their handwriting. Her typology distinguishes four hands, from the least skilled to the relatively experienced, as follows: 1) zero-grade hand, 2) alphabetic hand, 3) evolving hand, and 4) rapid hand. Accordingly, students with zero-grade hands would be beginners, barely able to write the letters of the alphabet and often getting confused about their shapes; whereas those with rapid hands would be advanced students, able to write quickly, confidently, and rather beautifully.[15]

Cribiore uses this typology to classify the texts copied by students. Especially interesting is an anomaly which she discovers, if the usual assumption about students learning to write in the same sequence as they were learning to read is maintained. She finds that texts dealing with the later stages of the reading sequence, such as sentences or short passages, which should display evolving or rapid hands, in fact also betray zero-grade and especially alphabetic hands.[16] In other words, Cribiore suspects that sentences and short passages functioned as texts for students to practice their handwriting skills before they were able to read these texts. For example, a wooden tablet from Tebtunis from the second or third century CE (T. Phoebe Hearst Museum 6-21416) has on side one a maxim by the teacher which is copied five times by a student, whose "increasing mistakes and omissions," Cribiore says, "indicate that he could not read it".[17] In other words, when practicing their handwriting students would skip the combinations of syllables and lists of words and move on to the next steps in the sequence, sentences and short passages. Hence the appearance of zero-grade and alphabetic hands on texts copied from these later stages in the sequence.

The importance of finding zero-grade and alphabetic hands on texts copying sentences and short passages is that it is precisely here that chreiai appear in the primary curriculum. Accordingly, chreiai which appear on texts that have been written by alphabetic hands would thereby point to their being used as a means to improve writing skills; chreiai written by rapid hands, in contrast, would suggest an older student who would be able to read the chreiai he was copying.

In fact, both alphabetic and rapid hands appear on the papyri and ostraca from Greco-Roman Egypt that contain chreiai and thereby suggest that chreiai functioned in both reading and writing instruction. At least ten texts document the chreia in primary education,[18] but only three will illustrate these twin educational functions. One text contains chreiai in the context of a reading sequence and hence confirms its use in teaching students to read. Two texts that contain only chreiai will be assigned their function through a consideration of their handwriting.

Text 1. P.Bour. 1.141-68 (=P.Sorb. inv. 826) (=Pack² 2643=Debut 206=Cribiore 393)

P. Bour. 1 is an extremely valuable papyrus codex because it includes nearly every step in the reading sequence. It was first published at the beginning of this century by P. Jouguet and P. Perdrizet, then again in 1926 by Paul Collart, and several times since.[19] The first editors dated the codex to the fourth century CE, but say nothing about its provenance.[20] The fourth century dating is still accepted,[21] but recently Alain Blanchard has attempted to identify the provenance more specifically. He notes the presence of numerous names from Menander's plays in the lists of words in this codex (lines 2-140) as well as in the lists of another textbook, the Chester Beatty papyrus published by Willy Clarysse and Alfons Wouters.[22] In particular, Blanchard draws attention to the names of characters and titles that come from the famous Bodmer papyrus codex of Menander that included the *Samia*, *Dyskolos*, and *Aspis*,[23] and argues that the Chester Beatty papyrus and, to a lesser extent, P. Bour. 1 are closely related to the same school setting, a post-Constantinian school in Egypt which was Christian but not necessarily monastic.[24]

At any rate, P. Bour. 1 contains eleven sheets, all of which, except for the last, have writing on both sides. The contents are clearly those of the primary curriculum. On the first five sheets are lists of words in vertical columns—213 words in all, having one, then two, then three, and finally four syllables (lines 2-140). These words functioned as examples of words for students to write and pronounce correctly. Indeed, pronunciation seems to have been a primary concern, as some of the words are rare and difficult to pronounce: ῥώξ (line 7:

either "breach," or, if ῥάξ, then "grape"), λύγξ (line 12: "lynx"), and ῥηξήνωρ (line 110: "breaker of armed ranks," epithet of Achilles; cf. *Il.* 7.228). Another function may have been to introduce students to Greek history and culture, for the polysyllabic words in particular are mostly proper names taken from philosophy (Thales [line 24]), mythology (Herakles [line 76]), history (Xenophon [line 92]), and literature (Achilles [line 57]), not to mention the Menandrian characters, noted above: for example, Demeas (line 74) and Moschion (line 100) from the *Samia*, and Gorgias (line 51) and Sikon (line 45) from the *Dyskolos*.[25] The elementary teacher probably commented on the identity and significance of these people at the same time as the students were copying and pronouncing their names.[26]

Following these lists of words on the sixth and on a portion of the seventh sheet are five complete sayings-chreiai (lines 141-68), all with Diogenes as the speaker and all with the same form: "On seeing ..., Diogenes said: ...".[27] The appearance of these five chreiai immediately after the lists of words means that they were the first experience students had of writing and reading a series of words that made connected sense. What is especially noteworthy about these chreiai, however, is that they are presented in the same vertical format as the preceding lists of words (with two columns per page). To illustrate the format, the first chreia is written as it appears on the papyrus:

ΙΔΩΝ	ΔΙΟΓΕΝΗΣ
ΜΥΙΑΝ	ΠΑΡΑ-
ΕΠ-	ΣΙΤΟΥΣ
ΑΝΩ	ΤΡΕΦΕΙ
ΤΗΣ	
ΤΡΑΠΕΖΗΣ	———-
ΑΥΤΟΥ	(next
ΕΙΠΕΝ	chreia
ΚΑΙ	follows)

This unusual format—perhaps an innovation, since it occurs nowhere else[28]—has been plausibly explained as forming a transitional stage for students who were moving from recognizing lists of individual words to reading series of words having connected sense.[29] The format facilitated these first steps in reading, as did the repetition of the chreia form, which would have given students some confidence when encountering the same sentence structure five times.

Once the students had learned to read these relatively easy sentences, they could then proceed to sentences in the traditional format, that is, written horizontally and in *scriptio continua*. The next material in P. Bour. 1, in fact, is presented in this traditional format. Thus on the remainder of the seventh sheet and continuing through the ninth are twenty-four maxims, arranged alphabetically and written two lines per maxim (lines 169-239). To illustrate the increased difficulty of reading these maxims in comparison with the columnar-formatted chreiai, the first maxim (lines 169-70) is given below in *scriptio continua*, as they occur on the papyrus:

ΑΡΧΗΜΕΓΙΣΤΗΤΟΥΦΡΟ
ΝΕΙΝΤΑΓΡΑΜΜΑΤΑ.[30]

After the maxims comes a longer continuous passage—the first twelve lines from the introduction to the fables of Babrius—which appears on the tenth sheet and the recto of the eleventh (lines 240-72). This reading passage concludes the materials in P. Bour. 1 and represents the most advanced lesson.

To return to the chreiai: Having all five chreiai attributed to Diogenes calls for further comment. In one sense his presence in P. Bour. 1 simply confirms what the other texts also indicate: chreiai attributed to Diogenes outnumber all others put together. In another sense, however, his presence is especially apt to the structure of P. Bour. 1. As already mentioned, the lists of words preceding the Diogenes chreiai progressed from one to two to three to four syllables. In the case of the words of one, two, and three syllables the lists are complete, beginning with A and going through to Ω, and each letter is typically illustrated with four words (lines 2-127). The list of four-syllable words, however, is far from complete, as only the letters A, B, and Γ are represented (lines 129-40) before the papyrus shifts, rather abruptly, to the Diogenes chreiai (lines 141-68).

Scholars have tended to explain this abrupt shift as evidence for a sizable lacuna in the material copied into P. Bour. 1, perhaps amounting to the loss of four sheets in order to fill out the four syllable words through Ω.[31] Such an explanation, however, seems unnecessary, once we recognize that the name "Diogenes" accords well with the logic of the lists. Diogenes begins with the letter Δ, the next letter in the list, and his name has, like the list, four syllables. In addition, other philosophers had appeared earlier—e.g., Zeno (line 16), Thales (line 24), and Socrates' student Xenophon, who was identified in the imperial period, perhaps surprisingly, as a philosopher in order to distinguish him from the historian Xenophon, the romance writer.[32] In any case, Diogenes' name is consistent with use of other philosophers' names in these lists, and Diogenes fits the logic of the list precisely where it occurs, beginning with the letter Δ and having four syllables. Seemingly, students had had enough single words to learn and were deemed ready to encounter their first sentences.

We thus come to the chreiai themselves (written horizontally rather than in the columnar format of the codex):

α. Ἰδὼν μυῖαν ἐπάνω τῆς τραπέζης αὐτοῦ εἶπεν·
    Καὶ Διογένης παρασίτους τρέφει.
β. Ἰδὼν γ[υν]αῖκα διδα[σκ]ομένην γράμματα εἶπεν·
    Οἷον ξίφος ἀκουνᾶται.
γ. Ἰδὼν γυν[αῖ]κα γυ[ν]αικὶ συμβουλεύουσαν εἶπεν· 5
    Ἀσπὶς παρ᾽ἐχίδνης φάρμακον πορίζεται.
δ. Ἰδὼν Αἰθίοπα καθαρὸν τρωγόντα <εἶπεν>·
    Ἰδού, ἡ νὺξ τὴν ἡμέραν πνίγει.
ε. Ἰδὼν Αἰθίοπα χέζοντα ε[ἰ]πεν·
    Οἷον λέβης τέτρηται.   10

7 εἶπεν addidi. **9** δέ post Αἰθίοπα addiderunt Jouguet et Perdrizet, unde Ziebarth; papyro deest.

1. Seeing a fly on his table, he said:
    "Even Diogenes keeps parasites!"
2. Seeing a woman being educated, he said:
    "Wow! A sword is being sharpened".
3. Seeing a woman giving advice to a woman, he said:
    "An asp is being supplied venom from a viper".
4. Seeing an Ethiopian eating white bread, <he said>:
    "Look! Night is swallowing day".
5. Seeing an Ethiopian defecating, he said:
    "Look! A kettle with a hole in it".

We cannot leave these chreiai without commenting on their content. The first, of course, attributes a self-deprecating wit to Diogenes, who comes to the realization that it is very hard to live up to the Cynic principles of independence and self-sufficiency, for even he has something left over for parasites.[33] The next four, however, make their humorous point at the expense of others, first women and then Ethiopians. Scholars have often registered their amazement at the inclusion of these chreiai in a school text, noting that the primary curriculum, in principle, was intended to inculcate morals along with reading and writing skills, and by today's standards all four chreiai would meet nobody's idea of the morally appropriate. Nevertheless, the sentiments expressed here are not atypical by the standards of the ancient and medieval worlds, as they appear elsewhere—in other school texts,[34] in various medieval or Byzantine collections of chreiai,[35] even in Arabic gnomologia.[36]

Statements against women are particularly widespread, both in educational texts and in the culture at large.[37] In fact, we need not go farther than P. Bour. 1 itself, whose maxims sometimes express the same sentiment: for example, "the savagery of a lioness and a woman is the same" (lines 194-95). The school system, it seems, simply reinforced the social structure. Still, whatever the contents of these chreiai, their columnar format and placement after lists of words and a series of maxims shows that the chreia functioned here as the first occasion for students to read words having connected sense.

Text 2. P.Vindob.G. 19766
(Pack[2] 1989=Debut 313=Cribiore 192)

After discussing a text in which chreiai played a role in teaching students to read, we turn now to several texts that used chreiai to teach students to write. The first such text is the back of a small scrap of papyrus (8 cm x 6 cm) (whose front preserves a document of the first half of the second century). Known as P.Vindob.G. 19766, it was first published in 1939 by Hans Oellacher[38] and again in 1980 by Gallo.[39] Its provenance is unknown but its dating is secure, fixed by Oellacher to the second half of the second century CE and assigned by him to the classroom on the basis of its unsteady, timid hand.[40] Gallo agrees on both counts,[41] but Cribiore is more precise in its educational use, identifying the hand as alphabetic and thus the hand of a very young student who was just learning to write and not yet having learned to read.[42] We thus have a handwriting exercise.

Only a part of this student's exercise, however, has survived. The papyrus preserves parts of nine lines, and Oellacher was able to restore three of them (lines 3-5). These lines, he recognized, contain a chreia, as indicated by the remains of a portion of a formal feature that is characteristic of a subtype of sayings-chreiai. Specifically, the letters OTI NOC (line 4) point to the formula ἐρωτηθεὶς ὑπ]ό τινος ("on being asked by someone").[43] In addition, the name of the person to whom the chreia is attributed is partially preserved. Even though only two letters HC are visible, the following appositive OK ΥΝΙΚΟCΦΙ ΛΟCΟΦ makes identification considerably easier, for ὁ κυνικὸς φιλόσοφ[ος ("the Cynic philosoph[er") typically points in chreiai to the main representatives of Cynicism: Ἀντισθέν]ης, Διογέν]ης, or Κράτ]ης. Other preserved words, however, enabled Oellacher to identify the specific Cynic and even to allow restoration of the entire chreia. Line 4 preserves the word χρυσίον ("gold") and line 5 the words πολλοὺς ἐπιβο<ύ>λο]υς ("many plotters"). These words point, as Oellacher recognized, to a chreia attributed to Diogenes that appears in Diogenes Laertius, *Lives of Eminent*

Philosophers 6.51 and elsewhere,[44] so that Oellacher could restore lines 3-5 of the papyrus to read as follows:

Διογέν]ης ὁ κυνικὸς φιλόσοφ[ος ἐρωτηθεὶς ὑπ]ὸ τινος διὰ τί τὸ χρυσίον χ[λωρόν ἐσ-
τιν, "ἐφη,]"ὅτι πολλοὺς ἐπιβο<ύ>λ[ο]υς ἔ[χει.   5

Diogen]es the Cynic philosoph[er, on being
asked b]y someone, "Why [is] gold p[allid?"
said,] "Because it h[as] many who plo[t against it".

    The student who copied this chreia probably could not read what he was copying, although his teacher may have told him what it said. In any case, this short passage functioned primarily to provide practice for this student who, having learned how to write the letters of the alphabet, was now trying to write them with increasing confidence and skill.

Text 3. SB 1.5730
(=Pack² 1988=Debut 205=Cribiore 215)

In 1912 Herbert Thompson published an ostracon that he had purchased, along with many others, a few years earlier in London; it contained two complete chreiai, both attributed to the Cynic Diogenes.[45] Thompson accepted the seller's claim that the ostracon had come from Thebes, since others in the collection confirmed the claim, and he tentatively dated it to the third or fourth century CE,[46] a dating accepted by Gallo and Cribiore.[47] Thompson did not attempt to assign the ostracon to any particular setting. Preisigke, however, described it as a *Schulübung*,[48] a characterization which Gallo accepts[49] and Cribiore refines by classifying it as an exercise of an advanced primary student on the basis of his rapid hand.[50] In other words, the student copied these two chreiai in order to increase his confidence and skill with the alphabet and could also probably read what he was copying. The text of these chreiai is as follows:

Διογένης ὁ κυνικὸς φιλό-
σοφος {ἐρωτηθεὶς ὑπό τινος}
ἰδὼν Αἰθίοπα καθάριον
ἐσθίοντα εἶπεν ἡ νὺξ τὴν
ἡμέραν τρώγει   5
Διογένης ὁ κυνικὸς φιλό-
σοφος ἐρωτηθεὶς ὑπό τινος,

19

ποῦ αἱ Μοῦσαι κατοικοῦσιν,
ε(ι)πεν· ἐν ταῖς τῶν πεπ[αι
δευμένων ψυχαῖς.   10

2 {ἐρωτηθεὶς ὑπὸ τινος} ostracon per errorem; delevit Oldfather **3** Αἰθίοπα correxit Thompson; Αἰτίοπα ostracon **4** ἐσθίοντα correxit Thompson; "εσθοντα ostracon **8** κατοίκουσιν Thompson sic **9-10** πεπ[αι]δευμένων supplevit Thompson.

> Diogenes the Cynic philos-
> opher,{on being asked by someone}
> on seeing an Ethiopian eating
> white bread, said: "Night is
> devouring the day".   5
> Diogenes the Cynic philos-
> opher, on being asked by someone
> where the Muses dwell,
> said: "In the souls of the
> educ[a]ted".   10

Both chreiai require comment. In copying the first chreia the student made a mistake when he wrote ἐρωτηθεὶς ὑπὸ τινος ἰδών in lines 2-3. Thompson tried to correct the text by changing ἰδών in line 3 to ἰδόντος so that the participle would agree with τινος in line 2.[51] W. A. Oldfather, however, correctly recognized that the words ἐρωτηθεὶς ὑπὸ τινος do not belong at all to this chreia and that the case of the nominative participle ἰδών need not be changed to the genitive; hence, he deleted ἐρωτηθεὶς ὑπὸ τινος,[52] a solution accepted by Gallo.[53]

Neither Oldfather nor Gallo, however, attempts to explain the mistake. The problematic words—ἐρωτηθεὶς ὑπὸ τινος and ἰδών—are formal signs of two different sub-types, or εἴδη, of sayings chreiai. The former signals the εἶδος αποκριτικὸν κατὰ πύσμα, or chreia that provides an answer to a question (see Theon 61-66), whereas the latter is typical of the εἶδος ἀποφαντικὸν κατὰ περίστασιν, or chreia that is a saying prompted by some circumstance (see Theon 40-41). In other words, the student has probably copied many chreiai before, as suggested by his rapid hand, so that he may have written down ἐρωτηθεὶς ὑπὸ τινος after copying Διογένης ὁ κυνικὸς φιλόσοφος without looking at his model; then when he did look to see what came next he saw ἰδών in the model and proceeded accordingly through to the end. It seems that the student was also becoming familiar with the chreia, as he already instinctively knows its formal features.

In any case, Thompson also assumed that both chreiai were "unrecorded elsewhere".[54] But, as we have seen, the first chreia appears in P. Bour. 1 (lines 157-66),[55] where, incidentally, we read ἰδών, and even the second occurs elsewhere. Gallo refers to the probable restoration of this chreia in a first century papyrus fragment (P. Mich. inv. 41, lines 5-6),[56] but even he is unaware that this chreia, although now attributed to Plato, occurs elsewhere in the educational tradition, specifically in the *Progymnasmata* of Hermogenes and Nicolaus.[57] In any case, this chreia is quite appropriate in an educational setting, and it is fortunate that the student who copied it onto the ostracon was able to read what he was copying.

The Use of the Chreia in the Secondary Curriculum

The use of the chreia in the primary curriculum carried over into the secondary instruction of the γραμματικός, or teacher of grammar and literature. The secondary curriculum was an extension of the previous one, in that it, too, progressed from letters to syllables, then to words, and then to extended poetic works. But the progression was now more complex and sophisticated. Thus, instead of merely learning the names and shapes of the letters of the alphabet, students began now to classify them, distinguishing consonants from vowels and further classifying both into various sub-categories, such as vowels into long and short. Likewise, instead of merely pronouncing lists of syllables, they started now to learn the metric values of syllables. Again, instead of merely reading lists of words of ever increasing numbers of syllables, they began now to classify those words according to the parts of speech–nouns, verbs, participles, articles, and so forth. And instead of merely reading short connected passages, they started now to read and interpret lengthy literary works, primarily Homer.

As brief as this summary of the secondary curriculum is,[58] it does allow us to identify where in the curricular sequence the chreia was used. Specifically, the chreia played a role at the point where words received extended analysis. In primary instruction, the lists contained only nouns, often proper names and always in the nominative case. Under the teacher of grammar, however, students moved on to the more challenging task of classifying words according to the eight parts of speech.[59] In addition, they learned the three genders of nouns, their five case endings, and their three numbers. Verbs likewise received attention, as students now learned to distinguish their various forms—for example,-ω, -ῶ, and -μι verbs—, not to mention the endings which indicate person, number, tense, voice, and mood.[60]

The teacher of grammar taught his students the noun and verbal systems by means of a formal exercise called κλίσις (=Lat. *declinatio*), or the systematic presentation of a noun's declension or a verb's conjugation.[61] Teachers' manuals were slow to incorporate model κλίσεις. Indeed, the full conjugation of the regular verb τύπτω was not added to Dionysius' standard grammar until the fifth century.[62] Nevertheless, numerous texts on papyrus, ostraca, and tablets provide many earlier examples of κλίσις, ranging from declensions of articles, adjectives, and nouns to conjugations of verbs in their various tenses, voices, and moods.[63] One text, for example, contains a noun group (article, adjective, and noun) for all three genders—ὁ χρηστὸς πατήρ, ἡ ἀγαθὴ παρείνεσις, and τὸ φιλάνθρωπον ἦθος—and declines them through the singular, dual, and plural and through all five cases.[64]

Such a κλίσις is quite long and complex, but an even more advanced form of κλίσις is what interests us. This form of κλίσις asked students to inflect not only articles, adjectives, and nouns but also verbs and participles—and all of them at the same time—which is precisely what is required of anyone who composes in Greek. This advanced form of κλίσις made use of the chreia, one of the short passages students were already familiar with from lessons in reading and writing in primary school. To carry out the κλίσις of a chreia, however, the teacher of grammar[65] had to supply certain formulae in order to require changes in the cases and numbers of the noun groups and verbs in the recitation of a chreia. Four texts will illustrate this use of the chreia in the secondary curriculum.[66]

Text 4. T. Brit. Mus. Add. MS 37533
(Pack² 2712; Debut 336; Cribiore 385)

The first text that illustrates the use of the chreia in the secondary curriculum is a schoolbook made up of eight wooden tablets (9.5 cm x 27 cm), which Frederic G. Kenyon published in 1909.[67] The provenance of this schoolbook is not known, but at the top of the first tablet (line 1) is the name of its owner Epaphroditus, whose hand on the first three tablets and a second hand on the next two date the schoolbook to the end of the third century CE.[68]

The contents of this schoolbook belong to the secondary curriculum. The first four tablets contain a list of 207 verbs and the cases they govern (lines 2-227), a classification of the letters of the alphabet (lines 228-51), a series of gnomic questions and answers (lines 252-73), and a complex classification of nouns with examples (lines 281-319). On the fifth tablet appear formulae for the κλίσις of a chreia (lines 320-29). The remaining tablets are blank.

Kenyon, however, did not connect the formulae in lines 320-29 to the κλίσις of a chreia, for he merely described them, rather vaguely, as "a set of formulae for the use of the various cases with verbs".[69] It was Adolf Brinkmann who soon made the connection, although some scholars still seem unaware of it.[70] At any rate, he correctly pointed to similar formulae used in the κλίσις of the chreia in Theon's and Nicolaus' *Progymnasmata* and hence identified these formulae as belonging to the grammatical exercise of κλίσις.[71] The formulae are as follows:

ὀρθὴ εἶπεν   320
     γενική· λόγος ἀπομνημονεύεται εἰπόντος
     δοτική· ἔδοξεν εἰπεῖν
     αἰτιατική· φασὶν εἰπεῖν
     κλητική σὺ ποτε εἶπας

καὶ δυικῶς   325
     ὀρθη· εἰπάτην
     γενική· λόγος ἀπομνημονεύεται εἰπόντον
     δοτική· ἔδοξεν εἰπεῖν
     αἰτιατική· φασὶν ἐιπεῖν

     Nominative: He said
     Genitive: The saying is recalled of the one saying
     Dative: It seemed best (to him) to say
     Accusative: They say that he said
     Vocative: You once said

And in the dual
     Nominative: The two said
     Genitive: The saying is recalled of the two saying
     Dative: It seemed best (to the two) to say
     Accusative: They say that the two said

The formulae break off abruptly, omitting the dual vocative and all the plural formulae. Since the accusative dual comes at the bottom of the fifth tablet and the remaining tablets are blank, it is reasonable to assume that the student, for whatever reason, did not finish his task. Indeed, he may even have intended to go on and include the κλίσις of an actual chreia on the blank tablets and thus make use of the formulae he had started to copy.

We will never know, of course, what those blank tablets were intended for, but we do have two other tablets that fill in what may have been left out. One text contains the full complement of formulae and another provides a fully worked-out example of the κλίσις of a chreia.

Text 5. T. Bodl. Gr. Inscr. 3019
(Pack² 2732=Debut 335=Cribiore 388)

In 1970 Peter J. Parsons edited another late third century CE schoolbook of unknown provenance; its seven wooden tablets (11 cm x 23.8 cm) are all devoted to grammatical exercises and preserve the work of more than one student.[72] Among the exercises are three examples of κλίσις. One student copied the conjugation of the verb ποιεῖν ("to make") (tablet 7a), while another copied out the declension of the personal pronouns (tablet 1a) as well as a complete set of formulae for the κλίσις of a chreia (tablet 5b). The complete set is as follows:

ὀρθή εἶπεν
γενική· λόγος ἀπομνημονεύεται εἰπόντος
δοτική· ἔδοξεν εἰπεῖν
ἀιτιατική· φασὶν εἰπεῖν
κλητική· σὺ ποτε εἶπας

καὶ δυικῶς
ὀρθή· εἰπάτην
γενική· λόγος ἀπομνημονεύεται εἰπόντον
δοτική· ἔδοξεν εἰπεῖν
αἰτιατική· φασὶν εἰπεῖν
κλητική· ὦ σφώ ποτε εἴπατον

καὶ πληθυντικῶς
ὀρθή· εἶπον
γενική· λόγος ἀπομνημονεύεται εἰπόντων
δοτική· ἔδοξεν εἰπεῖν
αἰτιατική· φασὶν ἐιπεῖν
κλητική· ὑμεῖς ποτε εἴπατε

Nominative: He said
Genitive: The saying is recalled of the one saying
Dative: It seemed best (to him) to say
Accusative: They say that he said
Vocative: You once said

And in the dual
Nominative: The two said

    Genitive: The saying is recalled of the two saying
    Dative: It seemed best (to the two) to say
    Accusative: They say that (the two) said
    Vocative: You two once said

And in the plural
    Nominative: They said
    Genitive: The saying is recalled of those saying
    Dative: It seemed best (to them) to say
    Accusative: They say that they said
    Vocative: You (pl.) once said

Text 6. T. Brit. Mus. Add. MS 37516
(Pack² 2711=Debut 336=Cribiore 364)

A final text that illustrates the use of the chreia in secondary education is a single wooden tablet (41.5 cm x 13.5 cm), which Frederic G. Kenyon published in 1909.[73] This tablet, which, like the previous two texts, is of unknown provenance and datable to the third century CE, has been whitened, ruled lengthwise, and written on both sides. On one side is the κλίσις, or conjugation, of "the optative and participles of the verb νικάω ["I conquer"] in all its moods".[74] On the other side is another κλίσις, the one of interest to us, namely the κλίσις of a chreia attributed to the well-known philosopher Pythagoras.[75]

The κλίσις of a chreia involved copying it fifteen times—that is, through all five cases and all three numbers. Such an exercise was a demanding, if also mechanical, one, but either way it amounted to, to use Peter J. Parson's description, "a grammatical mind-twister".[76] Consequently, it should not surprise us to find that the student who worked through this κλίσις made numerous mistakes. For example, in the genitive singular he wrote ἀποβάντες rather than ἀποβάντος.[77] But it is just as clear that such a κλίσις certainly taught the student what changes he needed to make in the inflection of noun groups and verbs as he encountered them in ever new cases and numbers.

The value of this text is that it clearly shows how the formulae, which are familiar from the two previous texts (T. Brit. Mus. Add. MS 37533 and T. Bodl. Gr. Inscr. 3019), actually function in the κλίσις of a chreia. The chreia used in this κλίσις reads, in the nominative, as follows: ὁ Πυθαγόρας φιλόσοφος ἀποβὰς καὶ γράμματα διδάσκων συνεβούλευεν τοῖς ἑαυτοῦ μαθηταῖς ἐναιμόνων ἀπέχεσθαι ("Pythagoras the philosopher, once he had disembarked and was teaching letters, advised his students to abstain from red meat").

Now, when the student uses the formula for the genitive—λόγος ἀπομνημονεύεται, or "the statement is remembered"—he must recast portions of the chreia to fit the syntax required by this formula. Thus the nominative ὁ Πυθαγόρας φιλόσοφος must be changed to the genetive τοῦ Πυθαγόρου φιλοσόφου in order to depend on λόγος, thereby making: "The statement *of* Pythagoras the philosopher …". Similarly, the attributive participles—ἀποβάς and διδάσκων—must also be changed to the genitive so as to modify τοῦ Πυθαγόρου φιλοσόφου. Accordingly, the student must write: τοῦ Πυθαγόρου φιλοσόφου ἀποβάντος καὶ γράμματα διδάσκοντος. In addition, the main verb in the nominative recitation must also be recast now as a genitive participle in order to depend on τοῦ Πυθαγόρου. Consequently, the chreia plus the genitive formula will read as follows (the changed words and formula are underlined to illustrate what the student has done to recite this chreia in this case): τοῦ Πυθαγόρου φιλοσόφου ἀποβάντος καὶ γράμματα διδάσκοντος λόγος ἀπομνημονεύεται συμβουλεύοντος τοῖς ἑαυτοῦ μαθηταῖς ἐναιμόνων ἀπέχεσθαι (*"The statement of Pythagoras, once he had disembarked* and *was teaching* letters, *is remembered for advising* his students to abstain from red meat"*).

The difficulty and pedagogical value of this grammatical exericise should now be clear, but providing the text of the singular of the κλίσις through all five cases will suffice to illustrate the various other changes the student needed to keep in mind when using all the formulae.[78] The following text has been tacitly corrected, but only the formulae used to require the changes are underlined.

Nominative: ὁ Πυθαγόρας φιλόσοφος ἀποβάς καὶ γράμματα διδάσκων συνεβούλευεν τοῖς ἑαυτοῦ μαθηταῖς ἐναιμόνων ἀπέχεσθαι.

Genitive: τοῦ Πυθαγόρου φιλοσόφου ἀποβάντος καὶ γράμματα διδάσκοντος λόγος ἀπομνημονεύεται συνβουλεύοντος τοῖς ἑαυτοῦ μαθηταῖς ἐναιμόνων ἀπέχεσθαι.

Dative: τῶ Πυθαγόρῳ φιλοσόφῳ ἀποβάντι καὶ γράμματα διδάσκοντι ἔδοξεν συνβουλεῦσαι τοῖς ἑαυτοῦ μαθηταῖς ἐναιμόνων ἀπέχσθαι.

Accusative: τὸν Πυθαγόρον φιλόσοφον ἀποβάντα καὶ γράμματα διδάσκοντα φασιν συνβουλεῦσαι τοῖς ἑαυτοῦ μαθηταῖς ἐναιμόνων ἀπέχεσθαι.

Vocative: ὦ Πυθάγορε φιλόσοφε ἀποβὰς καὶ γράμματα διδάσκων σὺ ποτε συνεβουλεύσατον τοῖς ἑαυτοῦ μαθηταῖς ἐναιμόνων ἀπέχεσθαι.

Nominative: Pythagoras the philosopher, once he had disembarked and was teaching letters, advised his students to abstain from red meat.

Genitive: The statement of Pythagoras the philosopher, once he had disembarked and was teaching letters, is remembered for advising his students to abstain from red meat.

Dative: To Pythagoras the philosopher, once he had disembarked and was teaching letters, it seemed best to advise his students to abstain from red meat.

Accusative: They say that Pythagoras the philosopher, once he had disembarked and was teaching letters, advised his students to abstain from red meat.

Vocative: O Pythagoras, you philosopher, after you had disembarked and were teaching letters, you once advised your students to abstain from red meat.

Evidence for this grammatical exercise with the chreia is not limited to these tablets from the classrooms of Greco-Roman Egypt. Other examples, in the handbooks of both the grammatical and rhetorical traditions, show that the κλίσις of a chreia was a standard part of grammatical instruction throughout antiquity and beyond. Κλίσεις of various chreiai appear in the Latin tradition in Diomedes' *Ars grammatica*[79] but especially in the Greek tradition where it appears in rhetorical writers from the first to the thirteenth century: Aelius Theon of Alexandria,[80] Nicolaus of Myra,[81] John Doxapatres,[82] and Maximus Planudes.[83]

Conclusion

To sum up: It should now be clear that a rather unassuming Hellenistic literary form, the chreia, was also rather remarkable for its versatility. This versatility is evident in the many uses to which it was put, and we have focused on some of its lesser known uses in primary and secondary education. We have seen that in the primary curriculum chreiai could function as the first sentences students encountered when learning to read or as sentences they were assigned for practice in learning to write fluidly, quickly, and beautifully. In the secondary curriculum chreiai could function in an advanced form of the grammatical exercise called κλίσις in which students now learned to make the requisite changes in case and number that noun groups and verbs needed to conform to a variety of syntactical arrangements. (Older students, long familiar with the chreia, then used it once again in the pre-rhetorical stage of the curriculum as a subject for developing a complex argument known as an elaboration.)

The chreia, in other words, became a habitual way of thinking for every educated person from the early Hellenistic period to the end of antiquity and beyond. It is not surprising, therefore, that the chreia became a vehicle for preserving—in a succinct and recognizable style—the wit and wisdom of the past. Indeed, one beneficiary of this literary form was the very inaugurator of the Hellenistic world, Alexander the Great. He is said to have regretted not having a Homer to record his exploits, as had Achilles.[84] Alexander, however, may have been placated somewhat to know that over a thousand years later, thanks to the chreia form, the following astute advice was still attributed to him by the Aphthonian commentator, John of Sardis: Alexander, on being asked how he had acquired such great power, said: "By not putting anything off until tomorrow".[85]

Notes:

¹ On these three stages of education, see further H.-I. Marrou, *A History of Education in Antiquity*, trans. G. Lamb (1956; repr. Madison, WI, 1982), pp. 142-85 and 265-91, and Stanley F. Bonner, *Education in Ancient Rome: From the Elder Cato to the Younger Pliny* (Berkeley, CA, 1977), pp. 165-249.

² For the variation and fluidity in the primary curriculum, see Alan D. Booth, "Elementary and Secondary Education in the Roman Empire," *Florilegium* 1 (1979), 1-14. He points out that the primary curriculum was often taught at home or by the secondary teacher (in order to insure that these primary students would continue on for his secondary teaching); that the time spent at the primary level varied according to ability, perhaps only two years for bright students; and that primary instruction under a γραμματιστής was more often reserved for children of poor and marginalized parents—such as Kottalos, the son of a blind fisherman, in Herodas' third mime. Agreeing with Booth, but also stressing local variations in education, is Robert A. Kaster, "Notes on 'Primary' and 'Secondary' Schools in Late Antiquity," *Transactions of the American Philological Association* 113 (1983), 323-46. Finally, William V. Harris (*Ancient Literacy* [Cambridge, MA, 1989]) has shown that literacy in the Hellenistic and imperial periods never exceeded 15%, hovered around 10%, and was largely the preserve of aristocrats.

³ I refer, of course, to the Institute for Antiquity and Christianity project, the Chreia in Ancient Education and Literature, directed by Edward N. O'Neil and me. The first of three projected volumes of this project has appeared: Ronald F. Hock and Edward N. O'Neil, eds., *The Chreia in Ancient Rhetoric*, Vol. 1, *The Progymnasmata*, Society of Biblical Literature: Texts and Translations 27 (Atlanta: GA, 1986).

⁴ On the rhetorical education provided by the chreia and other progymnasmata, see Heinrich Lausberg, *Handbuch der literarischen Rhetorik. Eine Grundlegung der Literaturwissenschaft*, 2 Vols., 2nd ed. (Munich, 1973), 1:532-46 (=§§1106-39); Herbert Hunger, *Die hochsprachliche profane Literatur der Byzantiner*, Handbuch der Altertumswissenschaft 12.5.1-2 (Munich, 1978), 1:92-120; George Kennedy, *Greek Rhetoric under Christian Emperors* (Princeton, NJ, 1983), pp. 54-66; Bernard Schouler, *La tradition hellenique chez Libanios*, 2 Vols. (Paris, 1984), 2:51-138; and Burton L. Mack, *Anecdotes and Arguments: The Chreia in Antiquity and Early Christianity*, Occasional Papers of the Institute for Antiquity and Christianity 10 (Claremont, CA, 1987), pp. 9-28. See also *The Chreia in Ancient Rhetoric*, Vol. 2, *Classroom Exercises* (Leiden, 2002), chap. 3.

⁵ See *Hermogenis Progymnasmata*, ed. Hugo Rabe (Leipzig, 1913), p. 7, line 10 – p. 8, line 14, and Hock and O'Neil, *Progymnasmata*, pp. 153-81.

⁶ See further Hock and O'Neil, *Progymnasmata*, pp. 3-9.

⁷ The earliest evidence is a reference to three books of chreiai by Aristippus of Cyrene, an older contemporary of Alexander (see Diogenes Laertius, *Lives of Eminent Philosophers*, 2 Vols., trans. R. D. Hicks [Cambridge, MA, 1925] 2.85; cf. 4.40). This reference is not at all clear; other references to books of chreiai include: Demetrius of Phalerum, a student of Aristotle (5.81); the Stoics Persaeus, Ariston of Chios, and

Cleanthes (7.36, 163, 175); and the Cynic Metrocles (6.33). Cf. Jan Fredrik Kindstrand, "Diogenes Laertius and the Chreia Tradition," *Elenchos* 7 (1986), 219-43, esp. 226-29. For a lengthy and diverse collection of chreiai, see esp. *Gnomologium Vaticanun e codice Vaticano Graeco 743*, ed. Leo Sternbach (Berlin, 1963).

8   See, for example, the various chreiai attributed to Alexander preserved in the *Gnomologium Vaticanum* (pp. 34-49 Sternbach), and new ones keep coming to light (see Michael Gronewald, "Hesiod, Xenophon, Psalmen und Alexander-apophthegma in Berliner Papyri," *Zeitschrift für Papyrologie und Epigraphik* 115 (1997), 117-20, esp. 119-20.

9   See esp. Dionysius of Halicarnassus, *Comp.* 25; *Dem.* 52; and Quintilian, *Inst. or.* 1.1.24-37.

10 See Marrou, *History*, pp. 150-59, esp. p. 150: "... the first thing to be learned was the alphabet; then syllables, then words, then sentences, and finally continuous passages;" and likewise Bonner, *Education*, pp. 165-77, esp. p. 165: "Instruction was based on a logical and orderly progression from letters to syllables, from syllables to words, and from words to sentences and short continuous passages".

11 Raffaella Cribiore, *Writing, Teachers, and Students in Graeco-Roman Egypt*, American Studies in Papyrology 36 (Atlanta, GA, 1996). Cribiore's collection of this documentary evidence (ibid., pp. 173-284), which includes 412 texts on papyri, ostraca, and tablets, supercedes the previous surveys of Roger A. Pack, *The Greek and Latin Literary Texts from Greco-Roman Egypt*, 2nd ed. (Ann Arbor, MI, 1965), and Janine Debut, "Les documents scholaires," *Zeitschrift für Papyrologie und Epigraphik* 63 (1986), 251-78. Cribiore's collection is so superior in scope and methodology that it becomes less crucial to have Pack 3 which is being prepared by Paul Mertens and Pack (as announced in Hermann Harrauer and Pieter J. Sijpesteijn, eds., *Neue Texte aus dem antiken Unterricht*, Mitteilungen aus der Papyrussammlung der Österreichischen Nationalbibliothek der Wien, n.s. 15 [Vienna, 1985], p. 9 n. 2). For the sake of convenience, however, the texts discussed below will carry the names and numbers of all three collections.

12 See Cribiore, *Writing*, pp. 40, 45, and esp. pp. 146-48.

13 See Marrou, *Education*, p. 155: "Writing was taught in the same way as reading. There was ... the same progression from the simple to the complex, from single letters via syllables and words to short sentences and continuous passages".

14 Such is the description of a chreia attributed to Euripides written on an ostracon by Paul Collart, "A propos d'un ostracon Clermont-Ganneau inédit de l'Académie des Inscriptions," *Comptes Rendus de l'Académie des Inscriptions et Belles-Lettres* (1945), 249-58 (description on p. 250).

15 For this typology, see Cribiore, *Writing*, pp. 111-12.

16 For the statistics, see Figures 3 and 4 in Cribiore, *Writing*, p. 132.

17 Cribiore, *Writing*, p. 206. See also Raffella Cribiore, "A Schooltablet from the Hearst Museum (Plates VIII and IX)," *Zeitschrift für Papyrologie und Epigraphik* 107 (1995), 263-70.

18 For discussion of all these texts, see Hock and O'Neil, *Classroom Exercises*, chap. 1.

[19] See P. Jouguet and P. Perdrizet, "Le Papyrus Bouriant no. 1: Un cahier d'écolier grec d'Egypt," *Studien zur Palaeographie und Papyruskunde* 6 (1906), 148-61 (text: pp. 150-56), and Paul Collart, *Les Papyrus Bouriant* (Paris, 1926), pp. 17-27 (text: pp. 21-26). References to this papyrus will be according to the line numbers of Collart's edition.

The whole text is reprinted in Erich Ziebarth, *Aus der antiken Schule: Sammlung griechischer Texte auf Papyrus, Holztafeln, Ostraka*, 2nd ed. (Bonn, 1913), pp. 21-24. The chreiai only appear in Gotthard Strohmaier, "Diogenesanekdoten auf Papyrus und in arabischen Gnomologien," *Archiv* 22/23 (1974), 285-88 (text: pp. 286-87); Italo Gallo, *Frammenti biografici da papiri*, Vol. 2, *La biografia dei filosofi* (Rome, 1980), pp. 377-90 (text: pp. 385-86); and Gabriele Giannantoni, *Socraticorum Reliquiae*, 3 Vols. (Naples, 1983-1985), 2:489-90 (=V B 173), 498-99 (=V B 204-5), and 583 (=V B 466).

[20] See Jouguet and Perdrizet, "Cahier d'écolier," p. 148.

[21] For recent discussion, see Gallo, *Frammenti*, p. 378, and Cribiore, *Writing*, p. 276.

[22] See Willy Clarysse and Alfons Wouters, "A Schoolboy's Exercise in the Chester Beatty Library," *Ancient Society* 1 (1970), 201-35.

[23] See Colin Austin, ed., *Comicorum Graecorum Fragmenta in papyris reperta* (Berlin, 1973), pp. 123-24.

[24] See Alain Blanchard, "Sur le milieu d'origine du papyrus Bodmer de Ménandre," *Chronique d'Égypte* 66 (1991), 211-20. The provenance of the Bodmer Menander codes was long unknown (see, e.g., *Menander, Samia*, ed. D. M. Bain [Wilts, England, 1983], p. xxiii). Recently, however, at least the last specific provenance of the Bodmer codex, which was written in the third century, has been identified. It eventually became the property of the Pachomian monastery in Upper Egypt, perhaps as the gift of a member on entering the Order (see further James M. Robinson, *The Pachomian Monastic Library at the Chester Beatty Library and the Bibliothèque Bodmer*, Occasional Papers of the Institute for Antiquity and Christianity 19 (Claremont, CA, 1990), pp. 2-5, 14, and 19). It is likely that it previously was in the same Upper Egypt region, although its giver may have come from afar as well. In any case, it looks as if P. Bour. 1, like the Chester Beatty papyrus, made use of the Bodmer Menander codex, and presumably in Upper Egypt.

[25] See further Blanchard, "Milieu," pp. 214-18.

[26] See Janine Debut, "De l'usage des listes de mots comme fondement de la pedagogie dans l'antiquité," *Revue des Études Anciennes* 85 (1983), 261-74, esp. 263-69. Cribiore (*Writing*, p. 44 n. 53) is not convinced, however, that lists of words served this additional function.

[27] This form (ἰδών ... ε"ιπεν ...) has the name ἀποφαντικὸν κατὰ περίστασιν (so Theon in *Rhetores Graeci*, 9 vols., ed. Christianus Walz (Stuttgart, 1832-36), 1:203, lines 6-9 =Hock and O'Neil, *Progymnasmata*, p. 84).

[28] So Marrou, *Education*, p. 154.

[29] See Jouguet and Perdrizet, "Cahier d'écolier," p. 149; P. Beudel, *Qua ratione Graeci liberos educerint, papyris, ostracis, tabulis in Aegypto inventis illustratur* (diss. Münster, 1911), p. 16; and Ziebarth, *Schule*, p. 23.

30 On the difficulty of reading *scriptio continua*, in which words were written without
    spaces between them, see Cribiore, *Writing*, pp. 47-48, 148-49. (Incidentally, the
    maxim cited above in *scriptio continua* reads in the style to which we are
    accustomed as follows: ἀρχὴ μεγίστη τοῦ φρονεῖν τὰ γράμματα, or "Letters
    are the best beginning of becoming wise".)

31 So argue Jouguet and Perdrizet, "Cahier d'écolier," p. 149; Collart, *Papyrus
    Bouriant*, p. 18; and Gallo, *Frammenti*, p. 378.

32 On this Xenophon, see the *Suda*, s.v. Ξενοφῶν (3.495 Adler). On the confusion
    over these two Xenophons, prompting the identification of the Socratic as a
    philosopher and the other as an historian, see James H. Oliver, "Xenophon of
    Ephesus and the Antithesis Historia-Philosophia," in *Arktouros: Studies presented
    to B. M. W. Knox*, ed. Glen W. Bowersock et al. (New York, NY, 1979), pp. 401-6.

33 This chreia appears elsewhere. See Diogenes Laertius, *Lives of Eminent
    Philosophers* 6.40; *Gnom. Par.* 30 (in *Gnomologium Parisinum ineditum*, ed. Leo
    Sternbach [Cracow, 1893], p. 40), and Arsenius in *Arsenii Violetum ex codd. mss.
    nunc primum editit etc.*, ed. Christianus Walz (Stuttgart, 1832), p. 206

34 Chreia 4 reappears on an ostracon which is discussed below (see Text 3).

35 For chreia 2, see *Gnom. Par.* 4 and 27 (pp. 2 and 40 Sternbach). For chreia 3, see
    Antonius Melissa, *Serm. XXXIV (De improbis mulieribus et adulteris omnique
    vitro plenis)*, (PG 136:1092A); and Arsenius (p. 197 Walz). For chreia 4, see
    previous note. Only chreia 5 seems unattested elsewhere; see also Strohmaier,
    "Diogenesanekdoten," p. 287: "Dieser Geistesblitz scheint in der Überlieferung
    untergegangen zu sein, was kein Schade wäre". But this chreia was hardly the
    invention of a school teacher either (see Gallo, *Frammenti*, p. 390).

36 For parallels, see Strohmaier, "Diogenesanekdoten," pp. 286-88, and esp. Dimitri
    Gutas, "Sayings by Diogenes preserved in Arabic," in *Le Cynisme ancien et ses
    prolongements*, ed. Marie-Odile Goulet-Cazé and Richard Goulet (Paris, 1993), pp.
    475-518.

37 Attacks on women are especially prominent in the monostichoi attributed to
    Menander, which often were used in schools (see nos. 342, 371, 502, 591, 700 in
    Menandri Sententiae, ed. Siegfried Jaekel [Leipzig, 1964]). Note also the
    collection of quotations against women collected from comedy and history by the
    γραμματικός Leonidas as reported in Athenaeus, *Deipnosophistae* 13.558e-560f.

38 Hans Oellacher, *Griechische Literarische Papyri II*, Mitteilungen aus der Papyrus-
    sammlung der Österreichischen Nationalbibliothek in Wien, n.s. 3 (Vienna, 1939),
    pp. 52-53.

39 Gallo, *Frammenti*, pp. 341-48 (text: p. 345) and Tavalo XIII.1. See also
    Giannantoni, *Reliquiae*, 2:505 (=V B 227).

40 Oellacher, *Literarische Papyri*, p. 52.

41 Gallo, *Frammenti*, pp. 341-42.

42 Cribiore, *Writing*, p. 218.

43 For the formula, see Theon in *Rhetores Graeci*, 1:202, line 21-203, 2, lines 17-
    19=Hock and O'Neil, *Progymnasmata*, p. 84.

44 See *Gnomologium Vaticanum* 172 (p. 71 Sternbach); Antonius Melissa, *De avar.* 127 (PG 136.896a); and Arsenius (p. 197 Walz).

45 See Sir Herbert Thompson, "A Greek Ostracon," *Proceedings of the Society of Biblical Archaeology* 34 (1912), 197 and Plate XXII. The ostracon was then taken up into Preisigke's *Sammelbuch* and hence has become known as SB 1.5730 (see Friedrich Preisigke, ed., *Sammelbuch griechischer Urkunden aus Ägypten*, 5 vols. [Strassburg, 1915-50], 1:629). The text has also been edited by Gallo, *Frammenti*, pp. 369-75 (text: p. 371).

46 Thompson, "Ostracon," p. 197.

47 See Gallo, *Frammenti*, p. 369, and Cribiore, *Writing*, p. 223.

48 See Preisigke, *Sammelbuch*, 1:629.

49 See Gallo, *Frammenti*, p. 369.

50 See Cribiore, *Writing*, pp. 112 and 223.

51 See Thompson, "Ostracon," p. 197, where he then translates: "... when questioned by one who saw ...". Preisigke (*Sammelbuch*, 1:629) simply prints the text as the student copied it.

52 See W. A. Oldfather, "Preisigke, *Sammelbuch* 5730," *Aegyptus* 14 (1934), 496-97.

53 See Gallo, *Frammenti*, 369 and 373.

54 See Thompson, "Ostracon," p. 197.

55 Gallo (*Frammenti*, p. 370) points out that P. Bour. 1 was published six years before Thompson published his ostracon.

56 For this text, see Gallo, *Frammenti*, pp. 325-45 (text: pp. 331-33) and Tavola XII. Gallo (ibid., p. 328) says that this papyrus, which contains fragments of at least eight chreiai, was compiled for scholastic use; Cribiore, however, does not include it in her collection of educational texts.

57 See *Hermognenis Progymnasmata* (p. 6, lines 9-10 Rabe), and Hock and O'Neil, *Progymnasmata*, pp. 174-75; and *Nicolai Progymnasmata*, ed. Iosephus Felten (Leipzig, 1913), p. 23, lines 3-5, and Hock and O'Neil, *Progymnasmata*, pp. 258-59.

58 On the secondary curriculum, see further Marrou, *History*, pp. 160-85, and Bonner, *Education*, pp. 189-249. The standard grammatical textbook, or *Ars grammatica*, was that attributed to Dionysius Thrax from the second or first century BCE, although it may not have been compiled until the third or fourrth century CE (see Vincenzo DiBenedetto, "At the Origins of Greek Grammar," *Glotta* 68 [1990], 19-39; for the text, see Gustaf Uhlig, ed., *Dionysii Thracis Ars Grammatica*, Grammatici Graeci 1.1 (1883; repr. Hildesheim, 1965), pp. 3-100; English translation in Alan Kemp, "The TEKHNÊ GRAMMATICKÊ translated into English," in *The History of Linguistics in the Classical Period*, Amsterdam Studies in the Theory and History of Linguistic Science 46 (Philadelphia, PA, 1987), pp. 169-89. For related grammatical texts on papyri, see Alfons Wouters, *The Grammatical Papyri from Graeco-Roman Egypt. Contributions to the Study of the 'Ars Grammatica' in Antiquity* (Brussels, 1979). See also the historical survey of Robert H. Robins, *The Byzantine Grammarians: Their Place in History*, Trends in Linguistics Studies and Monographs 70 (New York, NY, 1993).

59 For discussion of the eight parts of speech—noun, verb, participle, article,

pronoun, preposition, adverb, and conjunction—, see Dionysius Thrax, *Ars grammatica* 11-20 (pp. 22-100 Uhlig).

60 For further discussion of nouns and verbs, see Bonner, *Education*, pp. 192-97. For discussion of all eight parts, see Robins, *Grammarians*, pp. 53-86.

61 See Robins, *Grammarians*, pp. 113-20.

62 Marrou, *History*, p. 172.

63 For illustrative texts and discussion, see Cribiore, *Writing*, pp. 263-69, and Wouters, *Grammatical Papyri*, pp. 225-73.

64 For the text of this complete κλίσις, see Ziebarth, *Schule*, p. 32. Cf. also Cribiore, *Writing*, p. 272.

65 Teachers of rhetoric also taught the κλίσις of the chreia, as is clear from an example in Theon in *Rhetores Graeci*, 1:210, line 9-212, line 12=Hock and O'Neil, *Progymnasmata*, pp. 94-98]), but the comments in *Nicolai Progymnasmata*, p. 18, line 1 - 19, line 6=Hock and O'Neil, *Progymnasmata*, pp. 252-254 show that they gave this exercise over to teachers of grammar and focused instead on the elaboration.

66 For full discussion, see Hock and O'Neil, *Classroom Exercises*, chap. 2.

67 See Frederic G. Kenyon, "Two Greek School-Tablets," *Journal of Hellenic Studies* 29 (1909), 29-40 (text: pp. 32-39) and Plate VI. The text is also available in Ziebarth, *Schule*, pp. 24-29. Further bibliography: Adolf Brinkmann, "Aus dem antiken Schulunterricht," *Rheinisches Museum* 65 (1910), 149-55; Paulus Beudel, *Qua ratione Graeci*, pp. 49-51; Paul Collart, "A l'école avec les petits grecs d'Égypte," *Chronique d'Égypte* 21 (1936), 489-507, esp. 501-2; K. Painter, "Greek and Roman Wooden Writing Tablets in the British Museum," *British Museum Quarterly* 31 (1967), 103-10, esp. 109; Alfons Wouters, "The Grammatical Term ἀπολελυμένον in the Schoolbook Brit. Mus. Add. MS. 37533 (=Pack² 2712)," *Chronique d'Égypte* 68 (1993), 168-77; and Cribiore, *Writing*, pp. 54, 79-80, 171, 272-73.

68 On the name, see Kenyon, "School-Tablets," p. 32 n. 4. Cribiore (*Writing*, pp. 54, 171, 272) identifies two hands, one for the first three tablets (presumably Epaphroditus) and another for the fourth and fifth. The dating is Kenyon's (ibid., p. 32), but accepted ever since: Ziebarth, *Schule*, p. 24; Painter, "Tablets," p. 109; and Cribiore, *Writing*, p. 272.

69 Kenyon, "School-Tablets," p. 32.

70 See Brinkmann, "Schulunterricht," pp. 152-55. For those who are unaware of Brinkmann's identification, see, e.g., Collart, "A l'école," p. 502, and Painter, "Tablets," p. 109.

71 See Brinkmann, "Schulunterricht," pp. 152-53.

72 Peter J. Parsons, "A School-Book from the Sayce Collection," *Zeitschrift für Papyrologie und Epigraphik* 6 (1970), 133-49 (text of formulae for the κλίσις of a chreia: pp. 143-44). Parsons identified three hands and assigns them to teachers (ibid., pp. 134 and 147), but Cribiore (*Writing*, p. 274) prefers to see here the hands of two students.

73 See Kenyon, "School-Tablets," pp. 29-31 and Plate V. Text also in Ziebarth, *Schule*,

pp. 16-17. Bibliography: Brinkmann, "Schulunterricht," pp. 152-53; Beudel, *Qua ratione*, p. 50; Collart, "A l'école," pp. 501-2; Marrou, *History*, p. 175; Painter, "Tablets," p. 110; Parsons, "School-Book," p. 144; Bonner, *Education*, p. 257; and Cribiore, *Writing*, pp. 94, 264-65.

[74] Kenyon, "School-Tablets," p. 29 (text: p. 31).

[75] Kenyon, "School-Tablets," pp. 29-31 (text: p. 30).

[76] Parsons, "School-Book," p. 144.

[77] For a fuller, but by no means a complete, list of mistakes, see Kenyon, "School-Tablets," p. 29.

[78] For the complete text, see Kenyon, "School-Tablets," p. 30.

[79] Diomedes in *Grammatici Latini*, ed. Heinrich Keil (Leipzig, 1855-68), 1:310, lines 1-29.

[80] Theon in *Rhetores Graeci*, 1:210, line 9-212, line 12=Hock and O'Neil, *Progymnasmata,* pp. 94-98).

[81] See *Nicolai Progymnasmata*, p. 18, line 1-19, line 6=Hock and O'Neil, *Progymnasmata*, pp. 252-54)

[82] See John Doxapatres in *Rhetores Graeci*, 2:192, line 14-193, line 8, and 264, line 8-265, line 12.

[83] See Maximus Planudes in *Rhetores Graeci*, 2:21, lines 7-13.

[84] See Cicero, *Pro Archia* 24.

[85] See *Ioannes Sardianus Commentarium in Aphthonium*, ed. Hugo Rabe (Leipzig, 1928), p. 40, lines 6-8.

Jon Ma. Asgeirsson

THE CHRIA AS PRINCIPLE AND SOURCE FOR LITERARY COMPOSITION

This essay focuses on the tension between defining rhetoric as a useless form of art or the mere technical support for philosophical argumentation on the one hand and the art of literary composition on the basis of rhetorical logic (persuasion) on the other. The transformation of this conflict is explained in the useful application of anecdotes as an efficacious principle of literary construction (*chria*) and as a source of literary elaboration (*ergasia*). This accomplishment in terms of rhetoric of the late Hellenistic period is reminiscent, indeed, of nothing less than a renaissance of the amalgamation of knowledge and passion characteristic for art in the Greek world of Pericles.

Effete Rhetoric or Practical Art

The initial tension between philosophy and rhetoric, traditionally attributed to Plato and resulting in a rupture between the two,[1] clearly emerges again in the last two centuries BCE as attested for instance in the writings of the Epicurian philosopher Philodemus of Gadara (first century BCE).[2] At the center of any discussion about the nature of rhetoric and its relationship with philosophy is the very question of its claim to be ranked among the arts of science— differently as they were understood in ancient Greek culture and its subsequent developments through the centuries.[3]

The extent of the propagation of a re-kindled interest in rhetoric may be detected in the fact that Philodemus cuts rank with his peers in the very undertaking of writing about rhetoric.[4] Again, art becomes the fundamental criterion applied to the question of rhetorical technic by Philodemus in his *De rhetorica*[5] at the core of which is the Platonic imperative of its practical dimensions. In Plato's *Ion*, the rhapsodist becomes a mockery for being moved by an inexplicable afflatus and not knowledge according to Socrates who, thus, cuts poetry from the realm of true art.[6] Similarly, in *Phaedrus*, Socrates alienates rhetoric from the arts on the basis of what differentiates dialectic from rhetoric.[7] Rhetoric is described as a self-contained world: the "residue" of which is nothing but an exercise of persuasion.[8] Thus, the nature of poetry (being divinely inspired) and the nature of rhetoric (not depending on any reference outside of itself) are without reason and serve no practical purpose: they are art for art's sake alone, and an idle art is no art at all.[9]

Philodemus would seem to follow this trend of Platonic argumentation when he himself attempts at eradicating the two most influential manners of rhetorical speech. Thus, he claims that neither forensic nor deliberative rhetoric are worthy of the arts by applying to them the principle of usefulness, Philodemus says:

> The arguments of philosophy are not conjectural but rigorous. Speeches may be pleasing and beautiful, but one would not care for them unless they are *useful* [emphasis added].[10]

Philodemus can even go so far as to compare the unskilled laymen with the trained orator–stating the blunt question: "What is the loss incurred by the inability to speak rhetorically?"[11] Indeed, Philodemus identifies rhetoric with what is "deceitful" and consisting of "ignoble tricks".[12] Having such qualified the forensic orator, he then identifies the hortatory speaker as one not only using deceptive language but one being, indeed, himself a "magician" whose performance will in any case bring nothing of value to his audience. However, demonstrative speech is only less "profitable" in comparison to philosophy.[13]

In this many words, Philodemus has, indeed, dismantled the core of the rhetorical foundation in Aristotle's *Ars rhetorica*: the persuasive logic (*logos*) is less resultful than that of the unskilled person; the motivation (*ethos*) of the speaker is corrupt; and the reaction (*pathos*) of the apprehending audience is dull.[14]

He, thus, contends that rhetoric is little less than effete and auxiliary a tool at best in terms of its most common application. In employing the criterion of art to the forensic (judicial) and hortatory (deliberative) mode of speech (which he labels rhetorical enterprise) as well as to political oration (which he labels political business), he concludes that they do not qualify for a seat among the arts for the fact that they are useless or as Philodemus claims in his chapter on defining art, "the essence of art is to accomplish the *result* always".[15] More specifically, he declares art as the result of recurring "elementary principles" in contradiction to such common claims as "experience" or "practice".[16] However, in terms of demonstrative (epideictic) writings (which he labels sophisticated composition), Philodemus is able to make an equation with art on the basis that such writings is built on principles of knowledge (and in this case practice as well): It is method versus confusion.[17]

Of the contemporaries of Philodemus writing on rhetoric in Latin, Cicero and the unknown author of the seminal work for a certain Herennius are of immense importance for the understanding of how Greek rhetoric was being adopted in Latin during the first century BCE. But, as Kennedy points out, these authors develop and depend on rhetorical traditions less related to Aristotle.[18]

From *Gnome* to *Chria*: A Useful Principle

The Ciceronic heritage was to culminate in the magnum opus of Quintilian (first century CE), *Institutio Oratoria*. Not, however, as a non interrupted evolution, as noted by Kennedy, who describes this period as one of conflicting schools in rhetorical education where archaic tendencies and innovative efforts take center stage. Thus, while Dionysius of Halicarnassus attempts at turning education back to the standards of Attic style, Seneca the Elder advocates the style of declamatory speech in which maxims (*sententiae*) emerge as the most beneficial tools of speech. A later expansion of this tendency may be observed for instance in the writings of Seneca the Younger in his utilization of paradigms from Socrates (*exempla Socratis*).[19] The increasing impact of rhetorical devices is further noted in literary composition inside the Roman empire.[20]

With the exception of Egypt, the model of Greek and Hellenistic education was adopted in geographical areas affected by the political influences of Alexander the Great and his successors.[21] The Athenean model encompasses both an educational institution (private or public) (as early as the sixth century BCE) as well as itinerant tutors (as early as the fifth century BCE) who often would be hired by well to do individuals for educating their children in their homes. The basic division of elementary, secondary and military or advanced education remains in place through the sixth century CE in which musical subjects, literature (poetry) and sports are the key categories of teaching.[22]

The cultural integrity of Egypt, finally, suffers a significant setback under Roman rule during which Greek becomes the language taught to native Egyptians at the expense of Demotic. Yet, all during the Ptolemaic period, Greek elementary and advanced schools were established not only in the predominantly Greek cities of Egypt but even in small villages as well. As Herwig Maehler has shown, there is no extant evidence for elementary instruction of Greek to non Greek speaking individuals (children) before Roman reign in Egypt.[23] At the same time the intellectual activities of Alexandria continue to expand and from there derive some of the most important sources on rhetorical education in Late Antiquity.

While several references to introductory manuals on rhetoric (*Progymnasmata*) are known from the ancient world (mostly Late Antiquity), the earliest preserved manual is that of Theon of Alexandria from the first century CE.[24] From references to such manuals prior to Theon, it may be assumed that they became ever more popular in teaching rhetoric and literary composition during the last decades BCE and they are prominent tools of education in the Roman empire and beyond. Kennedy observes that the insistence of composing reach back to the early sophists who had challenged the traditional principles of literary education consisting in reciting existing poetry and their interpretation.[25] The *Progymnasmata* of Aphthonius became the model manual in the Byzantine period and was later adopted in the west as well (around fourteenth hundred CE), as Hock observes.[26]

In distinction to the technical handbooks (*Technai*) on rhetoric that are based on theoretical definitions such as the *Ars rhetorica* by Aristotle and that are aimed at specialists in the field of rhetoric, the *Progymnasmata* were class room manuals for teachers, as explained by Burton L. Mack, giving instructions to students who had completed secondary education and were starting their rhetorical training.[27] The extant manuals share some basic characteristics but differ in number of categories for exercises, as well as to the levels of explanation or expectations with regard to individual exercises. Mack observes how different "forms" are described at the beginning of each chapter as well as is a listing of the most common "types". He further notes how smaller rhetorical units are explained as principle for a larger literary construction: An inherent sequence of the material in the *Progymnasmata* themselves is from simple forms to a fully constructed speech—a process during which the student moves from imitating and reciting rhetorical units to applying various technical devices for the purpose of constructing a complete argument following a deliberative pedagogical pattern.[28]

Among the first listed exercises in the *Progymnasmata* is the one on "useful sayings" or *chriae*.[29] Implied in this very curious terminology chosen for the concept and applied to this category is its *usefulness* weather understood in an abstract or a practical sense.[30] The *chria* is a literary form (genre) related to maxims (*gnome*) and recollections (*apomnemoneumata*) but distinct from them at the same time as carefully explained by Theon. In comparison to a maxim, a chria is always attributed to an individual of distinction (most often a philosopher or an official of a state[31]) and it can either contain a saying (as maxims always do) or an action or a combination of both. Compared to recollections, a *chria* is always concise and charged with a characteristic wit.[32] Yet, as Mack points out, in context of the classroom, not all *chriae* were equally applicable to the many exercises recommended for the *chria* but had to be evaluated and applied on the basis of their authoritative value, as well as on the basis of how suitable they were to the individual exercises. The reputation of the model character is, as Mack explains, a key function for accomplishing a transformation of the audience itself—a metamorphosis through imitation (*mimesis*)–by virtue of the speaker's choice and ability to argue the case successfully. As such the *chria* proves its usefulness: It reflects something useful (desirable) for an audience; when properly argued it authenticates (legitimizes) the speaker through its very own construction (logic). In this, then, come together again the principles of characters of speech as outlined by Aristotle: Principles that, according to Mack, could easily be applied to imaginary characters of literary construction as well. It is a period when "deeds" of heros are being replaced with "sages and their sayings" or a new concept of virtue (*arete*).[33]

The emphasis on the authority of the person to whom a *chria* is attributed (the characteristics of whom the speaker imitates), as well as on the reception of the audience as a practical consequence of the content of the *chria* and the persuasive power of the argumentation, reveals a fundamental change from the disposition held by Philodemus a few decades earlier. In reducing rhetoric to mere play with words, Philodemus had concluded that such useless enterprise did, indeed, not make rhetoric worthy of the arts at all. Theon's discussion of the nature of the *chria* demonstrates the radical changes taking place within the field of rhetoric during the turn of the calendar. That rhetoric is a useful means for presenting practical matters—matters that are based on philosophical findings in general is expressed already at the very beginning of Theon's Introduction to his manual in which he criticizes those orators who practice rhetoric without proper knowledge of philosophy and rhetorical training (and thus create questionable reputation for rhetoric):[34]

> The ancient orators, and especially the renowned ones, did not usually think it proper to approach rhetoric in any way, until in some way or another they had touched upon philosophy and from it were filled with elevated thought. But nowadays the majority of orators are so far from knowing teachings, that even though they have received absolutely none of the so-called general lessons, they turn eagerly to speaking.[35]

Theon's comments reflect a historical situation which is the subject of Philodemus' critic: Circumstances that the systematic teaching of the *Progymnasmata* was to change for centuries to come. The "useful saying" (*chria*) encompasses these changes in its own components of artistry and pointed sagacity which never can rest on timeless maxims alone but a transformation of an intellectual scenario all by itself in appealing to the tradition of old and testing the sage of a forthcoming age.

From *Chria* to *Ergasia*: A Source of Elaboration

Collections of *chriae* are not only a task for the student in the course of a study. Anthologies of various types are referred to as early as in Plato but the oldest *chriae* collection goes back to the 3rd century BCE. Similar collections of recollections (*apomnemoneumata*) and maxims (*gnomologia*) are attested from the same period.[36] As a corpus, the *chriae* collections form a concise counterbalance to the lengthy traditions of disputation in the history of Greek philosophy. At the same time they attest to an oral tradition of conflicting philosophical schools, as noted by Mack, in contrast to the written traditions[37] (which often are presented, however, in an oral fashion such as the dialogue tradition of Plato). Mack further emphasizes the ostensible character of wisdom in the *chriae*. While some follow the course of *sophia* or conventional wisdom (the "stable systems"), other *chriae*—in particular those of the Cynics—express the very challenge to the establishment in the fashion of "street-smarts" or *metis* (the "sagacity necessary to survive in threatening and competitive circumstances").[38]

The prominence of this genre, thus, has a long history while the application of *chriae* for rhetorical instruction is predominantly (as it appears) a development during the Roman empire. Theon offers by far the most extensive account of the *chria* in comparison to the other extant *Progymnasmata*.[39] Of the many exercises suggested for manipulating the *chria*, the more extensive way of elaborating it as known in the works by Hermogenes and Aphthonius is missing in Theon (or the extant versions of his manual). It is in these patterns of elaboration that the *chria* emerges as a rhetorical principle and source of literary composition: the ultimate merger of rhetoric and literature. This important factor has largely been ignored in classical approaches to rhetoric and has been worked out most extensively by scholars in the field of Hellenistic texts (such as the biblical apocrypha and the New Testament).[40] Mack says:

> The chreia and the elaboration are forms of composition that bridge between rhetorical speech on the one hand and discursive, narrative literature on the other. They are also rhetorical and literary activities that combine interpretation with composition.[41]

While the patterns of elaboration are best explained in the *Progymnasmata* of Hermogenes and Aphthonius, traces of them are already attested to in the rhetorical treatise attributed to Herennius as well as in the *Progymnasmata* of Theon.[42] As will be demonstrated below Philodemus provides a first example of an elaboration of a *chria* in the first century BCE.

Thus, under the heading "thesis" Theon lists several units (maxims, *chriae*, proverbs etc.) that may be used for expanding into a full argument—a last exercise listed in the chapter on the *chria*. In addition to the categories listed for elaboration, Theon provides three major lists of topics (*topoi*), i.e., various supportive means to argue a case in full.[43]

The exercises applied to the *chria* in Theon are for the most part oriented towards its inner elastic nature or capacity for manipulation.[44] In Hermogenes, the focus has shifted from its inner qualifications to its ability to become subject for a clearly defined elaboration based on its inherent potential for being expanded beyond its inner self. In this process the *chria* becomes source for any kind of literary composition in which skilled techniques and innovative composition work towards a new literary unit.[45]

Mack observes a tendency in this change to reduce the number of the many and various topics listed in the rhetorical handbooks and manuals to a compact level of the most important elements for persuasive argumentation.[46] Yet, within the limits of the basic structure of the three main types of speech consisting of: introduction (*exordium*); statement of facts (*narratio*), arguments (*argumentatio*), and conclusion (*conclusio*).[47]

Pattern(s) of an Elaboration

In view of the development of elaboration patterns discernable from the first century BCE into the second century CE, literature and documentation from the same period and beyond it is subject for a careful search after any such patterned units as the manual tradition testifies to. Thus, wherever a model, consisting of recognizable parts of the extant components such as in the *Ad Herennium* or *Hermogenes,* is detected, a literary construction unfolds showing the hand of a skilled author.

In the context of any given kind of literature, the first task is to identify such a "rhetorical unit"[48] that may be analyzed as following a given pattern of elaboration, as well as in the application of the various topics (*topoi*).

When applied to the rhetorical manuals themselves, the objectives of the very instruction emerges from the hand of the author as may be discerned in the way Theon presents many of his exercises and illustrations. Mack shows how Theon applies topics (*topoi*) to his own discussion of the exercise on commenting or criticizing a *chria*. The three topics he recommends applying to the *chria* in this particular case are derived from the list of topics labeled "final categories" consisting of "conventional values" that were considered useful for any type of speech: on truth, ethics and appropriateness. In addition, Theon suggests yet another means of argumentation in the form of support by reference to an "ancient authority".[49] Through the sequence in which Theon presents this illustration, emerges a logical pattern consisting of applied rhetorical techniques and an original set of mind for expansion of the *chria*. Thus, Mack rightly claims to discover in this very illustration a variation of an elaboration pattern even though Theon does not present it as a separate exercise in his *Progymnasmata*.[50]

Collections of *chriae* are not only found in practical lists for educational purposes or imbedded in literary works such as Lives of Philosophers. They constitute themselves a literary genre and while some certainly serve the sole purpose of a depository for practical purposes, others are arranged in such a way as to constitute smaller or larger literary units based on rhetorical construction (patterns of elaboration).[51] The Coptic *Gospel of Thomas* is a Hellenistic text that has frequently been identified as a random collection of aphorisms or sayings.[52] Yet, when viewed in its own right, a premeditated structure of composition reveals itself in various patterns of elaboration of which the rhetorical unit of logia 10-13 is an example: an argument about the disappearance of the present world order and what will remain or return— exemplified in Jesus and his role in these sayings.[53]

The same proves to be the case within larger genres of literature or anywhere from theological treatises and homilies to large scale literature such as attested in various genres of Jewish and Christian writings and other Hellenistic literary texts such as romances.[54] Indeed, the educational pattern laid out in the instructional manuals on rhetoric may be seen as penetrating compositional activities throughout the Hellenistic world.

In returning to Hermogenes, his suggested model for elaborating a *chria* will have contained common components for elaboration as well as certain modifications by his own hand. The pattern unfolds as follows with only a brief instruction about each step: 1) *Praise* of the person to whom the *chria* is attributed in order to better establish the authority behind the statement and at the same time the claim of the speaker who seeks to identify with that person (*exordium*); 2) then the *chria* is cited but not "bare," as Hermogenes claims but adopted towards the objective of the argument (*narratio* a); 3) *proofs* take the third seat to be presented according to direct evidence (*narratio* b) or the statement of the argument, 3b [4] by its contrast (*narratio* c), 3c [5] with metaphoric illustration (*confirmatio* a), 3d [6] with an exemplary character (another *chria*) (*confirmatio* b), and, finally, 3e [7] by reference to historical "authority" (*confirmatio* c) by which the logical argumentation comes to a conclusion, the last step 4) [8] consisting of an exhortation (*conclusio*) aimed at an approval from the audience.[55]

The pattern itself is an expansion of the traditional four components of speech as defined by Aristotle.[56] Yet, not an arbitrary addition of argumentative elements but, as Mack concludes, a way to apply the most basic topics (*topoi*) and to address "all the orders of human perception, experience and discourse" evolving into a literary composition.[57]

Aristotle's first listed general topic (*topos*) is that of an "oppostie"[58] or the device to prove a statement by what contradicts it, thus, "to be temperate is a good thing, for to lack self-control is harmful".[59] Perhaps this very sample might be applied to the personality of Philodemus himself in his bitter resentment against rhetoric. However, the usefulness of rhetoric may equally be tested against this principle of opposites. The application of elaboration patterns for arguing a certain case, thus, should equally be applicable in arguing against a case if, indeed, the model is true, up to its promises and useful in every sense: In Philodemus, the case against the usefulness of rhetoric.

One of the persons who suffers the most from the attacks of Philodemus is the natural philosopher Nausiphanus (fourth century BCE), who will have attempted at drawing a correspondence between the laws or logic in nature and speech and, thus, favored the study of rhetoric as a discipline in its own right.[60] Philodemus launches his attack both on Nausiphanus and Aristotle by citing a chreia attributed to each.[61]

The *chria* attributed to the former is as follows:[62]
1) [2] "He (Nausiphanes) said that the natural philosopher and the 'wise man' will persuade their audience".

Philodemus, in accordance with his contempt for Nausiphanus, does not have a word of praise for him and the *chria* is left "bare" or verbatim without an attempt at paraphrasing.

The statement of the *chria* (rationale) is elaborated as follows:
2) [3] "He [that is, Nausiphanus] left no doubt that by 'wise man' he meant himself. But the essence of method lies in concealing the method".

In this scorning remark, Philodemus underscores his further disdain for Nausiphanus whose claim to wisdom and weight (in terms of persuasion) becomes the basic statements or theme of the argumentation.

The statement is followed by contrasting Nausiphanus' "task" to what would seem to make him different from others (the opposite):
3) [4] "Certainly he [that is, Nausiphanus] will not expect such a task to belong to the rhetorical sophists or the statesmen".

Philodemus, here, adds a sarcastic argument comparing Nausiphanus with others who practice rhetoric—as if he was better than all the rest of them. If true, Philodemus would be proven wrong and if false as Philodemus attempts at proving, Nausiphanus is no better than the other charlatans disliked by Philodemus. On this principle the thesis either fails or succeeds.

A first proof against Nausiphauns is launched by claiming that he is wrong in his assumption (analogy):
4) [5] "If the hearer comprehend with sufficient intelligence and zeal the one who knows how to lead the argument in any direction he chooses, there is a science and faculty [of guiding the argument] not whither the speaker, but whither the hearer wishes".

In this proof Philodemus appeals to the audience as a decisive factor in an encounter with a speaker: It is its ability to comprehend that is decisive and not the intelligence of the speaker or the persuasive power of the same.

Another proof is supplied in the form of a question to provide for an example:
5) [6] "Who can persuade with the help of natural philosophy? Nausiphanus says, 'Rhetoric strengthens and supports in time of trouble'".

The sarcasm in Philodemus' argumentation escalates in supplying an example from Nausiphanus himself in which he would seem to contradict his own contention.

A final proof is supplied by reference to attested truths:
6) [7] "A man blames his neighbor for his own troubles".

Nausiphanus' application of common wisdom in respond to the question posed by Philodemus tops the sarcasm in suggesting that Nausiphanus is an incapable philosopher who seeks other avenues than philosophy when his mind goes blank. In this case, rhetoric.

In conclusion, Philodemus states:
7) [8] "Consequently people will hate the rhetor for his political ills".

To this conclusion Philodemus immediately adds the following comments before starting an overall commentary on the short elaboration of the *chria*:

"Nausiphanes did not dodge this; for he says that the philosopher will practice rhetoric or statesmanship [if his audience is intelligent]. [This method then applies] only to the intelligent and interested".

"The majority of people are not interested in all methods of persuasion, and they have not the patience to wait for the great blessing promised by the rhetor, but want something immediately".

Philodemus contends that neither does Nausiphanus' claim for persuasion hold by means of an intelligent speaker (because it implies an equally intelligent audience) nor does the audience express interest or patience to listen to such a "skilled" speaker as Nausiphanus.

What immediately precedes the elaboration discusses the question of truth and what follows is a commentary by Philodemus on the interaction between the speaker and the audience and then a section on philosophers and politics in relation to rhetoric. A new section starts with a *chria* attributed to Aristotle.

Conclusion

In this somewhat crude elaboration of the *chria*, Philodemus states the elements of his commentary and, thus, the elaboration itself serves as an introduction to the commentary. In applying rhetorical patterns to even argue against rhetoric, Philodemus' method establishes the pattern as a useful means even if what he says against rhetoric as such would seem the very opposite of what it is capable of accomplishing. In other words, if Philodemus has not succeeded in arguing against rhetoric without using it, his claim about its usefulness falls short. Thus, also in reversing the value of the main topics (*topoi*) of truth, honor and expedience in the elaboration, Philodemus has, again, proved the usefulness of rhetoric for the argumentation of practically any case possible. In this case, the false claim of Nausiphanus, his questionable honor, and apparent inability, all add to the credibility or lack there of in Philodemus' argumentation in which also the character of Nausiphanus is made into a theme of worthlessness.

Dionysius of Halicarnassus (first century BCE) describes the decline of respect and reputation that rhetoric suffered subsequent to Alexander's death:

> In the epoch preceding our own, the old philosophic Rhetoric was so grossly abused and maltreated that it fell into a decline. From the death of Alexander of Macedon it began to lose its spirit and gradually wither away, and in our generation had reached a state of almost total

extinction. Another Rhetoric stole in and took its place, intolerable shameless and histrionic, ill-bred and without a vestige either of philosophy or of any other aspect of liberal education.[63]

What a far claim from Alexander's mentor, Aristotle. Yet, also here Alexander's Revenge was to strike again in defense of his mentor if the impact rhetoric was to have both on literary construction and philosophy, and, indeed, education in general from the turn of the calendar into the modern period, may be attributed to the cultural consequences following his reconstruction of the ancient world.[64]

Notes:

1   For a brief introduction into this matter, vide e.g., Harry M. Hubbell, "Excursus," in idem, "The Rhetorica of Philodemus: Translation and Commentary," *Transactions of the Connecticut Academy of Arts and Sciences* 23 (1920), 364-82; on Plato, Hubbell refers to *Gorgias* 501A; for earlier bibliographical information on the issue vide Hubbell, ibid., pp. 367-68.

2   Hubbell observes that contemporary sources on this debate have, for the most part, not been preserved and that the main knowledge about this period must be deferred from later sources which are: Philodemus of Gadara and Cicero (from the 1st century BCE) and Qunitilian and Sextus Empiricus (from the 1st and 2nd centuries CE), ibid., p. 367. The leading figure is Hermagoras (mid 2nd century BCE) whose work are influenced by Isocrates (436-338 BCE) and known from the writings of Quintilian and Hermogenes (2nd century CE). For a discussion of the main individuals and schools of the Hellenistic period to the Roman Empire, vide George A. Kennedy, *A New History of Classical Rhetoric* (Princeton, NJ, 1994), pp. 81-101. For a recent introduction to Philodemus, vide Marcello Gigante, *Philodemus in Italy: The Books from Herculaneum*, trans. D. Obbink (Ann Arbor, MI, 1995).

3   This is certainly true from Plato through the 18th century CE as exemplified in the seminal work on philosophical rhetoric by George Campbell, vide his *The Philosophy of Rhetoric,* Edited with a New Introduction by L. F. Bitzer, rev. ed. (Carbondale, IL, 1988). For the history of the early development of rhetoric(al theory), vide e.g., Kennedy, *A New History of Classical Rhetoric*; for the medieval development e.g., James J. Murphy, *Rhetoric in the Middle Ages: A History of Rhetorical Theory from St. Augustine to the Renaissance* (Berkeley, CA, 1974); for a contemporary application of the term rhetoric, e.g., Wayne C. Booth, *The Rhetoric of Fiction*, 2nd ed. (Chicago, IL, 1983); for a comprehensive list of works in the field of rhetoric—in particular classical and biblical, vide James D. Hester, ed., "The Rhetorical New Testament Project: Working Bibliographies," Prepared by Members of the Project and Duane Watson (MS kept at the Institute for Antiquity and Christianity, Claremont, CA, 1992), passim.

4   Cf. Kennedy, *A New History of Classical Rhetoric*, p. 94.

5   For publications of the fragmentary Greek text, vide Siegfried Sudhaus, ed., *Philodemus. Voluminia rhetorica*, 2 Vols. (Leipzig, 1892 and 1896) and *Philodemus. Volumina rhetorica. Supplementum* (1895; repr. Bibliotheca scriptorum graecorum et romanorum teubneriana [Amsterdam, 1964]); for a more recent edition vide Francisca Longo Auricchio, ed. and trans., "Philodemou PERI RHETORIKES. Libros Primum et Secundum," in R. Sbordone ed., *Ricerche sui papiri Ercolanesi*, Vol. 3 (Naples, 1977); for an English paraphrase of the text vide Hubbell, "The Rhetorica of Philodemus," pp. 265-364.

6   Cf. *Ion* 533d-e (on divine inspiration) and 536 (about different knowledge of the various arts).

7   *Phaedrus* 269b. On this tractate, vide Kennedy, *A New History of Classical Rhetoric*, pp. 39-43. Behind the different application of dialectic and rhetoric is

Plato's idea of the former being applied to "general" truths as the subject of philosophy whereas rhetoric is considered limited to matters of specific nature. Aristotle rejects this definition in the very first chapter of *Ars rhetorica* in which he claims that they complement each other. While not equating the two, Aristotle emphasizes their common element of logic. George A. Kennedy observes that this is, indeed, the only component present in dialectic and that the role of the speaker and the audience as part of persuasion is what sets rhetoric apart from dialectic, vide his, "Chapters 1-3: Introduction," in *Aristotle on Rhetoric: A Theory of Civic Discourse*, Newly Translated with Introduction, Notes, and Appendixes (New York, NY, 1991), pp. 25-27.

[8]   Ibid., 260a.

[9]   Hubbell compares this position of Plato (particularly with examples from *Gorgias*) with that of Aristotle and points out that while Aristotle argues that rhetoric is art, he does not apply the criterion of it being "beneficial" or not: the decisive criterion for art in Aristotle is that of observing "the persuasive elements in any case," "Excursus," p. 366. It is to be added here, that in this sense rhetoric is at the same time useful, cf. *Ars rhetorica* 1.12-14.

[10] *De rhetorica* VII: I, 330, col. VIII, Hubbell's translation in "The Rhetorica of Philodemus," p. 333. *De rhetorica* consists of 7 chapters: Chapters 1-2 deal with the issue of rhetoric and art; chapter 3 is lost; chapter 4 (very fragmentary) deals with Philodemus' view of rhetorical instructions; chapter 5 contains his critique of forensic and deliberative rhetoric; chapters 6-7 deal with his critique of different rhetorical schools and the use of rhetoric in politics. Cf. the brief introductions in Kennedy, *A New History of Classical Rhetoric*, pp. 94-95; Patricia P. Matsen et al., eds., *Readings from Classical Rhetoric* (Carbondale, IL, 1990), p. 201; for the more detailed descriptions vide Hubbell, ibid., passim.

[11] *De rhetorica* V: II, 134, fr. V, Hubbell's translation in "The Rhetorica of Philodemus," p. 306.

[12] Ibid., and V: II, 136, fr. VI. In this context Philodemus states that "More men are acquitted because of the lack of rhetoric than by means of it; nay even stammering is more persuasive than any form of speech," and in the following fragment, "Speeches of this sort are no disgrace, if the object of forensic oratory be to set forth the facts, and not to show one's power," ibid., V: II, 138, fr. XVI, Hubbell's translation in ibid., p. 307.

[13] Cf. his statement, "A rhetor is like a magician; able to bring down the moon, but what good does he get from it?" Ibid., V: II, 157, fr. XVII and V: I, 225, fr., Hubbell's translation, ibid., pp. 310-11.

[14] Cf. ibid., praesertim II, VI-VII, passim and *Ars rhetorica* I.2.2-6.

[15] Ibid., II: Section II-a, Hubbell's translation, ibid., p. 277 [emphasis added]. The words applied for forensic and deliberative speech is *rhetorike* and for political speech *politike*. The one form of speech dignified by Philodemus as worthy of the definition rhetoric, he calls *sophistike*. Cf. ibid., II, passim, and Hubbell's "Introduction," in ibid., pp. 254-55.

[16] Ibid., Hubbell's translation, ibid., pp. 276-77.

[17] Ibid., II: Section II-b, I, 103, 13=Suppl. 50,17, cf. Hubbell, ibid., p. 282. In this section Philodemus argues that "sophisticated writings" as art are in accordance with Epicurean teaching which as the Section reveals may not have been understood the same way by some of his peers. Hubbell observes the irony of this claim in view of the fact that demonstrative (epideictic) writings are traditionally less concerned with "thought" than pure matters of "style," in his "Introduction," ibid., p. 251.

[18] *A New History of Classical Rhetoric*, pp. 117-127. Kennedy observes that these authors follow more closely traditions exemplified in Anaximenes' (384-322 BCE) *Rhetorica ad Alexandrum* and that they do not pay "much attention to logical proof and neither discusses ethos and pathos as means of persuasion," p. 127.

[19] Cf. Klaus Döring, *Exemplum Socratis. Studien zur Sokratesnachwirkung in der kynisch-stoischen Popularphilosophie der frühen Kaiserzeit und im frühen Christentum*, Hermes. Zeitschrift für klassische Philologie 42 (Wiesbaden, 1979), praesertim pp. 1-42. Döring discusses in particular the significance of the teaching of Socrates or any teaching attributed to him within the circles of Cynic and Stoic philosophers. In commenting about the genre employed, he observes the relationship with *chriae* collections and the importance of identifying an utterance (saying) with a person of authority. Döring finds this especially true among Cynic philosophers of the first two centuries CE during which the person of Socrates becomes a moral example: "Vor allem in der Popularphilosophie war Sokrates unter den zahlreichen Gestalten aus Mythos und Geschichte, die man herbei-zitierte, wenn man das Gesagte oder Gemeinte durch ein autoritatives Zeugnis belegen oder die Erörterung durch die Beibringung eines oder mehrerer Beispiele anschaulicher und abwechslungsreicher gestalten wollte, von Anfang an eine der beliebtesten und blieb es bis zum Schluss. ... In den Chriensammlungen, die als Fundgrube bei der Suche nach Beispielen dienten, haben die Sokratesanekdoten und -apophthegmen gewiß von Anfang an einen erheblichen Raum eingenommen," ibid., pp. 12-13.

[20] Cf. Kennedy, *A New History of Classical Rhetoric*, pp. 166-200. For a discussion of Graeco-Roman influence on Semitic culture, vide e.g., Henry A. Fischel, "Prolegomenon," in Harry M. Orlinsky, ed., *Essays in Greco-Roman and Related Talmudic Literature,* Selected by H. A. Fischel (New York, NY, 1977), pp. xii-xxix.

[21] Cf. G. W. Bowersock, "Greek Literature in Egypt," in idem, *Hellenism in Late Antiquity*, Jerome Lectures 18 (Ann Arbor, MI, 1990), pp. 55-69.

[22] For a brief discussion of education in Greece and the Hellenistic world, vide e.g., Oswyn Murray, "Life and Society in Classical Greece," in J. Boardman et al., eds., *Greece and the Hellenistic World*, The Oxford History of the Classical World (Oxford, 1988), pp. 221-26. Murray informs that elementary education would have started at the age of seven for some four years (for basic reading and writing skills), secondary education would have lasted for a few more years (?) and citizens' sons would then have advanced to the *gymnasion* after some break from learning. In literature, Murray explains, the basic emphasis was on reading and writing, grammar and poetry interpretation from a moral perspective; as for music,

he lists vocal training and instruments; and finally the many sports of value in the Greek world, occupied the physical education, ibid.; Robin L. Fox, "Hellenistic Culture and Literature," in *Greece and the Hellenistic World*, pp. 336-37. Fox observes that from the late second century BCE, literature played an increasing role in the formal educational system. He also notes that secondary education was sometimes complemented with further training in classics and composition, and that upon completion of military training (*gymnasion*) some students would continue reading philosophy and rhetoric with a tutor, ibid. For a brief discussion of education in the Roman world, vide e.g., Elizabeth Rawson, "The Expansion of Rome," in J. Boardman et al., eds., *The Roman World*, The Oxford History of the Classical World (Oxford, 1988), pp. 57-58. Rawson notes that Greek teachers (tutors) started going to Italy already in the second century BCE whereas students from Italy would have started going to Athens to study from the beginning of the first century BCE, ibid. For a comprehensive discussion on education in these periods, vide e.g., Henri-Irenée Marrou, *A History of Education in Antiquity*, trans. G. Lamb (New York, NY, 1956). On the impact of rhetoric on education, e.g., Donald L. Clark, *Rhetoric in Greco-Roman Education* (New York, NY, 1957).

[23] Vide his, "Griechische Schule in Ptolemäischen Ägypten," in E. Van 'T Dack et al., eds., *Egypt and the Hellenistic World: Proceedings of the International Colloquium Leuven – 24-25 May 1982*, Studia Hellenistica 27 (Leuven, 1983), pp. 191-203. Maehler describes the cultural isolation of native Egyptians, i.e., those at the grassroot level during the Ptolemaic period. He further explains how the scribal elite (traditionally connected with the temple cults) and government officials will have had access to advanced Greek education in Egypt at the many and dispersed centers of Greek education in Egypt at this time—resulting in Greek being used by the literary elite, governmental offices and even in private correspondence. He neither finds evidence of elementary Greek instruction in Ptolemaic Egypt nor of private tutors for the general native public. Maehler contributes the increasing Greek language influence and competency to the more difficult Demotic (script in particular) which would have made Greek more appealing to learn—a process that may have penetrated the cultural scene informally (through a daily exposure to Greek speaking individuals), ibid., passim.

[24] Kennedy informs that the earliest reference to *Progymnasmata* is found in the *Rhetorica ad Alexandrum* 28; that the author of *Ad Herennium* 1.12 mentions "narrative" for the practicing in composition; that Cicero talks in *De Oratore* 1.154 about Crassus' method for paraphrasing; that Quintilian talks about "exercises in composition". The other extant manuals in Greek are those by Hermogenes (2nd century CE); Aphthonius (4th century); and Nicolaus (5th century), *A New History of Classical Rhetoric*, p. 202. For a discussion of references to other authors of *Progymnasmata* whose works are no longer available, vide Ronald F. Hock and Edward N. O'Neil, *The Chreia in Ancient Rhetoric*, Vol. 1, *The Progymnasmata*, SBL: Texts and Translations 27, Graeco-Roman Religion Series 9 (Atlanta, GA, 1986), pp. 10-11. Hock considers the reference from Anaximenes' work "ambiguous" and explains that the title *Progymnasmata* may be secondary

applied to the works of Theon and Hermogenes as they themselves refer to works of this kind as *Gymnasma(ta)* whereas *Progymnasmata* first become the dominant term by the time of Aphthonius and more specifically that of Nicolaus, ibid., pp. 10, 11-15. Kennedy further notes that the earliest manual known in Latin derives from the 6th century CE, that of Priscian, but that the influence of the manuals is obvious long before that in "Roman schools of grammar and rhetoric". In addition, Kennedy explains that coinciding with the disintegration of the Roman Empire in the 4th century CE, the Ciceronic tradition was to dominate in the west and that of Hermogenes in the east, ibid., pp. 202 and 201.

[25] Kennedy, ibid., p. 202. On the ancient sophists (Gorgias through Isocrates) and the second sophistic (from the 1st century CE), vide ibid., pp. 230-33.

[26] Cf. Hock who adds that the influence of the *Progymnasmata* of Aphthonius continued in western education well into the 17th century CE, *The Chreia in Ancient Rhetoric*, p. 11. In addition, Hock notes that the *Progymnasmata* of Aphthonius became a source of two distinct literary traditions: "Model compositions" based on the categorized exercises in the manual and commentaries on the "nature and role" of the manual as well, ibid., pp. 15-16. Kennedy observes that handbooks on writing letters may also date back to the Hellenistic period, *A New History of Classical Rhetoric*, p. 208; cf. Abraham J. Malherbe, referred to by Kennedy, "Ancient Epistolary Theorists," *Ohio Journal of Religious Studies* 5 (1977), 3-77.

[27] Vide his, "Elaboration of the Chreia in the Hellenistic School," in idem and Vernon K. Robbins, *Patterns of Persuasion in the Gospels* (Sonoma, CA, 1989), pp. 33-35. Mack lists the main theoretical handbooks, in addition to *Ars rhetorica*: *Rhetorica ad Alexandrum*; *Rhetorica ad Herennium*; Cicero's, *De inventione*, *De optimo genere oratorum*, *Topica*, *De oratore*, *De partitione oratoria*, and the *Orator*; Qunitilian's *Institutio oratoria*, and *Techne rhetorices* by Hermogenes, ibid., p. 33, n. 1.

[28] Ibid., pp. 34-35, "… the collection [of exercises] ranges from small literary units, through sub-units of the rhetorical speech, to exercises having to do with complete speech forms," p. 34.

[29] Hock points out that it may most likely have been the first exercise (chapter) in Theon's *Progymnasmata* but that a later editor of his manual may have changed the order in accordance with the one found in Aphthonius where the category comes in third place. This contention he bases on the discrepancies between Theon's Introduction to his manual (in which Hock identifies fifteen categories of exercises) and the actual number and sequence of the exercises in the extant versions of the manual, *The Chreia in Ancient Rhetoric*, pp. 17, 63-66; cf. also Mack, ibid., pp. 35-36. Mack lists the ten chapters in Theon's *Progymnasmata* which he labels as follows: "fable, historical episode, anecdote [*chria*], commonplace, praise and blame, comparison, speech-in-character, description, thesis, and introduction of law," ibid., p. 34. For a short introduction into the chapters in Aphthonius' *Progymnasmata*, vide Kennedy, *A New History of Classical Rhetoric*, pp. 203-207.

[30] Hock notes that Theon applies its usefulness to situations in life as do Nicolaus

whereas for Hermogenes it is less specific, ibid., pp. 25-26. Their use in context of education is described by Hock as one applicable for preparing rhetorical education at the third level, ibid., p. 21. Cf. Mack, who notes that, "... during this period first century teachers used the chreia to introduce the basic notions and skills necessary for the practice of rhetoric. The chreia functioned in this way because it had to do with a particular case in which a specific person was challenged to respond to a certain situation, The saying or action of that person could therefore be viewed rhetorically," "The Elaboration of the Chreia," pp. 35-36. Mack further adds that exercises connected with the *chria* are oriented towards "rhetorical skills". Theon provides eight such exercises: recitation, inflection, commentary, critique, expansion, abbreviation, refutation and confirmation—that Mack reduces to "four sets of complementary pairs," to which students were trained in applying series of rhetorical proofs, ibid., pp. 36-41.

[31]   Cf. Hock, *The Chreia in Ancient Rhetoric*, pp. 6, 24-25.

[32]   Vide the *Progymnasmata* of Theon, in James R. Butts, "The Progymnasmata of Theon: A New Text with Translation and Commentary" (PhD Diss., Claremont Graduate School, 1987), p. xx; cf. Hock's discussion, ibid., pp. 23-26. Hock further analyses the main subcategories of *chriae* most specifically listed by Theon. Thus, saying-*chriae* are divided under two major headings: one being that of "statements" (again, divided into two types) and the other of "responses to questions" (again, divided into four types); another subcategory is that of "double" *chriae*, i.e., those which consist of "two [opposing] characters". Another means of dividing saying *chriae* is by means of formal characteristics (such as a maxim etc.) or at least twelve in all. Finally, action-*chriae* are divided into two subcategories according to an active or a passive role of the character of the *chria*, ibid., pp. 27-36.

[33]   "Elaboration of the Chreia," pp. 41-44.

[34]   Butts mentions Hermagoras as an example of a rhetorical instructor who taught rhetoric without philosophical basis, "The Progymnasmata of Theon," p. xx, n. 2.

[35]   *Progymnasmata* I, 1-8, transl. by Butts, in ibid., p. xx.

[36]   Hock lists several attestations to oral but mostly written collections of *chriae*: Private collections by e.g., Plutarch and Seneca; Lives (*bioi*) of philosophers are one of the most common depository of *chriae*; Collections of Recollections and "Successions" will also have contained chriae or been the source for them; finally, Chriae Collections are frequently cited and used by Diogenes Laertius— collections attributed to various individuals, ibid., pp. 7-9. Cf. also on collections of this kind, K. Horna and K. von Fritz, "Gnome," in *Pauly Wissowa* Supplement 6 (1935), pp. 74-90; J. Barns, "A New Gnomologium: With some Remarks on Gnomic Anthologies," *Classical Quarterly* 44 (1950), 126-137 & 45 (1951), 1-19; John S. Kloppenborg, *The Formation of Q: Trajectories in Ancient Wisdom Collections*, Studies in Antiquity and Christianity (Philadelphia, PA, 1987), pp. 289-316. Kloppenborg notes that anthologies of various kinds date back to the time of Plato of which anthologies of "poetic sayings" may be the oldest. Collections of *chriae* date to the fourthth or third centuries BCE—the first one being attributed to Metrocles of Maroneia. Earliest anthologies of maxims (*gnomologia*), likewise, go

back to the third century BCE. Yet another collection of sayings, epigrams (*stephanoi*), commonly labeled the "Greek Anthology" listed by Kloppenborg, dates to the first century BCE., ibid., p. 290; and Mack, "Elaboration of the Chreia," pp. 45-51.

37 Vide his, *Anecdotes and Arguments: The Chreia in Antiquity and Early Christianity*, Occasional Papers of the Institute for Antiquity and Christianity 10 (Claremont, CA, 1987), p. 5.

38 Ibid., pp. 8-9. The tension between the established wisdom and the spontaneous one is the subject of a study by Marcel Detienne and Jean-Pierre Vernant, referred to by Mack, *Cunning Intelligence in Greek Culture and Society*, trans. J. Lloyd (Sussex and New Jersey, NJ, 1978).

39 Vide Butts, "The Progymnasmata of Theon," p. xx; Hock and O'Neil, *The Chreia in Ancient Rhetoric*, pp. 82-107; for a schematic overview of Theon's discussion of the chriae, vide Vernon K. Robbins, "Introduction: Using Rhetorical Discussions of the Chreia to Interpret Pronouncement Stories," in *The Rhetoric of Pronouncement*, ed. Vernon K. Robbins, Semeia 64 (Atlanta, GA, 1993), pp. vii-xvi.

40 Kennedy discusses the theoretical development of the rhetorical tradition from various perspectives but he barely makes mention of the *chria* and its importance for understanding literary composition (but he does refer to the works by Hock and O'Neil and Mack and Robbins). In the context of his discussion of the *Progymnasmata*, Hermogenes' contribution on *stasis* and style are given most of the weight, *A New History of Classical Rhetoric*, pp. 201-16. For a brief history of research into the chria and its application in literary composition, vide e.g., Mack, *Anecdotes and Arguments*, pp. 1-4; Robbins, "Introduction," pp. vii-xi and Mack, "Persuasive Pronouncements: An Evaluation of Recent Studies on the Chreia," in *The Rhetoric of Pronouncement*, pp. 283-287. Mack observes that a *chria* may itself be analysed in terms of its own rhetorical components; its pedagogical dimensions in terms of building character; and its ability to be amplified: internally by expanding the narrative components and externally by "developing its theme or logic into a literary unit known as an 'elaboration,'" "Elaboration of the Chreia," p. 32.

41 Ibid., p. 32. Mack notes that the very procedure of the exercises in the *Progymnasmata* show how instruction in rhetoric is being "integrated" with literary composition, ibid., p. 34. He further adds that the inherent rhetorical character of the *chria* is that of a "situation" to which the character (speaker) of the *chria* reacts or responds to," ibid., p. 36; cf. note 30 above.

42 *Ad Herennium* 4.44, 56-57. Hock notes that the elaboration found in the *Ad Herennium* is not that of a *chria* but of a "maxim," *The Chreia in Ancient Rhetoric*, p. 10. Indeed, Hock and others consider the first evidence of an elaboration of a *chria* to be found in the second century CE (Hermogenes), cf. his article in this volume, "The Chreia in Primary and Secondary Education," p. 25. Mack, on the contrary, argues that the elaboration patterns found in *Ad Herennium*, as well as various indicators in the *Progymnasmata* of Theon must be seen as precursors to the elaboration pattern established by Hermogenes, *Anecdotes and Arguments*, pp. 21-22. The *De rhetorica* of Philodemus provides an example of a *chria*-elaboration

from the first century BCE that not only supports the contention of Mack about there existing some kinds of roots of an elaboration of a *chria* in the first century BCE but, indeed, that of a chria itself (*pace* Hock).

[43] Vide Butts, "The Progymnasmata of Theon," p. xx; cf. Mack, *Anecdotes and Arguments*, pp. 13-14. Mack further explains how some of these lists were even given names such as "Final Arguments," but they differ in number: Anaximenes, e.g., provides a list of three topics (to add a similar argument, a contrasting argument and a referral to a person of authority); Hermogenes lists six categories which he calls an elaboration of an argument (analogy, example, what is less, what is greater, what is identical, and a contrast), ibid., p. 20. On Hermogenes' elaboration of arguments, vide also, Kennedy, *A New History of Classical Rhetoric*, p. 212.

[44] Cf. the eight recommended exercises, in "The Progymnasmata of Theon," (ed. Butts), p. xx.

[45] For a translation of the chapter on the *chria* in Hermogenes' *Progymnasmata*, vide Charles S. Baldwin,"Chreia," in idem, *Medieval Rhetoric and Poetic* (New York, NY, 1928), pp. 26-27. The same is the case in Aphthonius.

[46] *Anecdotes and Arguments*, p. 22. Mack supports this finding by two lists of argumentations in *Ad Herennium*: The first example is about "the full argument" [2.18.28] consisting of five components (*propositio, ratio, confirmatio, exornatio, and complexio*) of which the first three correspond to the *narratio* of the typical speech. For *exornatio* four elements are suggested (analogy, example, amplification, and judgment). Taken together these would seem like a precursor to the pattern found in Hermogenes as does the second example referred to by Mack on "the development of a thesis" [4.43.56]. There seven categories constitute the argumentation (statement, reason, paraphrase, opposite statement, analogy, example, and conclusion), ibid., pp. 21-22.

[47] Ibid., pp. 7, 21. Mack adds how the forensic and hortatory types of speech constitute the main models for argumentations due to their target audience whereas the demonstrative speech does not consist of stern rules of argumentation but style in particular, ibid., p. 18.

[48] Cf. Robbins, "Progymnastic Rhetorical Composition and Pre-Gospel Traditions: A New Approach," in C. Focant, ed., *The Synoptic Gospels: Source Criticism and the New Literary Criticism*, Bibliotheca ephemeridum theologicarum lovaniensium 110 (Leuven, 1993), pp. 111-147.

[49] "Elaboration of the Chreia," pp. 37-39.

[50] Ibid., p. 39.

[51] Cf. Kloppenborg, *The Formation of Q*, pp. 306-16. On his application of the genre to part of the source of sayings in the so-called Synoptic gospels, vide ibid., pp. 322-25.

[52] Cf. e.g., Helmut Koester, *The Ancient Christian Gospels: Their History and Development* (London, 1990), pp. 80-84.

[53] Cf. Jon Ma. Asgeirsson, "Components and Composition of the Gospel of Thomas" (Paper Presented at the Annual Meeting of the Society of Biblical Literature, November, 1996), passim.

[54] Cf. e.g., Burton L. Mack, "Decoding the Scripture: Philo and the Rules of Rhetoric," in F. E. Greenspahn et al., eds., *Nourished with Peace: Studies in Hellenistic Judaism in Memory of Samuel Sandmel* (Denver, CO, 1984), pp. 81-115; Mack and Robbins, *Patterns of Persuasion*, passim.

[55] Cf. the text in Baldwin, *Medieval Rhetoric and Poetic*, pp. 26-27; cf. also Mack, numbers in brackets refer to his numbering and speech components in parentheses refer to his analysis of the steps of the elaboration, *Anecdotes and Arguments*, pp. 16-18. The eight components are listed by Mack as follows: praise, chreia, rationale, opposite, analogy, example, judgment, exhortation, ibid., pp. 16-17.

[56] *Ars rhetorica* 3.13.1-19.6.

[57] *Anecdotes and Arguments*, pp. 27-28. Mack explains that: "Such include the arena of logic or dialectic (argument from the opposite), the worlds of nature and human activity (analogy), history and its institutions (example) and literary tradition (judgment)," ibid., p. 27.

[58] *Ars rhetorica* 2.23.1. Kennedy observes that the common topics (*topoi*) are applicable to any type of speech whereas others (such as *koina* and *idia*) are employed for specific kind of speech (such as syllogisms and enthymemes), *Aristotle on Rhetoric*, pp. 45, 190.

[59] Ibid., Kennedy's translation, in ibid., pp. 190-91.

[60] Cf. Hubbell, "The Rhetorica of Philodemus," pp. 318-20.

[61] *De rhetorica* VI: II, I, col. XI and VI: II, 59, col. 36. Cf. Hubbell, ibid., pp. 321, 329.

[62] Ibid., VI: II, I, col. XI-XII, 5, col. XIV. Cf. Hubbell, ibid., pp. 321-22. The following quotes are all from this section in Hubbell's edition. Numbers in brackets refer to Mack's listing of the components of elaboration in Hermogenes, *Anecdotes and Arguments*, pp. 16-17.

[63] *On the Ancient Orators* 1.1, in Stephen Usher, trans., *Dionysius of Halicarnassus: The Critical Essays in Two Volumes*, Vol. 1 (Cambridge, MA, 1974), p. 5. Cf. Kennedy, ibid., p. 162.

[64] On the impact of rhetoric on literary construction, vide e.g., Francis Cairns, *Generic Composition in Greek and Latin Poetry* (Edinburgh, 1972). On philosophy, e.g., George L. Kustas, *Studies in Byzantine Rhetoric*, Analekta Vlatadon 17 (Thessaloniki, 1973), praesertim pp. 5-26; Kennedy, ibid., pp. 217-24. Both authors emphasize the importance of rhetoric on the works of Neoplatonic philosophers for whom rhetoric became a standard prolegomena to writing about philosophy. Kennedy observes an important shift in this direction when Hermogenes introduces the idea of applying specific styles to the different types of speech and that *stasis* should precede the issue of style. With this idea emerges the "view of rhetoric as a logical discipline," ibid., p. 210.

James D. Hester

RHETORIC AND THE COMPOSITION
OF THE LETTERS OF PAUL

Introduction

The genesis of the topic of this paper goes back some 25 years to the Seminar on the Form and Function of the Pauline Letter that was conducted under the auspices of the Society of Biblical Literature in the early 1970's. In that forum, scholars like Robert W. Funk,[1] Nils A. Dahl,[2] Hans Dieter Betz, M. Luther Stirewalt,[3] John L. White[4] and Chan-Hie Kim[5] introduced some of us to ancient epistolography, and in that forum we explored the complexities of the letter form used by Paul. It was also in that forum that Betz proposed, building on a paper that he had done while on sabbatical in Sweden, that the argumentative structure of Galatians could be analyzed by using speech genre and style from categories found in Greco-Roman rhetoric.[6]

That proposal, which was yet another development in rhetorical critical study of Hebrew and Christian scriptures in the line of work already done by Amos Wilder[7] and James Muilenberg,[8] was the catalyst for a flood of works describing rhetorical analysis of New Testament texts, and in particular the letters of Paul.

It didn't take long for reaction to occur. David Aune[9] and Hans Hübner,[10] for example, in reviewing Betz's commentary on Galatians, weren't convinced that genre analysis worked, particularly when Betz couldn't fit the last chapters of Galatians into the topics found in forensic speeches and described Galatians as a magical letter. But cautionary voices were muted a bit when George Kennedy, the great classicist and historian of rhetoric, weighed in on the side of rhetorical analysis of the New Testament with his book, *New Testament Interpretation through Rhetorical Criticism.*[11] Thus it was by the first third of the 1990's, the Rhetorical New Testament Project of Institute for Antiquity and Christianity, and Duane Watson of Malone College, could independently identify over a thousand articles, essays and monographs that used some kind of primarily ancient rhetorical analytical method in the study of New Testament texts.[12]

The Seminar also contributed to the already established interest in studying the form and function of the Pauline letter. Scholars had long since recognized that the model for Paul's letters was to be found in the Greek letter writing tradition,[13] and some important studies of the that tradition were known and used by a handful of New Testament scholars, but the work of the Seminar made it clear that earlier studies needed to be expanded and updated.[14]

That task was taken up, in part, by the Ancient Epistolography Group, which worked for six years on collection and analysis of Cuneiform, Aramaic, and Greek letters. They attempted to identify and describe epistolary types and sub-types; conventions and formulae in the opening, body and closing sections of letters; and, epistolary clichés. In the end, they were not able to investigate, as planned, letters embedded in other literature or letters appended to other literature.[15]

Heightened interest in the study of letters has meant that in the last twenty five years several major studies of ancient letter writing have appeared in English that significantly enhanced our understanding of that means of communication. Major studies of the Greek letter tradition, including New Testament letters, have been done by David Aune, William Doty, Jerome Murphy-O'Connor, Stanley Stowers and John L. White, and dozens of articles have analyzed parts of the letter and formulae used in those parts. [16]

In this essay I want to describe two ways to understand the composition of Paul's letters: on the one hand as a product of Greco-Roman, or, if you will, Hellenistic culture, a process informed by the practice of letter writing as illustrated primarily in the private letter tradition; and on the other hand, as a product of a theory of argumentation, shaped by Paul's understanding of the world and situation of his audience. That theory of argumentation allowed him to create what we should understand to be a new type of letter, a hybrid product of epistolary and rhetorical theory, that is highly contextual in its argumentation.

Historical Background: Development of the Letter

Correspondence as such seems to have developed in the ancient near and middle east as oral messages delivered by couriers.[17] As written correspondence was formulated, the writer's name was sometimes appended to the beginning of the message, but the absence of the identity of sender and recipient on many letters suggests that the messenger greeted the recipient in the name of the sender and then read the message, perhaps adding to it or providing explanation if requested.

Early letter writing was carried out in order to maintain communication between kings and is often referred to as "diplomatic" correspondence.[18] In addition to maintaining friendly contact,[19] royal correspondence was also used to convey military orders or transmit reports. Letters could also be used to address issues of management of internal affairs.

Postal service was first developed in Mesopotamia in the sixth century BCE, but it was used for official purposes, and ordinary citizens from that time through the end of the Roman empire had no organized delivery system available to them.[20] While official postal service was speedy and efficient, private delivery was haphazard and unreliable, depending on the integrity and goodwill of unofficial messengers from friends to river boat captains and disinterested travelers passing through on the way to the territory of the intended recipient.[21]

Once the letter form had developed to the point that it was not dependent on a messenger to supply parts of its formulae, a fairly standard arrangement of topics, found even in letters from the ancient near east in Cuneiform or Aramaic, was set. Refreshingly free of jargon, the major parts of a letter are referred to as the letter opening, body and closing.

The opening contains the greeting, which usually identifies the sender and recipient, and a word of greeting. This is usually followed immediately by a so-called "health wish," which typically expresses hope for the good health of the recipient, undergirded by assurances that the sender has offered prayers in support of that hope. Expressions of joy or frustration, both of which act to maintain contact by reminding the recipient of an earlier circumstance shared by the sender and receiver, are sometimes substituted for the health wish.

The body contains those topics that express the purpose of the letter.[22]

The closing can consist of a single word, "farewell," or be left off entirely. In some letters, however, it can serve as a kind of epilog that summarizes or re-states the major topics found in the body. It might also contain greetings (ἀσπάζεσθαι) for persons other than the recipient, and occasionally a date.

This arrangement became so standardized during the Hellenistic era that Doty tells us that Theophrastus said one of the traits of Arrogance is that he "deviated from normal letter practice"![23]

The discovery in the late 19th century in Egypt of thousands of private letters written on papyrus provided a source of non-literary, private correspondence for scholars to analyze. The creation of sheets of papyrus had provided the ordinary citizen a cheap and widely available medium on which to write messages and so enabled the practice of letter writing outside of official circles.[24] Private letters were used typically to handle business matters and to maintain lines of communication with one's family. If one were illiterate, he could turn to secretaries who could transcribe his message and would include a formula of authentication to guarantee that the recipient would view the secretary's work as a reliable expression of the intent of the author.

In the Greek papyrus letter tradition, there are formulaic words or phrases associated with each section of the letter. For example, the simplest form of greeting consists of three words—two if the name of the sender is left off! The name of the sender in the nominative case, the recipient in the dative, and the infinitive form of the verb, "greet," χαίρειν.[25] White has noted that it is customary to argue that placing of the name of the recipient first in the formula may indicate that the sender considered himself to be in an inferior relationship to the recipient or was asking a favor of some kind.[26] However, custom varied, and there are clear instances of greetings in which a letter from a superior would open by addressing the recipient before identifying the sender. The greeting could be elaborated by adding attributive terms to the names, such as phrases to indicate family kinship or relationships, or by qualifying the verb.[27]

Depending on the type of letter, the body may be introduced with the use of a disclosure formula or some expression of knowledge shared by the correspondents or an event experienced by them that the writer wants to make sure the recipient remembers. In Paul's letters, for example, you find phrases like, "You know ..." (I Thess. 2.1), "I want you to know ...," (Rom. 1.13; Phil. 1.12); or, "we do not want you to be ignorant..." (II Cor. 1.8). Another common introductory formula is connected to letters that function as petitions. In Paul one finds an "appeal" formula in I Corinthians (1.10) and Philemon (9). Terms of reproach or rebuking formulas appear most often in letters whose purpose is maintenance of contact. The use of θαυμάζω in Galatians 1.6 is analogous if we assume that one of Paul's concerns in writing is the breakdown of communication between himself and the churches of Galatia. Expressions of joy and reference to previous instructions also introduce the body of the letter.[28]

The single most characteristic formula of the letter closing was the use the word ἔρρωσο, "Farewell." White reminds us that this and other terms used in the final greetings can function as a kind of extension of the health wish.[29] Another common term is, "Prosper," again implying a hope for the welfare of the recipient. Almost all of the other statements found in the closing are determined by the selection of topics made by the writer and can't be standardized. [30]

Following the closing notes associated with docketing of the letter or the statement of a scribe noting his involvement because the senders were illiterate are often appended.[31]

Classification of Letters

Without elaborating on the function of official letters, and focusing attention on the Greek familiar letter alone, it is widely agreed that letters functioned as a substitute for the presence of the writer.[32] A letter is, "a written means of keeping oral conversation in motion".[33] Letters served to overcome the distance between sender and recipient and helped to convey a message that otherwise would have been delivered in person.[34]

In most instances letters were intended to nurture friendly relations (φιλοφρενήσις) with the recipient. When written between family members, they often have no discrete topic other than reporting recent activities or letting people know that the writer is well. But, letters could also be used to disclose or seek information, to make a request, or give instructions. Thus White describes the three main purposes of a letter as being: maintenance of contact; sharing or seeking information; and conveying requests or commands.[35]

Those general functions form the basis of different types of letters found in the non-literary letter tradition.

It is widely recognized in scholarship today that Adolf Deissmann's classic distinction between "real" and "non-real" letters, or "letters" and "epistles," was based more on his goal of demonstrating that Paul's letters were more like non-literary papyri letters than those written by the philosophers and the rhetoricians. He wanted to distinguish between letters that represented "conversation" and those that were self-consciously "literary".[36] He also tried to distinguish between letters that came from and dealt with "real life," and those that reflected universal topics meant for general audiences.

Deissmann's classification simply wasn't nuanced. He failed to take into account types of letters that are very real indeed despite their tendency to use epistolary conventions and vocabulary typically found in "literary" letters. He didn't appreciate the fact that private letters could be written with a more "public" audience in mind and that they could also be conventional and stylized.[37]

Recent scholarship, acknowledging the existence of literary letters, has created more useful categories based more on function than style. William Doty has suggested that there were five types of letters in the Greek letter tradition: Business Letters, Official Letters, Public Letters, "Non-Real" Letters (i.e., things like magic letters, heavenly letters, letters embedded in novels or historical narratives), the Letter Essay or Discursive Letter. In the "Index to Letter Writing" in *Light from Ancient Letters*, White lists: Administrative, Consolation, Contrition, Diplomatic, Family/Friendship (with a sub-type for Soldier's letters), Invitations, Literary, Memoranda, Petitions, and Recommendation. Stanley

Stowers describes six types: friendship, family, praise or blame, hortatory, mediation, and apologetic.[38] To those six David Aune adds: private, official, and literary letters.[39] An overview of these lists suggests that a synthesis of Stowers' and Aune's classifications would be inclusive enough to categorize most letters found in the tradition. On the other hand, that synthesis should also include Doty's category of "Non-Real Letters".[40]

Epistolary Theory

Education in the art of letter writing was a part of rhetorical education, provided mainly during early stages of education by the grammarians.[41] The rhetorical handbooks do not devote much attention to it, assuming, apparently, that the occasions for writing would be analogous to those of speaking and thus models for letters could be developed by example from one or more of the genre of speeches. Given the function of letters in maintaining and nurturing friendly relations, the genre most suitable for models would have been the epideictic.[42]

The earliest handbook on epistolary theory is that one falsely attributed to Demetrius of Phalerum, *Typoi epistolikoi*. Dating of it is difficult, but Abraham Malherbe suggests that it may have originated in pre-Christian times.[43] It is a commentary on twenty-one kinds of letters and was designed to be used by professional letter writers as examples of styles appropriate to a variety of situations, or what might be called in modern rhetorical parlance, exigencies.[44] Types include: friendly, commendatory, blaming, reproachful, consoling, censorious, admonishing, threatening, vituperative, praising, advisory, supplicatory, inquiring, responding, allegorical, accounting, accusing, apologetic, congratulatory, ironic and thankful.[45]

Assigning authorship of *Typoi epistolikoi* to Demetrius may not be surprising when one considers the fact that the first extensive discussion of letter theory is found in *De elocutione*, attributed to Demetrius and dated from the first century CE. Having expounded on the virtues of clarity and brevity in writing in that treatise, the author then says:

> We will next treat of the epistolary style, since it too should be plain. Artemon, the editor of Aristotle's letters, says that a letter ought to be written in the same manner as a dialogue, a letter being regarded by him as one of two sides of a dialogue. There is perhaps some truth in what he says, but not the whole truth. The letter should be a little more studied than the dialogue.[46]

He goes on to recommend that writers avoid including what might be considered oratorical displays in letters; that letters be relatively brief and reveal glimpses of character; and that the letter writer feel free to ignore concerns about structural features. Two statements seem most representative of his instruction: "A letter is designed to be the heart's good wishes in brief; it is the exposition of a simple subject in simple terms." And, "... the letter should be a compound of these two styles, the graceful and the plain".[47]

It may be that Apollonius of Tyana had this view of the style of a letter in mind when he wrote, during the same approximate time period, to Skopelianos the sophist indicating that one of the five kinds of speeches was "epistolary," that is, presumably, plain and graceful in style.

This view of letter writing is reiterated in Cicero, who nonetheless acknowledges that public letters may need a somewhat more refined style than private ones.[48]

It is evident, therefore, that there is a fairly consistent view among early theorists that two things should be true for the letter. On the one hand, its form should fit the occasion, with topics and formulae developed for everything from petition to consolation, from official correspondence to attempts to maintain contact among family members. On the other hand, the style of a letter should be, in so far as it meets the requirement of the occasion, conversational and unaffected. What that means for the critic is that the type of letter can often be identified by an analysis of topics and formulae, while style becomes a secondary consideration.

Over time epistolary theory became more elaborate. Forty-one types of letters are described in the handbook attributed to Libanius, *Epistolimaioi characteres*, dated from the 4th to the 6th centuries CE, and major treatises in the art of letter writing appeared in the 11th and 12th centuries, reaching a high point in the early 13th century. These manuals described the parts of a letter based on analogies from Cicero's parts of a speech.[49] It would seem that both rhetorical genre and topics dominated the art of letter writing during and after the so-called Second Sophistic.

The Composition of the Pauline Letter

It would be incorrect to insist that Paul's letters are a different type from those listed in the handbooks. After all, more than anything else the handbooks simply provided examples of how letter writers might respond to a variety of situations that could be addressed by means of a letter. Moreover, Paul paid attention to formal conventions and topics associated with letters and, like other more "literary" letter writers, did not hesitate to modify those conventions to serve the purpose of his argument.[50] However, it is clear, and a source of continuing frustration for scholars, that his letters are not like others, whether from the tradition of literary letters, official correspondence, or the private letter. They cannot be neatly categorized.

Structurally they are more complex, with at least four, perhaps five, major sections found in most: the opening greeting, which typically uses χάρις as a substitute for χαίρειν and as a substitute for the health wish; the thanksgiving period, which I take to be distinct from the opening itself; the body; a section of teachings or moral exhortations; and the closing greeting.[51] (Obviously no external address, docketing notes, or dates are present in the manuscript tradition.)

The opening greeting can be extensively elaborated, cp. Romans 1.1-7, e.g., and often makes mention of Paul's office or role in the life of his mission, i.e., "servant" of those to whom he writes.[52] It concludes not with a conventional word of greeting but with a kind of benedictory declaration of grace that supplants the health wish. In five of the seven undisputed letters Paul includes the names of others as sending the letter. It is my contention, building on an argument made in one session of the Seminar on Paul by M. Luther Stirewalt, that those mentioned either by name, or with the designation "brothers," should be understood to be the carriers of the letter.[53]

The greeting is followed by a thanksgiving period that usually contains reference to the topics that will be elaborated upon in the body.[54]

The body is designed to do more than maintain friendly relations, make a request, seek information, or give an order. In fact his letters may seek to do all those things and more! The body can have three parts to it, with opening, transitional and closing formulae marking the trajectory of the development of the message.[55]

Assuming that the letter is not primarily parenetic in function, Paul follows the body of the letter with a section of moral exhortations or instructions.

The closing greeting is often extensively elaborated and usually serves as a kind of epilogue.[56] Paul tends to ignore or adapt standard conventions and uses instead benedictions, greetings to various people, a personal "signature," doxology, exhortations and recommendations, or some combination of these.

The function of the letter as representing the writer's presence is given high prominence by the probability that the letter carrier was Paul's emissary and played an important role in its presentation to the audience, and by the inclusion of what Funk calls the "travelogue" as a discrete topic appearing at the end of the body of the letter.[57] There is a hint of Paul's importance or official status in that he used a secretary not because he was illiterate and needed such help, but because he was busy![58]

No matter to whom it can be attributed—Paul or his secretary—the fact is that the style of his letters is hardly plain, with dialog becoming diatribe and periods, enthymematic reasoning and amplification in evidence throughout.

Finally, whereas the letters of Cicero were anywhere from 22 to 2530 words long, averaging 295 words; those of Seneca, 150 to 4130, averaging 955; the seven undisputed letters of Paul run from 335 for Philemon to 7111 words for Romans, averaging 3442 words with Philemon, 3959 without![59] Clearly Paul's letters fail the stylistic test of brevity.

What frustrates and bedevils modern scholarship is how to explain how Paul's letters came to be what they are. It is to that task I turn now.

Composition: Rhetorical Description

Over the past two decades there have been attempts to understand and describe the integration of the Pauline letter form with the basic form of speeches.[60] These attempts usually deal with things like identifying the letter structure and the parts of a speech and then arguing that the elements of the letter structure and the formula that are associated with them are a harmonious part of the rhetoric of the letter. They are based largely on literary-historical methods or on what might be loosely described as a variation of neo-classical rhetorical analysis.[61]

Such analyses are problematic for me at at least three levels. In the first place they tend to limit rhetorical analysis to description of *dispositio* or arrangement, which then is used for claims of identification of genre (forensic, deliberative, epideictic or "mixed").[62]

Or, they reduce our understanding of rhetoric to the formulaic application of structural elements determined by the identification of place (or, perhaps, occasion)—i.e., is the argument designed for the law court, assembly or public ceremony?—and function—i.e., is the alleged purpose defense, deliberation, or examination of values. Finally, they focus heavily on analysis of style, which is usually identified through its association with genre, an analysis that is in the end circular.[63]

While those are clearly important considerations for rhetorical criticism, they are as clearly derivative of other, earlier rhetorical moments. These moments—the exigence, audience, speaker and rhetorical situation—are the engines which drive the inventional process. These moments exist within a context of cultural variables that may or may not be shared completely by both speaker and audience. They come to expression in a coding system that may or may not be able to represent details of the argument clearly. They use a channel of communication—in the case of Paul's letters both the text itself and the interpretation the letter carrier may have given it—that cannot necessarily shield out all the noise that affects the transmission of the message that the speaker/author has chosen to communicate. All of these and others occur and give shape to how the argument is presented, the nature of its content, and the way in which it is elaborated. And so, before the rhetorical critic should move to issues of genre and arrangement, she must try to reconstruct the inventional process.

In what follows I am going to try to describe a kind of inventional strategy that we may be able to ascribe to Paul, using both ancient and modern rhetorical theories.

Without developing an elaborate defense for this premise, let me just say that I look to Aristotle's theory of invention simply because I believe it to be foundational for almost every theory that appears subsequently, even when those theories view invention differently. Aristotle defined the art of rhetoric as the discovery of all available means of persuasion. Given situation, place and audience, it was the speaker's task to bring the audience from one understanding of something to the speaker's view of it, to gain the audience's adherence to the propositions presented by the speaker.

According to Aristotle, the most effective tool in argumentation was the enthymeme, a rhetorical syllogism which depended on the audience to supply one or more of the premises. In other words, the speaker had to discover and then create a syllogism that he could be confident could be completed by the audience, who drew from its stock of knowledge either the major or minor premise to complete it, thus becoming persuaded because of the truth they recognized in the syllogism. Unlike dialectical reasoning, rhetorical logic was situational and contextual.[64]

By the time Quintilian wrote *Institutionis oratoriae* at the end of the first century CE, the definition of rhetoric had changed and with it the central element of inventional theory. For Quintilian rhetoric was the art of speaking well and, refining Cicero's theory of topics, invention was, for the most part, the effective exercise of memory. Common places were conventional wisdom not unlike maxims, principles that could be elaborated, or techniques that had proven successful in times past. The good speaker was to be so attuned to the audience that if the argument he was developing appeared to be unsuccessful, thinking quickly on his feet he could dip into his stock of common places and re-direct it.

What is important to recognize in both of these theories of invention is the central role the audience plays. Indeed even in Aristotle's three modes of persuasion—*logos, ethos, pathos*—the audience is central to two and involved in the other. In *logos*, reasoning is completed by the audience; appeal is not made to foundational truths. In *pathos*, the speaker must discover and tap into the emotion of the audience; he is not displaying his own. Even in *ethos*, the audience must recognize the traits of character in the speaker that they agree are admirable.

Modern rhetorical theory has increased our awareness of the fact that the speaker himself is a part of the audience. In situational or functional theories of rhetoric the point is made that the speaker comes out of the audience in order to offer a potential resolution of an exigence by means of discourse. Lloyd Bitzer calls this circumstance a "rhetorical situation," which he defines as "a complex of persons, events, objects and relations presenting an actual or potential exigence that may be completely or partially removed if discourse ..." can modify behavior or illicit action.[65]

The rhetorical situation also contains what Bitzer calls "constraints,"

> ... persons, events, objects, relations, rules, principles, facts, laws, images, interests, emotions, arguments, and conventions. Having the power to influence decisions and action needed to modify the exigence, these constraints are parts of the situation and influence both rhetor and audience. The rhetor's central creative task is to discover and make use of the proper constraints in his message in order that his response, in conjunction with other constraints operative in the situation, will influence the audience.[66]

In other words, the rhetorical situation is central to the inventional task.[67]

For Bitzer the audience is also integral to the process of argumentation. Discourse seeks to modify an exigence, something viewed by audience and speaker as a problem, something other than what it ought to be. The ability to modify the exigence lies with the audience. Put differently, an argument cannot be effective if it is addressed to an audience that has no ability to modify the exigence.[68] Just as in classical rhetoric the response must be "fitting," so in situational or functional rhetoric, the audience must be able, capable, empowered by its circumstance to be able to affect its environment.[69]

In their book, *The New Rhetoric*, Chaim Perelman and his associate Lucie Olbrechts-Tyteca define "audience" as all those who the speaker seeks to persuade.[70] They share Aristotle's view of the function of the audience, for it is the audience who processes the argument, rendering judgment on its effectiveness. The audience is an essential component of the process of argumentation. On the other hand, the speaker is the one who defines the audience.[71]

Audiences are basically one of two types: particular and universal. A particular audience is, "... those appealed to upon the basis of their value system."[72] This value system is based on the experience and the group affiliation of the audience, and the appeal made by the speaker will be based on his understanding of their beliefs and values.[73]

The "universal audience" is in fact a creation of the mind of the speaker, his conception of an audience most reasonable and most competent with respect to the issues under discussion.[74] It is used by him as the final arbiter for values or truths that he believes are shared by both him and the particular audience. It is "universal" in that it shares the universe of values common to them, not in the foundational or timeless sense. Because it transcends the particularity of the rhetorical situation, it can serve as a group to whom an appeal can be made for agreement in adherence to values advocated by the speaker. In other words, for Perelman the premises of an enthymeme are supplied not by the particular audience, nor by some kind of elite audience "endowed with exceptional and infallible knowledge,"[75] but by a more competent audience, who has a more inclusive world view, asked to pass judgment on the truth of what the speaker is saying. And, importantly, the speaker must be a member of the universal audience; because the universal audience is the final judge and arbiter of what the speaker is arguing, and because the speaker is a part of that audience, the argument itself cannot be manipulative.[76] To be so would be, among other things, self-deceptive!

Perhaps the most intriguing claim Perelman makes is that for the speech to be efficacious, the locus of argumentation must move from particular audience to universal audience.[77] If the universal audience can be shown to support, or to have been persuaded by, the propositions advocated by the speaker, or to share the values and beliefs of the speaker, and if the speaker can be shown to be a member of both the particular and universal audiences, then the particular audience, who lack the competence to render a reasonable judgment because of the parochial nature of their experiences, etc., must accept the propositions posed by the speaker or recognize that it shares the values of the speaker and, therefore, increase their adherence to his, and therefore by definition the universal audience's, beliefs or accept his resolution of the exigence they both face. In other words, the process of persuasion consists in adjusting and transforming the particularities of an audience into a universal dimension.[78]

Another inventional source is the argumentative situation. Perelman defines it as the goal the speaker sets for himself and the arguments he may encounter in trying to reach that goal.[79] These are related components because the topics the speaker chooses in the construction of the argument in order to reach the goal of adherence will be affected by the arguments he encounters in response to his. Perelman illustrates this by pointing to the preference of the Romanticists for the loci of quality in response to their recognition that the Classicists preferred the loci of quantity, but another way of thinking about it is Quintilian's expectation that the well-educated orator could react to the effects his argument was having on the audience and adjust his speech to meet the new expectations created in the audience by it. The argumentative situation moves along a trajectory from exigence to resolution, or from opposition or skepticism, to adherence.

In constructing an argument, therefore, a speaker is confronted by three different kinds of situations: the audience situation, which can be generally described as the complex of social, political, cultural and religious forces in which the audience exists and which shapes their world view, or, to use Bitzer's term, "constraints;" the rhetorical situation; and the argumentative situation, which takes shape and direction within the processes of argumentation. The speaker must also keep in mind two different audiences: the particular and the universal. The real art in rhetoric is the discovery of the means of persuasion that takes advantage of the resources of the audience situation in its effort to modify the exigence confronting a particular audience, and makes use of the speaker's imagination in order to anticipate the reaction of that audience as they are being persuaded by means of persuading the universal audience.

Combining features of epistolary theory and rhetorical theory to use in an analysis of Paul's letters produces what Johannes Vorster has called an "interactional model"[80] for doing rhetorical criticism. This model keeps in sharp focus the fact a letter was situational and assumed that the recipient would do something as a result of having received it. Understood rhetorically, a letter did not just convey information but, even when its purpose was as simple as maintaining contact, prompted decisions to be made. This was true even when the audience was a single interlocutor. The sender expected, at the minimum, a reply at some time in the future. In other words, an analysis of letter structures and speech *dispositio* are not enough to understand the process of persuasion of which a letter is a part.

Inventional Strategies in the Composition of the Letters of Paul

Keeping in mind that the primary purpose of private letters was to maintain friendly contact over distance, it is evident that when Paul was confronted with one or more exigencies involving one of his churches, he would turn to the letter as the medium of communication. On the other hand, it is also apparent from the letters we have that he needed to do more than fulfill the conventional purposes for which letters were used. He needed to develop discourse to modify behavior or to prompt action. Given the audience and rhetorical situation it seems likely he would turn to conventions and topics associated with Greco-Roman rhetoric to help him in the process of addressing the exigence, so he had two tools he could use: epistolary theory and rhetorical theory. He also had the advantage of having available trusted messengers who could be relied upon to interpret his thought.

He was faced with some very important constraints, however. Epistolary theory advocated careful wording and clarity of style in order to avoid misunderstanding that can arise when you can't see your audience. Furthermore, private letters rarely attempted to deal with more than one topic, and in most cases Paul had to deal with more than one exigence thus needing to elaborate on more than one topic. That meant that in all likelihood Paul had to mix letter types and very possibly instruct the letter carrier to elaborate on points when questioned about them, thus leaving himself open to misunderstanding.

Understanding the complexity of the interactional situation Paul faced in each of his letters is complicated. It would seem in some cases as though Paul quite deliberately privileges one or more exigencies defined by him but not fully experienced by the particular audience he had in mind. This is clearly the case for the Roman letter; the rhetorical situation there was less situated in his plans for the future or his need to describe his understanding of the gospel to those who didn't know him than it was in his recent experience with the Corinthians. It is also true for his argument for the Collection; it was the exigence of the audience in Jerusalem, and not the churches making the contribution, that Paul had to modify, and the contributors had to be persuaded by appeals to a universal audience whose values and beliefs came out of its experience with the gospel as Paul had preached it. There are other places where an aspect of an exigence important to his audience has a whole other importance for him; you can see that in the Corinthian correspondence or in Philippians, for example. In Galatians the exigence is experienced by the universal audience because there is more than one particular audience, all of whom are failing to adhere to the values of the universal audience in which Paul firmly places himself.

The multiplicity of audiences that could be a part of any given rhetorical situation meant that the argumentative situation in any one letter became more complex. Paul had to try to imagine the effect of his argument on both the particular audience and the universal audience and then make appropriate adjustments in its trajectory. (Examples of these changes can be seen in Galatians 3.1, I Thessalonians 4.1, and Romans 9.1, to cite some of the most evident.) This means that he might have to use enthymematic reasoning in one section of the argument, thus making appear to be more forensic-like, or argument from example in another, thus making it appear more deliberative. He might select topics from the genre of Greco-Roman speech, or from rabbinic argumentation, or even from arguments becoming common in the emerging Christian paideia.[81] These selections had to be made on his judgment of the degree of persuasion he had accomplished at the point he wanted to adjust the focus of his argument, and they had to be made without being able to do more than imagine the effect his argmuents were having. It is at these points in the shift in the argumentative situation that we see Paul's "art" at work.

A given rhetorical situation could be made complex by the audience setting. In Corinth, for example, there was more than one audience that had to be persuaded, but before that could happen one or more of these audiences had to be made competent to make a "reasonable" choice. For the Galatians one letter had to be addressed to audiences whose physical location and, most probably, spiritual understandings were different. Philemon, whose purpose can be thought of as maintaining friendly contact and whose topic can be described as an appeal for "family" members to the reconciled, clearly has a public tone to it and was undoubtedly meant to be read to the church meeting in Philemon's house; it has two audiences and expects action from both Philemon and the church. Again, more could be illustrated, but these few examples make the point.

There is ample evidence of the fact that Paul was conscious of his need to persuade a particular audience by appeal to the values of universal audience and by his membership in that audience. For example, in many places the use of "we" is clearly rhetorical. Depending on context "we" can refer to the particular audience, or at least to experiences he shared with that audience, or to the universal audience. Note the intermingling of audiences in I Thessalonians 2, for example, where in one sentence Paul can refer to the fact that "we have been approved by God to be entrusted with the gospel," (2.4) a reference to the universal audience already defined as a group worth of being imitated (1.6-10), and then almost immediately speak of his ministry among the Thessalonians, using "we" as the signifier (2.7). It is a powerful rhetorical device that links particular and universal audience through the agency of Paul! This interplay of audiences continues until the argumentative trajectory shifts at 4.1, when he takes up the practical side of the values of love, hope, and faith.

Finally, because issues of character are important exigencies in so many of the authentic letters, the establishment of his ethos often takes precedence as a mode of persuasion even in letters to those he knows well, the Thessalonians or Philippians, e.g.; and the topics of honor and shame, or blame and praise, are more common than those associated with logos; arguments in the Galatian and Corinthian correspondence are obvious examples of this, as are those found in I Thessalonians 2 and 3.

It is only after we have considered issues of invention that we can turn to analysis of the argument. Inventional strategy comes to expression in use of the private letter genre but also in forms, formulae, topics, tropes, figures of speech, elements of style, and issues of arrangement characteristic of Greco-Roman rhetoric. These derive their importance from the strategy of persuasion to adherence. They serve that strategy, and our analysis of them must look first to that strategy and only secondarily to the handbooks, which, even when they were written, were understood to be inventional in purpose.

Finally, when we try to describe the general content of Paul's arguments, we must be careful to keep before us the fact that the messages Paul chose to communicate to a variety of audiences are by definition situational and pragmatic, and that the task of harmonizing them requires us to construct a universal audience for the corpus.[82]

Conclusion

A number of recent attempts to describe the form and function of the Pauline letter beg the question of the inventional strategies, the earlier rhetorical moments, that inform issues of form and function. If modern rhetorical theorists are correct, rhetorical criticism of the letters of Paul should include description of evidences of not only the audience situation, often the provenance of historical critical and other methods loosely associated with it,[83] but also the rhetorical and argumentative situations. However, description of the interaction between and among those situations requires a description of problems that Paul faced associated with producing a universal audience and its value system in order to make effective use of the formulae of a letter and the topics of an argument. Then the critic must describe the argumentative interaction between letter form and discourse making it clear that both the epistolary and rhetorical theories available to Paul are resources in service of his inventional strategy and desired argumentative outcomes. In other words, the rhetorical critic must make it clear that ancient epistolary and rhetorical theories form only a part of the inventional resource used in pursuit of the goal of resolving the exigence confronting Paul and his audience in any given letter. To describe the practical evidence of those theories does not exhaust the rhetoric of a letter.

Notes:

1   Perhaps his best known early analysis of the form and function of the letter is found in *Language, Hermeneutic and Word of God: The Problem of Language in the New Testament and Contemporary Theology* (New York, NY, 1966), pp. 250-74.

2   In my opinion, his article on "Letter," in *The Interpreter's Dictionary of the Bible*, Supplementary Volume (Nashville, TN, 1976), pp. 538-40 is among the best brief introductions to epistolography in late antiquity available to students of the New Testament.

3   Stirewalt produced a number of important studies on epistolography, many of which did not find their way into broad distribution. He argued that the "Letter Essay" might be one letter type analogous to the letters of Paul. See "The Form and Function of the Greek Letter-Essay," in *The Romans Debate: Revised and Expanded Edition*, ed. K. P. Donfried (Peabody, MA, 1977), pp. 147-77. Some of his work was published under the title, *Studies in Ancient Greek Epistolography*, SBL: Resources for Biblical Study 27 (Atlanta, GA, 1993).

4   White's dissertation was published under the title, *The Form and Structure of the Official Petition* (Missoula, MT, 1972). He later chaired the Society of Biblical Literature's Ancient Epistolograghy Group.

5   His dissertation, *The Familiar Letter of Recommendation*, SBL Dissertation Series 4 (Missoula, MT, 1972), has become one of the standard references in study of the genre of the Greek papyrus letter.

6   That paper appeared as, "The Literary Composition and Function of Paul's Letter to the Galatians," *New Testament Studies* 21 (1975), 353-79. The full implications of the analysis were worked out in his commentary on Galatians for the Hermeneia series, *Galatians: A Commentary on Paul's Letter to the Churches in Galatia*, Hermeneia: A Critical and Historical Commentary on the Bible (Philadelphia, PA, 1979). He also used rhetorical analysis for his understanding of the arguments in II Corinthians 8 and 9, in another commentary for Hermeneia, *2 Corinthians 8 and 9: A Commentary on Two Administrative Letters of the Apostle Paul*, Hermeneia: A Critical and Historical Commentary on the Bible (Philadelphia, PA, 1985).

7   See, e.g., "Scholars, Theologians, and Ancient Rhetoric," *Journal of Biblical Literature* 75 (1956), 1-11; or, *Early Christian Rhetoric: The Language of the Gospels* (1964; repr. Boston, MA, 1971).

8   "Form Criticism and Beyond," *Journal of Biblical Literature* 88 (1969), 1- 8.

9   *Religious Studies Review* 7 (1981), 324-25.

10   "Der Galaterbrief auf der Hintegrund von antiker Rhetorik und Epistolgraphie," *Theologische Literaturzeitung* 109 (1984), 241-50.

11   George A. Kennedy, *New Testament Interpretation Through Rhetorical Criticism*, Studies in Religion (Chapel Hill, NC, 1984).

12   The Project's data base is maintained by Pro-Cite Bibliographic software at the Institute. Watson, and his collaborator Alan Hauser, published their database under the title, *Rhetorical Criticism of the Bible: A Comprehensive Bibliography with*

Notes on History and Methods (Leiden, 1994). In a section entitled, "Notes on History and Method," (pp. 101-25) Watson describes the use of the rhetorical critical methods by New Testament scholars from Augustine to the modern era. His overview deals mainly with work done by those representing historical or classical criticism, however, and only very briefly mentions literary critical or socio-rhetorical critical studies.

[13] That judgment was confirmed by studies done by Stirewalt, and later by the Ancient Epistolography Group of the Society of Biblical Literature. While examples of Jewish and other ancient near eastern letters are extant, analysis of them makes it clear that Greek letter writing traditions were dominant. That point will become important later in this paper.

[14] Among studies widely regarded as ground breaking are Adolf Deissmann, *Light from the Ancient East*, 4th ed., trans. L. R. Strachen (1965; repr. Grand Rapids, MI, 1978); and *Paul: A Study in Social and Religious History*, trans. W. E. Wilson (London, 1928); Francis Xavier J. Exler, *The Form of the Ancient Greek Letter: A Study in Greek Epistolography* (Washington, DC, 1923); Heikki Koskenniemi, *Studien zur Idee und Phraseologie des griechischen Briefen bis 400 n. Chr.* (Helsinki, 1956); and, C. Bradford Welles, *Royal Correspondence in the Hellenistic Period* (New Haven, CT, 1934).

[15] A review of their work was published in John L. White, ed., *Studies in Ancient Letter Writing*, Semeia 22 (Chico, CA, 1982). Specific articles in this issue will be referred to below.

[16] David Aune, *The New Testament in Its Literary Environment*, Library of Early Christianity 8 (Philadelphia, PA, 1987); William Doty, *Letters in Primitive Christianity*, Guides to Biblical Scholarship: New Testament Series (Philadelphia, PA, 1973); Jerome Murphy-O'Connor, *Paul the Letter Writer: His World, His Options, His Skills*, Good News Studies 41 (Collegeville, MI, 1995); Stanley Stowers, *Letter Writing in Greco-Roman Antiquity*, Library of Early Christianity 5 (Philadelphia, PA, 1986); John L. White, *Light From Ancient Letters*, Foundations and Facets, (Philadelphia, PA, 1986). The number of articles precludes any listing here; see references below, and bibliographies in the monographs cited, for representative studies.

[17] John L. White, "Ancient Greek Letters," in *Greco-Roman Literature and the New Testament*, ed. David E. Aune (Atlanta, GA, 1988), p. 87. Brent Knudson, "Cuneiform Letters and Social Conventions," in *Studies in Ancient Lettery Writing*, ed. John L. White, Semeia 22 (Chico, CA, 1981), p. 16, points out that cuneiform letters are the descendants of oral communication.

[18] According to Ernst Ruess, *Cicero's Letters* (New York, NY, 1912), p. xi, ancient tradition attributed the first letter to Queen Atossa, mother of Xerxes.

[19] William Doty, "Imaginings at the End of an Era," in *Intertextuality and the Bible*, ed. George Aichele and Gary A Phillips, Semeia 69/70 (Atlanta, GA, 1995), p. 92, notes the most recent scholarship assumes the position argued by Koskenniemi, *Studien zur Idee und Phraseologie des griechischen Briefen*, that letters were designed to cultivate friendship. Stowers, *Letter Writing*, pp. 28-31, argues that

while that purpose may have been prominent in Greek society, by Roman times the "ethos of family" is more characteristic and themes not typically associated with Greek male friendships are widely encountered.

[20] Stephen R. Llewelyn, "Sending Letters in the Ancient World: Paul and the Philippians," *Tyndale Bulletin* 46 (1995), 339-49, describes the major features of Persian, Hellenistic and Roman official postal systems, including the establishment by Augustus of professional letter carriers traveling by wagon, assuring that official letters would not pass through a number of hands on their way to the recipient.

[21] White, "Ancient Greek Letters," p. 87. See also *Light from Ancient Letters* where he provides numerous examples of letters mentioning the character of the postal system and the messengers.

[22] Stowers, *Letter Writing*, p. 22, makes the interesting argument that modern epistolary theorists tend to focus their analyses on formulae in the opening and closing sections of the letter and have little to say about the body. He claims that ancient theorists took the opposite view. They said little about those two sections and tended to treat the letter "holistically". John L. White, "Introductory Formulae in the Body of the Pauline Letter," *Journal of Biblical Literature* 90 (1971), 97, makes something of the same point, noting that careful attention has been paid to the analysis of formulae in the opening and closing elements of Paul's letters and then remarks that the same care needs to be addressed to the main argument(s) in the body of his letters. Stowers solution to the need to see letters as a unit is to turn to identification of them within rhetorical genre, thus tying their function to that of the three classical categories of oratory: forensic, deliberative and epideictic. He seems to associate most with the epideictic. We will see below the limitations of that approach.

[23] Doty, *Letters*, p. 14.

[24] Murphy-O'Connor, *Paul the Letter Writer,* describes the materials used in writing letters, particularly the production of papyrus sheets, in a section entitled, "The Tools of a Writer's Trade," pp. 1-6.

[25] According to Kim, *Recommendation*, pp. 11-12, who cites Exler (*Form of Ancient Letter*, p. 60), the basic greeting form—A to B, greetings—was used for almost 600 years, from the third century BCE into the third century CE.

[26] John L. White, "Greek Documentary Letter Tradition," in *Studies in Ancient Letter Writing*, p. 94.

[27] See the examples listed by Kim, *Recommendation*, pp. 14-21.

[28] Full analysis of body opening and closing formulae are provided by John L. White in his dissertation, "The Body of the Greek Letter" (published as *The Form and Function of the Body of the Greek Letter: A Study of the Letter-Body in the Non-Literary Papyri and in Paul the Apostle*, SBL: Dissertation Series 2 (Missoula, MT, 1972) and "Introductory Formulae in the Body of the Pauline Letter". These formulae are widely illustrated in White's, *Light From Ancient Letters*; consult the "Index of Letter Writing," pp. 237-38. All the formulae can be categorized under the topics of contact, petition, or commendation.

[29] "Documentary Letter Tradition," p. 14.

30   Jeffrey A. D. Weima, *Neglected Endings: The Significance of the Pauline Letter Closings,* Journal for the Study of the New Testament Supplement Series 101 (Sheffield, 1994), has done an extensive review of closing formulae in both the common letter tradition and the Pauline letters and argues that the typical Pauline letter closing functions as an epilogue, adapting conventional formulae to the purpose of pointing back to arguments made in the body of the letter. That is rhetorical move not found in the ordinary papyrus letter.

31   White, *Light,* pp. 216-17, provides rich illustrations of these in both the numerous letters he translates and in the commentary.

32   White, *Light,* pp. 191-92, reviews Stirewalt's argument in "Uses of Letter Writing," that the "familiar" letter in fact develops from the tradition of official letter writing; White accepts Stirewalt's contention.

33   White, "Documentary Letter Tradition," p. 91.

34   Jeffrey T. Reed, "Discourse Features in New Testament Letters," *Journal of Translation and Textlinguistics* 6 (1993), 230-32, claims that the primary function of ancient letters was, "to bridge the spatial separation between communicants". That function, according to Reed, drives the elements of epistolary forms, including the content of the letter opening, the topics in the body, and the need for a closing greeting. These "obligatory elements" are supplemented by "optional elements" added to the letter when the writer wants the letter to do more than simply "bridge spatial separation".

35   White, "Ancient Greek Letters," p. 95. See also, "Documentary Letter Tradition," p. 95; and, "Greek Letter Writing," p. 198.

36   See, e.g., his argument in *Paul,* pp. 7-15.

37   For fuller discussions of Deissmann's analysis, see, e.g., Murphy-O'Connor, *Paul the Letter Writer*, p. 44; Stowers, *Letter Writing*, pp. 17-20; and Greg Bloomquist, *The Function of Suffering in Paul*, Journal for the Study of the New Testament Supplement Series 78 (Sheffield, 1993), pp. 72-73.

38   In chapters on each of these in *Letter Writing*, Stowers provides descriptions of sub-types found in each category.

39   Aune, *Literary Environment,* p. 161, reports that A. N. Sherwin-White, *The Letters of Pliny: A Historical and Social Commentary* (Oxford, 1966), lists eight types of public affairs, character sketches, patronage, admonitions, domestic affairs, literary matters, scenic, and social courtesy.

40   J. Schneider, "Brief," in *Reallexicon für Antike und Christentum*, multiple vols. (Stuttgart, 1954), 2: 564-85, describes seven letter types: Public, Teaching, Poetic, Magic, Heavenly, Love, and Pseudonymous.

41   Abraham J. Malherbe, "Ancient Epistolary Theorists," *Ohio Journal of Religious Studies* 5 (1977), 12. See also Luther Stirewalt, "Chreia and Epistole," in *Studies in Ancient Greek Epistolography*, SBL: Resources for Biblical Study 27 (Atlanta, GA, 1993), pp. 43-66, who illustrates how the chreia elaboration exercise described in the *progymnasmata* were also used in writing *epistole*, non-real letters used in school exercises.

42   For a fuller discussion of education in letter writing, see Stowers, *Letter Writing*,

pp. 27-35, and "Greek and Latin Letters," in *The Anchor Bible Dictionary*, 6 vols. (New York, 1992) 4:291.

43   Malherbe, "Ancient Epistolary Theorists," p. 4.

44   Malherbe, "Ancient Epistolary Theorists," p. 4 says that this kind of handbook was not intended for use by grammarians to instruct students or to teach epistolary theory as such. If he is correct, then caution should be used in comparing the styles found in them to those found in the papyrus letters in an attempt to classify a particular papyrus letter.

45   White, *Light*, p. 203, argues that only four of the types listed by Demetrius— friendly commendatory, petitionary and consolatory—correspond to types found in the papyrus letter tradition.

46   Demetrius, *De eloc.* 233.

47   Ibid., 223-35.

48   Cicero, *Ad Fam.* 15.21.4.

49   James J. Murphy, *Three Medieval Rhetorical Arts* (Berkeley, CA, 1971), pp. xv-xvi. Murphy includes a translation of a letter writing manual published by an anonymous author in Bologna in the 12th century.

50   For a fuller illustration of this point, see, e.g., Abraham Smith, *Comfort One Another: Reconstructing the Rhetoric and Audience of I Thessalonians* (Louisville, KY, 1995), pp. 43-46.

51   Doty, *Letters*, pp. 32-33, and White, "Ancient Greek Letters," p. 97, provide descriptions of the structure and major characteristics of each part. Surprisingly, few other major studies, aside from that of Murphy-O'Connor, bother to review it.

52   For an epistolary and rhetorical analysis of Romans 1. 1-7, see, Samuel Byrskog, "Epistolography, Rhetoric, and Letter Prescript: Romans 1.1-7 as a Test Case," *Journal for the Study of the New Testament* 65 (1997), 27-46. Byrskog describes one potential rhetorical effect—establishment of *ethos*—of this particular kind of elaboration of the opening greeting.

53   Murphy-O'Connor, *Paul the Letter Writer*, makes an elaborate argument to the effect that those listed in the opening greeting should be understood to be "co-authors" of the letter. Among other things he points out in support of this is the use of "we" in various passages. I am not convinced. The inclusion of names in the greeting most likely serves as a truncated form of recommendation or introduction formula, and the "we," as I will argue below, is a rhetorical device.

54   The classic study of the Pauline thanksgiving period is Paul Schubert, *The Form and Function of the Pauline Thanksgivings*, Beihefte zur Zeitschrift für die neutestamentliche Wissenschaft 20 (Berlin, 1939). See also, Jack T. Sanders, "Transition of the Opening Epistolary Thanksgiving to the Body in the Letters of Paul," *Journal of Biblical Literature* 81 (1962), 348-62. Recently Jeffrey T. Reed, in an article entitled, "Are Paul's Thanksgivings Epistolary?," *Journal for the Study of the New Testament* 61 (1996), 87-99, has argued, *contra* P. Arzt "The 'Epistolary Introductory Thanksgiving in the Papyri and in Paul," *Novum Testamentum* 36 (1994), 29-46, that although the subject of the thanksgiving period in Paul doesn't conform in detail to those found in the familiar papyrus letter, the form, etc., does,

and the Pauline variation can be accounted for by, on the one hand, the flexibility of epistolary conventions and, on the other, adaptation of conventions to meet the need to communicate to a given audience.

[55] Stowers, *Letter Writing*, pp. 20-22, remarks that in contrast to ancient epistolary theorists, who had little to say about opening and closing formulae, modern authors have spent little time and effort on the analysis of the letter body in Paul. He attributes this to their focus on "epistolary" features rather than on the form and function of the letter as a whole.

[56] Weima, *Neglected Endings*, provides a full analysis of this use of the endings in Paul's argument.

[57] Funk, *Language*, pp. 264-70.

[58] E. Randolph Richards, *The Secretary in the Letters of Paul*, Wissenschaftliche Untersuchungen zum Neuen Testament 42 (Tübingen, 1991), pp. 169-89, presents a detailed discussion of evidence for Paul's use of a secretary.

[59] Martin R. P. McGuire, "Letters and Letter Carriers in Christian Antiquity," *The Classical World* 53 (1960), 148-53, 184-86, 199-200, gives the numbers for the classical writers; his count of the Pauline letters includes the 13 traditional letters, which he reckons as averaging 2500 words. Murphy-O'Connor, *Paul the Letter Writer*, p. 121, also provides a word count of each of the letters traditionally attributed to Paul, including Hebrews(!). According to his count, the average length of the seven undisputed letters is 3442. On the basis of a computer count I did, I corroborated his figures for the undisputed letters. Aune, *The NT In Its Literary Environment*, p. 205, gives word counts for each of the letters; using his figures, the average count for the undisputed letters is 3427. The difference could be explained by the use of different editions of the Greek text. In any case, it is hardly a significant variation.

[60] For a useful overview of major representatives of these attempts, see Duane F. Watson, "Rhetorical Criticism of the Pauline Epistles since 1975," *Currents in Research: Biblical Studies* 3 (1995), 219-48. Watson, *Rhetorical Criticism of the Bible*, p. 120, describes the controversy engendered by these attempts as a "vigorous debate" over the extent to which ancient rhetorical theory influenced the writing of letters. Among the more important voices cautioning against simple use of classical rhetorical theory in the analysis of Paul's letters has been that of C. Joachim Classen; see, e.g., "St. Paul's Epistles and Ancient Greek and Roman Rhetoric," *Rhetorica* 10 (1992), 319-44. Another is Jeffrey T. Reed, "Using Ancient Rhetorical Categories to Interpret Paul's Letters: A Question of Genre," in *Rhetoric in the New Testament*, ed. Stanley Porter and Thomas Olbricht (Sheffield, 1994), pp. 293-324.

[61] Lauri Thurén, *The Rhetorical Strategy of 1 Peter* (Åbo, 1990), pp. 50-51, warns of a "quasi-ancient conception of rhetoric" that appears in many studies and labels the misuse of classical rhetorical handbooks as analytical sources, "... one of the most perilous fallacies in the growing interest in rhetorical criticism." Later he describes such analyses as guilty of "oversimplification" (p. 52). Weima, *Neglected Endings*, pp. 23-27, briefly describes the problems arising from the failure of what he calls

an "epistolary camp" and the "rhetoric camp" to effect a synthesis of methods. However, in his own study he adopts what is essentially a neo-classical analysis.

62 Kathy Eden, *Hermeneutics in the Rhetorical Tradition: Chapters in the Ancient Legacy and Its Humanistic Reception* (New Haven, CT, 1997), pp. 28-32, shows that both Cicero and Quintilian picked up on and elaborated the Greek rhetoricians view that arrangement is not fixed but must always respond to the speaker's understanding of the circumstances of the case. The most effective arrangement is "economical". She cites at length Quintilian, *Inst. or.* 7.10.11-12.

63 Stanley Porter, "Rhetorical Categories in Pauline Literature," in *Rhetoric in the New Testament*, pp. 101-22, after reviewing arguments of those who give priority to the classical rhetorical tradition as the source for analyzing Paul's letters, insists that stylistic matters were the only things discussed concerning epistolary material in the handbooks. Therefore, he says, rhetorical criticism, properly conceived, should deal only with stylistic elements found in the letters. His discussion leaves out reference to genre issues, other than those that are raised by the critics whom he reviews.

64 Still among the best explanations of what Aristotle meant by a rhetorical syllogism is Lloyd Bitzer, "Aristotle's Enthymeme Revisited," *Quarterly Journal of Speech* 45 (1959), 399-408. Compare Richard Lanigan, "Enthymeme: The Rhetorical Species of Aristotle's Syllogism," *Southern Speech Communication Journal* 39 (1994), 207-22; and Lanigan, "From Enthymeme to Abduction: The Classical Law of Logic and the Post-Modern Rule of Rhetoric," in *Recovering Pragmatism's Voice*, ed. Lenore Langsdorf and Andrew Smith, (Albany, NY, 1995), pp. 49-70.

65 "The Rhetorical Situation," *Philosophy and Rhetoric* 1 (1968), 6.

66 Lloyd Bitzer, "Functional Communication: A Situational Perspective," in *Rhetoric in Transition*, ed. Eugene E. White (University Park, PA, 1980), pp. 23-24.

67 Dennis Stamps, "Rethinking the Rhetorical Situation," in *Rhetoric and the New Testament*, pp. 193-210, envisions the effect of the rhetorical situation slightly differently. He states that "... a text presents a selected, limited and crafted entextualization of the [rhetorical] situation" (p. 199). He goes on to argue that Paul's letters should be analyzed as a kind of epistolary narrative, viewing the rhetorical situation as part of a story. The problem with that proposal is that it empowers the kind of linearity that Bitzer's critics worried about, and it virtually ignores the central role of exigence and the audience's perspective of it. It may privilege the "speaker" in situations in which it is not warrented

68 Critics of Bitzer's definition of the rhetorical situation typically pointed to its tendency to imply an objective condition rather than a condition perceived by the audience and speaker, which may or may not be real or actual. Bitzer modified his notion of exigence to meet the objections of his critics, but for some his modifications still didn't credit the existence of the exigence to the perception of the audience or sufficiently acknowledge the ability of a speaker to create an exigence. Nevertheless, the rhetorical situation and the exigence should be understood as being objective because they are made real by the speaker and audience; they are simultaneously objective and subjective. For that reason, the

rhetorical situation cannot be fully described by historical criticism. For a more complete description of this point see, Craig R. Smith and Scott Lybarger, "Bitzer's Model Reconstructed," *Communication Quarterly* 44 (1996), 197-213.

69   Bitzer, "Functional Communication," p. 23. Smith and Lybarger, "Bitzer's Model," pp. 209-10, argue that in any communication there are in fact multiple audiences and multiple exigencies, and, therefore, there are audiences who lack the power to modify an exigence. Recognition of that fact allows for the situation model to be used in ideological criticism.

70   Ch. Perelman and L. Olbrechts-Tyteca, *The New Rhetoric: A Treatise on Argumentation*, trans. John Wilkinson and Purcell Weaver (Notre Dame, IN, 1969), p. 19.

71   Chaim Perelman, "The New Rhetoric and the Rhetoricians: Remembrances and Comments," *Quarterly Journal of Speech* 70 (1984), 191.

72   John R. Anderson, "The Audience as a Concept in the Philosophic Rhetoric of Perelman, Johnstone and Natanson," *The Southern Speech Communication Journal* 38 (1972), 41.

73   Because of his interest in arguing for the essential relationship between rhetoric and philosophy, Perelman does not devote a great deal of space to describing the particular audience. He comments in "Remembrances and Comments," p. 191, that he understands Aristotle's *Rhetoric* to be concerned with "... the means of persuading particular audiences".

74   Chaim Perelman, *The New Rhetoric and the Humanities: Essays on Rhetoric and its Applications* (Boston, MA, 1979), pp. 48, 58.

75   *New Rhetoric and the Humanities*, p. 35.

76   Perelman, "Remembrances and Comments," p. 194.

77   James L. Golden, "The Universal Audience Revisited," in *Practical Reasoning in Human Affairs*, ed. J. L. Golden and J. J. Pilotta (Dordrecht, 1986), p. 297, quotes the Committee on the Nature of Rhetorical Invention in their statement on the universal audience: "... the task is not ... to address either a particular audience or a universal audience but in the process of persuasion to adjust to and then to transform the particularities of the audience into universal dimensions". He goes on to say that Perelman agreed with this description of the inventional use of the universal audience.

78   Perelman, "Remembrances and Comments," p. 192, quotes with favor this characterization of his position found in *The Prospect for Rhetoric*, ed. L. Bitzer and E. Black (Englewood Cliffs, NJ, 1971), p. 235.

79   Perelman, *New Rhetoric and the Humanities*, p. 96.

80   "Toward an Interactional Model for the Analysis of Letters," *Neotestamentica* 24 (1990), 107-30. Vorester's model is more complex and more dependent on modern theories of communication than the one I have sketched out above. He combines Perelman and Bitzer with pragmatics inherent in conversational analysis, speech-act theory and a reconfiguration of *topos* theory in the context of inventional strategies. Dennis Stamps, "Rhetorical Criticism and the Rhetoric of New Testament Criticism," *Literature and Theology* 6 (1992), 268-79, argues that

rhetorical criticism cannot be seen as a variation of historical-literary criticism but as part of hermeneutics. That is the thrust of Vorster's point as well.

81   I am using *paideia* here not in the narrow sense of "education" or "training," but in the larger sense of aspects or features of a culture instilled by that teaching. Compare Burton L. Mack, *Myth of Innocence: Mark and Christian Origins* (Philadelphia, PA, 1988), pp. 159-60. See also Werner Jaeger, *Paideia: The Ideals of Greek Culture* (Oxford, 1986); or, *Early Christianity and Greek Paideia* (Oxford, 1961).

82   Doty, "Imaginings," pp. 96-103, suggests that careful attention should be paid to Paul's self-referential comments in his letters as a way of appreciating the intertextual nature of the letters. That appreciation leads to more insight if one looks at the collection of letters as a kind of "epistolary novel," the intertextuality of which permits the reader to fill in her half of the conversation with Paul with more competence.

83   In addition to, or perhaps as a supplement to, the interactional model mentioned above, socio-rhetorical criticism holds promise for helping us understand the dynamics of the argumentative process developed in the letters. See especially Vernon K. Robbins, *The Tapestry of Early Christian Discourse: Rhetoric, Society and Ideology* (London, 1996); and *Exploring the Texture of Texts: A Guide to Socio-Rhetorical Criticism* (Valley Forge, PA, 1996). In these two books he fully describes and illustrates the features and operation of the method.

Ernst F. Tonsing

FROM PRINCE TO DEMI-GOD: THE FORMATION AND EVOLUTION OF ALEXANDER'S PORTRAIT

Introducton

The portrait of Alexander the Great survives in many copies: in marble, bronze, and ivory statues, reliefs in gold and silver, on gem stones and especially coins, wall frescoes and miniature book illuminations, and even wood carvings and textiles.[1] Such images testify to the popularity of Alexander well into the Middle Ages, the Renaissance and as late as the nineteenth century. Alexander is the subject of works by such well-known artists as Verrocchio, Raphael, Giovanni Antonio Bazzi, Parmigianino, Pietro da Cortona, Ludovico Carracci, Paolo Veronese, Tiepolo, Poussin, Rembrant, Rubens, Watteau, Thorwaldsen, David, Delacroix, and Daumier.[2] Remarkable, too, is the variety of depictions of Alexander in legends. An illustration from a fourteenth-century French manuscript, *The Romance of Alexander,* Bodleian Library, Oxford, illustrates how the curiosity of Alexander led him to explore the depths of the seas in a glass bell-shaped bathyscope. He took a cock to indicate the days and nights, a cat whose breathing would purify the air, and a dog, so that if he got into difficulty he could kill it. It seems that the sea always gives up its dead, so the reason for the presence of the dog is that in case of mishap, the dead animal would guarantee that Alexander would be washed up alive on the shore along with it.[3]

In another popular legend, Alexander was inspired by the story of Bellerophon who tried to fly to the summit of Mt. Olympus on the winged horse, Pegasus. An early sixteenth-century woodcut by Hans Schäufelein recounts how Alexander tied two carnivorous birds (depicted in the woodcut as griffins) to a chariot, and holding up a horse's liver (shown as a decapitated corpse) on a pole, lured the beasts to fly up into the sky. He did not stay long in the air, for, in the story, an anthropomorphic bird, perhaps an angel, spoke to him and warned him of the dangers of such pride. In good Christian humility he returned immediately to earth.[4] The image of Alexander is evoked for other purposes, however. For example, a gold medallion of the

Renaissance pope, Paul the Third (1534 and 1549), shows that the Church could employ the image of Alexander against the Protestant reformers. The reverse of the medallion shows Alexander on his knees, worshipping the high priest Jaddus at the gates of Jerusalem. The implication of the scene is clear: the world, following the example of Alexander, must be subordinate to the Church of Rome.[5]

In Francesco Fontebasso's painting of the of *Alexander's Triumphant Entrance into Babylon*, 1761-62, one notes the political association between the Macedonian king and the artist's patron. Alexander holds a scepter, wears a cape over his armor, and on his head is a helmet with three feathers.[6] He is surrounded by his generals and rides into the city in a gold chariot pulled by two elephants. Painted for the French king, Louis the Fifteenth, Fontebasso's depiction of Alexander in all his grandeur was meant to recall to the mind of the viewer not only the ancient hero, but also the present ruler. Indeed, even the face of Alexander is sufficiently close to the idealized features of the monarch that the relationship between the two protagonists would not be missed.[7] In a Gobelin tapestry of the *Alexander's Entry into Babylon* designed by Charles Lebrun and Louis Testelin, 1664, Alexander is surveying his riches as well as his subjects. Elevated in his golden chariot and costumed in the finest materials, here, even more, in his elegance and grandeur, Alexander resembles Louis the Fourteenth. This tapestry, with its exotic architecture and grand scale, documents the purpose for which many portraits of Alexander were created, that is, the identification by a political ruler with the ancient hero's achievements.[8]

Portraits of Alexander

In view of the astonishing achievements of Alexander in the course of a short career, it is not surprising that the young son of a minor ruler in an obscure kingdom comes to be depicted by important European artists. But, one is prompted to ask, what did Alexander really look like, and how did the ancient artists who created so many objects take certain aspects of Alexander's physiogonomy and assemble, rearrange, disassemble and even add to them to create a portrait which could easily be recognized in the centuries following? Is it possible to reconstruct the steps by which the artists created a portrait which was able to evolve from that of a young prince of Macedonia to a successful general, a son of Zeus-Ammon and then to a demi-god? While others have discussed the political and social motivations in the transmission of the portrait of Alexander,[9] this study will concentrate on the creation of the elements of the portrayal and the additions which subsequent artists made to clarify the portrait. Furthermore, only the early part of the trajectory of the image will be reviewed, from the point of departure to the emergence of the portrait of Alexander in the Roman world.

This survey will examine only some the portraits themselves. But, the bases upon which even these portraits can be used in establishing the path of development are tentative, given the condition of some of the statues, the difficulty in dating them, and the fact that much of the evidence is late Hellenistic or Roman copies of earlier works which may or may not be faithful to the originals. Further, many of these may not even have been intended to depict Alexander, but, rather, of rulers who tried to associate their careers with this illustrious predecessor. Added to this is the accidental survival of these objects. Thus, the hazards are many in studying what works remain.[10]

The starting point is Alexander himself. There are only hints at Alexander's physical appearance. Arrian (ca. 90-145 CE) cites his great personal beauty,[11] and Plutarch (ca. 46-120 CE) criticizes Apelles who painted Alexander too dark-skinned, saying, "he was fair-skinned, with a ruddy tinge that showed itself especially upon his face and chest".[12] And Quintus Curtius Rufus (died 53 CE) writes that the Scythians were unimpressed with Alexander, "presumably because they judged a man's courage according to his physique and they thought Alexander's slight build entirely at odds with his reputation".[13] But these descriptions are late, and, almost independently of his physical characteristics, Alexander's portrait relies upon artistic, iconographic and even allegorical traditions for its creation and development.[14]

Alexander as Noble Prince

The earliest portraits of Alexander are those when he was crown prince in the palace of his father, Philip the Second, and his mother, Olympias. Created by court artists, his images attest not only to the style of portraiture acceptable to the court in Vergina but also to the self-image which the royal family held and the image which they wished others to view. There is no portrait of Philip the Second, the founder of the Macedonian Empire, on his own coins.[15] The only image is on one minted by the Roman Emperor Alexander Severus in the third century CE.[16] Philip is depicted in a corselet with Victories on the straps and breastplate. He wears a diadem and his hair and his beard are full and quite curly. His forehead has a pronounced bulge above the nose and his eyes are shaded. But, as will be seen below, these features may be components of the portrait of Alexander projected back to the father from a much later period and may not have been those of Philip himself.

87

A likely image of Philip is from the royal tombs at Vergina. Found as a relief decoration on the wooden couch or bier in the main chamber of the second tomb, this quite individualized ivory is small, only one and one-quarter inch high, and represents a bearded man with powerful, somewhat weary features.[17] Helping to identify the object is the treatment of the right eye. It appears to be deformed, and the right eyebrow shows a deep scar which cuts down into the eye socket, conforming to that which is known of an injury to the king himself.[18]

One reads of other depictions of Philip: a statue erected by the Athenians in front of the Odeum in the Agora after the battle of Chaeronea in gratitude for the mild terms of peace granted them by Philip;[19] the Philippeion at Olympia in which there were gold and ivory statues of Philip, his father Amyntas, and Alexander, sculptured by Leochares;[20] a portrait together with one of his son, Alexander, made by Chaereas (site unknown);[21] statues of Philip and Alexander mounted on a quadriga, sculpted by Euphranor;[22] a statue of Philip erected in the temple of Artemis at Ephesus;[23] and the statue which, along with the ones of the twelve Olympian gods, was being carried into the theater when Philip was assassinated.[24] Other statues certainly were made for Pella and Philippopolis, the city which he founded in 355.[25] However, all of these are now lost.

The mother of Alexander, Olympias, also has few portraits remaining. A gold medallion from Abukir, near Alexandria, Egypt, shows her profile. The drapery leaves exposed only her face and some hair, along with one hand which holds a scepter. In her hair is a diadem signifying her status as queen. However, this dates from the reign of the Roman emperor Caracalla in the early second century CE.[26] A late Roman Macedonian coin depicts the Olympias seated on a throne, her himation pulled over her head and left shoulder, and feeding a snake, her favorite pet.[27] On other coins she has the same carefully waved hair, noble profile, diadem and scepter, and, draped around her arm, a living snake.[28] But these images are late and reflect an association with the iconography of her son, Alexander.

Closer to Olympias' lifetime is a small ivory found in Vergina along with the one of Philip the Second. It shows the rather heavy features of a woman with the same wrinkled brow, deep-set eyes and prominent and full lips as Philip's. The latter features will be characteristic of the companion ivory portrait of Alexander which is discussed below.[29]

Later representations of Olympias appear on two large cameos in St. Petersburg. On one it is possible that both Alexander and his mother are depicted, although the features of Olympias show her much too young.[30] In the second cameo Olympias is alongside her son. A serpent coiling on the upper part of Alexander's helmet may refer to his divine ancestry and his miraculous birth, or even to the serpent which guided him through the Libyan desert to the Oracle of Ammon.[31] No longer extent is a chryselephantine statue of Olympias mentioned by Pausanias.[32] It had been exhibited in the Philippeion in Olympia, but was reinstalled in the Heraion.[33]

As son of the court it may be expected that Alexander would be treated by the same artists who produced images of his parents: Chaereas, Euphranor, and Leochares. The earliest known depiction of Alexander is the marble *Head of the Youthful Alexander* which was found near the Erechtheion and is now in the Acropolis Museum, Athens. Here Alexander is fifteen or sixteen year old, about the time he was a student of Aristotle, circa 340 BCE. He is shown as a serious, gentle, intelligent young hero. His hair stands up from his face with only a few strands falling down over his forehead and temples. The portrait seems to be closer to the style of Leochares and echoes the slender and youthful appearance of the *Apollo Belvedere*. Two other sculptures similar to this *Head* are known.[34]

The *Alexander Rondanini* statue was probably sculpted by Leochares about 338 BCE, after the battle of Chaeronea during which Alexander distinguished himself. It shows the powerful youth standing against a cuirass which identifies him as a general, his left foot upon a shield. This early statue is important in that it incorporates attributes which, once attached to the portrait of Alexander, became an iconographic "canon" for subsequent images of Alexander. These consist of the following: the figure is unclothed, which, in the iconography of Greek sculpture signifies that this is a hero.[35] The neck is bowed to the left while the head turns slightly in the other direction. The front of the hair, which is heavy and curly, stands up like a lion's mane, a feature called the *anastole* ["the rising"], and is peculiar to the portraits of Alexander. The curls descend to the sides and back. The eyes are deep-set and stare into the distance. The brow is extended out just above the beginning of the nose, and the nose is slightly bent. Beneath this, the mouth is determined and individual, and the chin is forward, resolute. In this statue these features are combined to give the portrait an intense expression.

In the same tradition as the *Alexander Rondanini* is an unfinished bust called the *Eubuleus* which was found in the Agora of Athens. Also possibly by Leochares, the attributes relating to the peculiar turn of the neck, the quantity of hair, the set of the brow, eyes, mouth and chin mentioned above are found here as well.[36] The massive head is turned slightly to the left,[37] and shows a quantity of hair above the gently protruding brow and strong chin. A great quantity of hair descends over the ears and down the back. The statue's large eyes gaze confidently ahead. Some ten replicas of this *Eubuleus* type have been found, all with the same huge mass of hair and wide face along with the other now-typical features.

The influence of the work of Leochares is to be seen in another image of *Alexander as Crown Prince*, a marble head now in Paris.[38] The youthful figure has the same abundant hair, the head turned slightly to the right, the forehead coming forward to meet the top of the nose, and the eyes rather large, staring forward. And similar to the Erechtheion head and the Rondanini statue is a coin issued later by Lysimachus which intensifies the wavy hair, the bulge of the brow, the nose and far-gazing eyes.[39]

There is a small ivory image of Alexander which was a companion to those of Philip the Second and Olympias found in the main chamber of the same royal tomb at Vergina.[40] Despite some damage, the one and three-eighths inch high miniature head reveals the essential features of the portrait of Alexander: the low, deeply grooved forehead, the aquiline nose, the deep-set eyes, the full lips, the long cheeks and prominent chin.

In the portraits of Alexander the hair is given special attention. For instance, nearly straight hair is to be seen in the so-called *Azara Herm*. Discovered by the eighteenth century Spanish ambassador José Nicolás Azara in Tivoli near Rome, it is probably a copy of a statue by Lysippus.[41] The head is turned partly to the right and the hair rises over the center of the forehead and falls alongside the temples in front of the ears. Conspicuous, also, are the slightly open mouth, the bulge over the nose and the eyes gazing into the distance. In the well-known mosaic of the *Battle of Alexander and Darius* found in the House of the Faun in Pompeii and now mounted on a wall in the National Museum in Naples, Alexander pursues Darius with a frightening ferocity.[42] Based upon a painting by the artist Philoxenos of Eretria, the battle of Issos is depicted at the decisive moment when Alexander races to attack the Persian king himself. Darius turns in his decorated chariot, wide-eyed in terror as his opponent rides forward. Alexander's head leans slightly forward, his mouth is set and his large eyes are fixed upon his foe. The mosaicist intensifies the countenance of the furious Alexander by showing straight hair streaming up and back in brown waves.

Neither the dates nor the artists of these portraits of Alexander can be assigned exactly, they do present a definite tradition of attributes for the portraits of Alexander as crown prince of Macedon, probably established by the same sculptors who were court artists for Philip the Second and Olympias. The attributes consist of the perfection and beauty of Alexander's features, which hint at immortality; youthfulness, a reference not only to his age at death but the strength and courage of his manhood; the nudity of a victorious athlete or a hero; the profusion of hair which is like a crown; the anastole on the forehead uncovering a broad head bulging in front to signify his great intelligence and comprehensive knowledge; the strong nose and chin, asserting his determination; and his enlarged eyes, read as not only surveying the vast domains which he conquered, but also his heavenly aspirations.[43] These formulae, which, in various configurations, enable the viewer to identify the portrait as that of Alexander and serve to proclaim that Alexander is more than an important man, that, as a prince, he belongs to a glorious lineage and family.[44] The "canon" of attributes is established already in the early stages of the development of the iconography of Alexander and serves as a core upon which later artists add certain elements further to clarify the image.

Alexander as Successor to Heroes

At the age of twenty, in 336 BCE, Alexander assumed the throne of Macedonia, and, continuing his father's efforts, soon he controlled much of the Greek territories as well. The victory over Darius at Issos in 333 BCE and Alexander's subsequent occupation of all of Asia Minor to Egypt and then Persia, concluding with the sack of Susa and Persepolis, secured his reputation as conqueror of Europe and Persia.

As king, Alexander chose only certain artists to make his images: Lysippus the sculptor, Apelles the painter, and Pyrgoteles the gem cutter. There is a statue which can be assigned to this period, the above mentioned *Azara Herm.*[45] Identifying it is an inscription written on the base: Αλεξανδρος Φιλιππου Μακε[δων] ["Alexander, Son of Philip of Macedon"].[46] Despite its poor condition, the character of the work of Lysippus is clear: the narrow proportions of the head; that one side is different from the other; that, like a lion's mane, the hair stands up over the forehead in the anastole; the subtleties of the movement of the muscles under the surface; and the general nervous interplay of the various parts of the face. Plutarch, writing more than four centuries after Alexander's death, probably had in mind a copy of this statue when he writes the following description: "The best likeness of Alexander which has been preserved for us is to be found in the statues sculpted by Lysippus, the only artist whom Alexander considered worthy to represent him. Alexander possessed a number of individual features which many of Lysippus' followers later tried to reproduce, for example the poise of the neck which was tilted slightly to the left, or a certain melting look in his eyes, and the artist exactly caught these peculiarities".[47]

The *Azara Herm* is likely a copy of the head of a statue by Lysippus of *Alexander with the Spear*, upon which Plutarch comments: "When Lysippus had finished the first statue of Alexander looking up with his face to the sky (as Alexander was wont to look with his neck slightly bent) he not improperly added to the pedestal the following lines: The statue seems to look to Zeus and say, 'Take thou Olympus; me let earth obey!'".[48] An epigram in *The Greek Anthology* has a different version: "Lysippus modeled Alexander's daring and his whole form. How great is the power of this bronze! The brazen king seems to be gazing at Zeus and about to say, 'I set Earth under my feet; thyself, Zeus, possess Olympus'".[49] The Louvre houses the so-called *Fouquet Alexander*, a statuette which reflects these descriptions. Found in lower Egypt, it is possibly modeled upon the one that Lysippus made for the city of Alexandria somewhere around the year 330 BCE when Alexander was in India.[50] Some of the features are obscured by damage, but enough remains to show that it depicts Alexander when he was some twenty-five years old, a bit younger than the *Azara Herm*. As in the herm, the head is long, turned sharply to its right, with the neck stretched out, but, at the same time, bent to its left. The left arm is extended horizontally and possibly held a spear. The right hand points down towards the earth which Alexander had conquered by his weapon, just as Plutarch recalled. The uplifted and turned right heel and the twisting movement in space animates the statuette in much the same way as other works by Lysippus. The J. Paul Getty Villa, Malibu, has a variant of the Lysippus' *Alexander with the Lance* from the second century BCE. The small statue is conceived frontally and is elegantly modeled and proportioned. The separately carved arms are missing. One would have held a lance, the other would have pointed down along the side of the statue. While the hair is full, it lacks the lion-like rising and mass of other portraits.[51] In these last two statues Alexander is depicted nude, the attribute of the heroes, but also of gods. However, Alexander is not yet a god. He employed the powers of his wit and strength to obtain on earth what Zeus ruled on high.

The great conqueror and king is also depicted with his horse, Bucephalus, in a bronze statuette found in Herculaneum, now in Naples. It is possibly a copy of the central statue from a group erected in Dion, below Mt. Olympus, which Alexander himself commissioned. Here Lysippus depicted the twenty-five companions of Alexander who fell in the first decisive battle on the river Granicus in 334 BCE. Metellus Macedonicus took the original statue of *Alexander on Bucephalus* to Rome in 146 BCE where this replica may have been created.[52] The rudder which extends down from the figure is a reference to the site of the battle, and the scarf over Alexander's corselet indicates that he is a general. He has a broad fillet in his hair, but it is not the diadem, which was adopted by Alexander after the death of Darius in 330 BCE.[53] The hair of Alexander is only slightly curled, almost straight, and it is tousled as the wind sweeps it back. His features are youthful, depicting a twenty-two-year-old warrior.

A bronze statuette found in Begram in Afghanistan depicts a rider who has the youthful characteristics typical of other sculptures by Lysippus.[54] Here, in a portrait much like previous images of Alexander, the rider wears Greek defensive armor and the leather greaves of the Macedonians. A scarf covers the cuirass indicating his rank as general.[55] The hair is straight and exhibits the usual anastole like other portraits of Alexander. He is presented as the noble prince and triumphant soldier whose deeds evoke astonishment and admiration. The portraits of Alexander created as he conquered Europe and Persia advance the depiction by bringing to it the iconographic attributes of equipment of a military man and general, and by emphasizing the might of this successor to heroes.

Alexander as Son of Zeus-Ammon

Lysippus views Alexander as a conqueror who won by the spear, and as a man, not a god. But, even at an early date two court artists move to a new level in the development of the iconography of Alexander in which the portraits assimilate aspects of divinity. The first attributes consist of the thunderbolt and goatskin aegis of Zeus. In St. Petersburg there is a gem cut from carnelian which depicts Alexander as Zeus, accompanied by the eagle, holding the thunderbolt in his right hand and the protective aegis in the left.[56] Plutarch describes the contrast between the intentions of Lysippus and that of the court painter, Apelles: "Lysippus the sculptor blamed the painter Apelles for drawing Alexander's picture with a thunderbolt in his hand. He himself had represented Alexander holding a spear, which was natural and proper for him as a weapon, the glory of which time would not rob him".[57] Apelles had painted this image for the temple of Artemis in Ephesus, and it was notable in that the finger of Alexander's hand seemed to project out from the painting as did the thunderbolt. The gem may be an early Hellenistic copy of this painting. The aegis dates the gem after 330 BCE, after Alexander had been deified, but the diadem and straight hair look back to earlier depictions.[58]

The third of the court artists to Alexander, Pyrgoteles the gem cutter, may have influenced this carnelian image. The ancient writers considered him as excellent as Lysippus and Apelles. Pliny wrote: "Alexander was presented with singular excellence in all his likenesses; so that in all statues, pictures and engraved gems he appears with the same vigorous aspect of a most intrepid warrior, the same genius of a mighty hero, the same beauty and freshness of youth, the same noble expansion of forehead".[59]

The next attribute was that of horns. According to Plutarch, Alexander visited the shrine of Ammon at Silwa in Libya during his visit to Egypt. Perhaps acknowledging Alexander as pharaoh by the usual title for the ruler of Egypt, the high priest greeted Alexander as "Son of Ammon". As Ammon was equated in the Greek mind with Zeus, Alexander took this to mean a prophecy that he was the "Son of Zeus".[60] Subsequently, the ram's horn frequently curls behind his ear in the portraits on coins.[61] Horns of animals had previously been employed in the representations of the gods. The bull was a common manifestation of the god Dionysus and its horns often projected from the sides of the heads in depictions of both male and female rulers.[62] Goat horns, small, high and close together on the top of the head also appear, and were associated with the Macedonian ruling family because of its origins in the "Goat City" of Aigai.[63] But ram's horns appear regularly only with Alexander's images, with the exception of the coin of Arsinoë the Second who is shown with a small ram's horn curling down behind her ear.[64]

While in Persia an incident occurred which showed Alexander's change in attitude concerning the relationship between him and his army. With the size of the conquered territories, and, consequently, the shortage of man-power, Alexander accepted Persian soldiers into his forces.[65] While to his Macedonian troops he was the first among peers, to the recently conquered Persians he was their king. Prostration (*proskynesis*) was the manner in which the Persians demonstrated their submission to their rulers, and to refuse to do so before Alexander meant that he was not a true monarch. At Bactria Alexander suddenly demanded prostration not only of the Persians but also of his own warriors. However, these veteran soldiers resented being placed on the same level as the Persians and interpreted prostration as worship of Alexander. After his Macedonian soldiers resisted, Alexander relented by allowing his Macedonians to ignore this order.[66]

With the subjugation of Persia, the Macedonian troops thought the campaigns at an end. Not so, Alexander. As he now considered himself Lord of Asia, he sought to conquer the whole of the Persian empire. His troops grumbled, friends betrayed him and were executed. Finally, Alexander pushed on to India, founding cities in the remote regions of Bactria and Sogdiana which were to be outposts of Greek civilization.[67]

Another attribute was that of an unusual helmet. Alexander already long had been identified with Heracles through his family and nation.[68] This hero was especially attractive to the Macedonians in that he had fought thieves and barbarians and thus won his way to heaven. The Macedonian rulers minted coins with the hero as a coin type. For example, on a tetradrachm minted in Sicyon about 330 BCE, Heracles wears the lion's head as his helmet.[69] But except for the heavy features and large curls of the hair, the image of the hero could just as well be that of Alexander himself, given the presence of the attributes of Alexander's portrait described above. On this and similar coins one sees the unruly hair, the anastole, the prominent forehead, bulging eyes, nose, chin, all of these being part of the iconography of Alexander by this time.[70]

While Alexander believed himself under the divine protection of Heracles and Zeus-Ammon, it is uncertain, however, whether he sponsored these images on his coins or simply allowed these depictions. Alexander's successors, however, followed Apelles and Pyrgoteles rather than Lysippus, and the portraits of Alexander retained the lion's scalp as a helmet and the ram's horns behind the ears.[71]

Alexander as Demi-God

At Alexander's death in 323 BCE, the successors, or "Diadochi," were eager to appropriate the realms and honors of their illustrious predecessor. At first it was enough to declare their association with the general. Thus, when Abdalonymos, ruler of Sidon, who had been made king by Alexander himself, commissioned a sarcophagus for himself, it depicted Alexander in hunting scenes and the battles between the Greeks and the Persians.[72] These representations of Alexander are similar to the coin minted in Sidon discussed above. One can recognize Alexander by the elongated cheeks, the full lips and rounded chin, and the large, radiant eyes. There is little emotion, and, despite the movement of the horses and gestures, the scenes are idealized and elegant. In one scene Alexander wears the lion's scalp as his helmet just as did Heracles, and as depicted on the tetradrachm minted in Sidon in 330 BCE.[73]

But in contemporary portraits, Alexander becomes more than a mighty warrior and defeater of the kings of the earth. On a marble head found in Sparta, now in the Boston Museum of Fine Arts, Alexander appears as Heracles. There are the swelling of the brow, large eyes, elongated cheeks, full lips, and short chin, all marks of the depiction of Alexander, but the identification with the mythical, deified hero is more strongly asserted.[74]

This "canon" of attributes of Alexander is augmented by his successors with the iconography of various deities. These include the symbols not only of Zeus, Ammon and Heracles, but even Helios. Based upon the colossal bronze statue which once stood in the port, one of the "seven wonders" of the ancient world, a silver didrachm of Rhodes from the third or second century BCE shows the spiked, radiant crown of Helios surrounding a head which is turned somewhat to the right of full front. But, the broad face, wide eyes and anastole is that of Alexander.[75]

In India Alexander became more and more possessed by romantic notions. Thus, when he was near the city of Nysa he discovered ivy growing. He declared the mountain upon which he had found the ivy sacred to Dionysus and asserted that the god had preceded him to India.[76] When the Hellenistic rulers themselves assumed the mantle of Alexander they also donned his image. This consisted of the expected marks of the portrait of Alexander: the bulge in the forehead, the heavy eyebrows and wide eyes, the high cheekbones, the full lips and the strong, rounded chin. But, in addition to these, on a coin of Ptolemy the First, Satrap of Egypt beginning 318 BCE, the ruler adds to the ram's horns of Ammon the elephant's head of the god, Dionysus.[77] This head is worn as a helmet with the trunk curling back and upwards on top, the tusks extending forward above the brows, and the elephant's ears hanging down behind the head. The elephant skin also recalls Alexander's triumphs in India, and high above the forehead but underneath the tusks of the elephant is a ribbon. It encircles his brow horizontally, more like the fillet of Dionysus than the royal diadem. Yet, the hint of a diadem is preserved in the fluttering ends of the cloth. Below the neck are the entwined serpents of the aegis of Zeus.

During the period of the Diadochi there are more developments in the iconography of Alexander. Alexander is not just associated with the gods Zeus, Ammon, etc., by bearing their attributes. Rather, he himself appears as a god, or, at least, a demi-god. An image of Alexander on coins issued by Lysimachus, King of Thrace, 306-281 BCE, has the horn of Ammon curling around the ear and the diadem worn in the customary fashion, descending from nearly the crown of the head to behind the neck, issuing in fluttering ends which are almost entangled in the great curls of the hair. All the features of Alexander are present, but the eyes are greatly enlarged, indicating god-like intelligence.[78] Absent is the human Alexander emphasized in the portraits by Lysippus. Here, the divinization in the depiction of Alexander has progressed to a great extent, the legacy of the gem cutter, Pyrgoteles.[79]

This can be seen also in the only full-length portrait of Alexander from this period, a statuette found in Priene one-third life-size, of which just the upper part remains. Created about 300 BCE, it depicts a muscular athlete, the head turned towards its right.[80] The hair is only roughly cut but is full like the other images of Alexander. The profile shows the features already seen on the coins of Lysimachus: the bulge of the brow, the heavy eyelids and large eyes, full lips and short, rounded jaw. The left hand was found separately and probably held a sword.[81] All these features combine in this statue to impress upon the viewer that here is no longer a mere human. Alexander is now represented as a demi-god, not just to be identified with his mythical forebear, Heracles, but a deified hero. Alexander now is worthy to bear the attributes of deity: the thunderbolt of Zeus, the ram's horns of Ammon, the solar rays of Helios and even the elephant skull of Dionysus.

Alexander as Patron of Hellenistic Rulers

Alexander's friend and general, Ptolemy the First, became satrap of Egypt upon the death of Alexander, and then in 306 BCE, king. His capital, Alexandria, later became a showplace for the Greek arts and sciences, especially with the founding of the museum and its large library. To secure his preeminence, Ptolemy stole the body of Alexander as it was on its way to Macedonia, taking it first to Memphis, and then a few years later to Alexandria. Placing the embalmed corpse into a glass coffin, he established a cult of Alexander and statues of the hero were set up in various sanctuaries.[82]

A small, marble head found in Egypt and now in the Museum of Stuttgart comes from this period and illustrates the accretion of the new elements in the portrait of Alexander. These consist of further idealizing the face and making the overall impression more monumental.[83] Falling within the Praxitelian tradition, these traits are seen in the rounding out of the structure of the head and the softened, delicate, languid appearance of the face. The lion-like hair is gone, the anastole barely present, the twist of the neck only slight, and, in general, the specific portrait characteristics of Alexander reviewed above tend to be lost. Yet, seen in relation to the previous images of Alexander, the impressive brows, nose and eyes, and the elongated cheeks and hair mass identify it as the likeness of Alexander. A large head from Alexandria now in the British Museum incorporates the new elements of the portrait: the bending of the neck and the head, the soft features, languid eyes, broad face, gently waving hair, and the overall idealization combined with monumentality.[84] And another large Alexandrian head, now in Cleveland, Ohio, is similar, but even softer and almost lethargic. The mouth is opened to suggest yearning, the eyes gaze out, as if to the heights of Mt. Olympus.[85] There are also traces of red in the hair, evidence that the curls were originally reddish blond.[86] These three statues all are meant to instill wonder and awe in the viewer.

Through the third and into the second century BCE the generalization of the features of Alexander as a deity continued. This can be seen on a coin from Cos, minted about 200 BCE, showing Alexander in three-quarter view, wearing the lion's scalp upon his head.[87] The broad face and bulging brows, nose and eyes are distorted, given the small surface and low relief upon which the artist worked. But the image is still impressive. More successful are a gold ring in the Metropolitan Museum of Art, New York, with Alexander in three-quarter view and the same iconographic features, the lion's skin, wide eyes and broad face,[88] and a number of coins, such as one minted about 250 to 200 BCE now at the Boston Museum of Fine Arts.[89] In these, Alexander is shown in profile, wearing the lion's scalp, with the divinized features as noted above. In the deification of Alexander the specific features of his canonical portrait tend to be suppressed by the idealization of the image, and attributes of other deities are emphasized. For example, the so-called *Alexander Aigiochos* bronze statuette from Alexandria now in London has Alexander draped to the knees with the apotropaic aegis of Zeus.[90] And another bronze statuette from Egypt kept in the Louvre also shows Alexander dressed in the aegis.[91] But in all of these representations the tendency is to generalize the image, to soften the hair, the upturned eyes and broad face, giving these early Hellenistic, Alexandrian portraits a dreamy, divine appearance.

The second century BCE saw the increasing influence of Rome and changes in the status of the various Greek states. The Ptolemies in Egypt were weakened to such an extent that they had to accept the Roman senate as warden. Antiochus the Third was defeated in the battle of Magnesia in 190 BCE, thus removing Syrian domination in Asia. However, Bactria increased in strength in Central Asia and even ruled the Indian Punjab for a time. The Attalids sided with the Romans, and were awarded with greater territories and power.[92] In all of these states, the archetype and standard for authority remained Alexander, so it is not surprising that his portraits continued to evolve.

Pergamum was the center of artistic activity as Alexandria decreased in its influence. A marble head found in Pergamun and now in the Archaeological Museum in Istanbul is thought to come from the same time as the construction of the great altar of Eumenes the Second (197-159 BCE).[93] Majestic, yet poignant, his brow is furrowed, his eyes lie in shadows, and the look is of sadness recalling the difficult campaign in India, the insurrections of his troops, the arduous return through the desert, and the tragic deaths of his friends. The statue is given straight hair originating in the anastole, similar to the *Azara Herm*. The countenance still holds the passionate drive which took Alexander to the very edges of the known world, but it is full of pathos, expressing the profound emotions depicted in the so-called "baroque" Hellenistic art. Ambition and longing here are moderated by a sense of grief.

The origin of the passionate, romantic conception of Alexander may have been Lysippus with his use of the "lion's mane" and twist of the neck, but this is remodeled in a purely Hellenistic manner. A Roman bronze statuette found in Grado near Aquileia in Northern Italy, reflects this tradition.[94] The figure probably held a spear in the left hand and perhaps a sword and scabbard in the right. Remarkable is the dramatic turn of the head to the left, the sway of the body, the feet in a walking position, and the left leg drawn considerably back from the right. Another example of this emotional depiction of Alexander is a small bust found in Egypt, now in the Brooklyn Museum.[95] An *akrolith*, that is, a statue with a stone head to be attached to a body of a different material, the head and one shoulder are of alabaster. It comes from the second century BCE and probably was created in Alexandria. The hair is full, wavy, ascending in the front like a lion's mane and descending to the back in curls. The upturned eyes are large and the mouth is slightly open, giving the statue a sense of passionate longing.

Also within this tradition is a marble statue of a youthful Alexander from Pella.[96] It shows him nude, gracefully turning the torso as he draws his left leg back a little and raises his right arm forward. He lifts his head and turns it to the right, and on the head is a band and two small, upright horns. These attributes of Pan, the companion of the god Dionysos, thus associate Alexander with the horned, goat-footed god of forests, flocks and shepherds.[97]

A heroic bronze head of Alexander from a private collection in Switzerland, said to have been found at Boubon (Bubon) in Lycia in a building dedicated to the Roman emperors, merges the splendor of the Lysippian model with the baroque passion of the Pergamum.[98] It seems to have been broken from a full-length statue, and the eyes, now lost, were inset with other materials. With the twist of the neck, the wrinkled forehead and pensive face, it reflects the romantic, middle Hellenistic productions. The expression is longing, sad, the embodiment of tragedy.

Many examples of the depiction in Hellenistic Asiatic traditions can be cited. For example, a marble head of the last quarter of the third century BCE from the excavations at Olympia also possesses characteristics of the Pergamum style.[99] Although the anastole is absent, the lion-like hair is suggested by its length and the thickness of the curls. While badly damaged, it is yet expressive, and the overall expression is animated, keen, tense. A large marble head of the late Hellenistic period, nearly twelve inches high (.30 m.), said to be from the Yannitsa area, now in the Pella Museum, depicts the heroic Alexander.[100] The slightly open lips, deep-set eyes and bend of the neck to the left are all from the canon of the portraits, but are brought together in a convincing image of the deified hero.

One of the most impressive sculptures of Alexander the Great is to be found at the J. Paul Getty Villa, Malibu.[101] Created shortly after the death of Alexander, it departs from the tradition of the court sculptor Lysippus to give an idealized portrait of the hero. Its larger-than-life size reinforces the idea that this is not just a human being but a deity, and not just Alexander but the god-Alexander. Found along with this head of Alexander was that of Hephaistion, the companion of Alexander, identified from a votive relief of about 300 BCE in Thessaloniki,[102] and a portrait head of a woman, possibly Alexander's wife, the Persian princess, Roxane.[103] Together with a group of other persons and animals, seem to have been part of a funerary group dedicated some time after the year 300 BCE.[104] The Hephaistion figure offers a contrast with the monumental treatment of the portrait of Alexander. The size of the head is slightly smaller, ten and one-quarter inches (27 cm.). The neck is straight forward, and the head, while idealized, is a series of gently rounded planes. There is no anastole. Rather, the top of the head is covered by tight curls. The visage is calm and focused. The female head, too, is smaller, a little over ten inches and one-eighth inches (25.7 cm.). The neck is long and inclines slightly to the statue's left. The head is almost oval and the nearly symmetrical features are idealized. The hair is carefully plaited in tresses which are gathered up in a cylinder and then braided in a coil around the top. In contrast, the statue of Alexander is more massive, nearly eleven inches (27.5 cm.) in height, and has billowing hair parted in the middle and flowing down on either side of the face. The bulging brow, and grave, deep-set eyes, the parted lips, the turn of the head to the left, and the strong, concentrated gaze are the usual attributes of Alexander. But the greater size and mass in contrast to the attendant male, female and animal figures set him apart from the other statues in the group.

The artists during the Hellenistic period created images of Alexander to maintain that he was more than extraordinary, more than heroic, that he was to be regarded as a powerful patron. The head and face are further generalized, and the emotional qualities of the features are modified with either a languid softness or "baroque" passion. The attributes of various deities, such as the aegis of Zeus or even the horns of Pan, are given greater prominence. Alexander could now serve as an able protector for his political successors

Alexander's Portrait in the Early Roman Period

Rome became ever more dominant during the first century BCE, and had only one last contest with the Hellenistic rulers. Mithridates the Sixth, Eupator, of Pontus, captured Paphlagonia and Bithynia in 100-99 BCE, but he was compelled by the Roman senate to retreat. Then with the help of the Greek cities he commenced his program to liberate all of Asia Minor from the tyranny of the Romans just as Alexander had removed the Persians. Throughout Asia Minor Mithridates was acclaimed as a new Alexander and was celebrated with statues and coins. A large marble head of Mithridates is in the Louvre. While it is recognizable as a portrait of the ruler, the lion-skin helmet, the bulging forehead and the long, tangled sideburns (the only part of his hair that shows) are attributes taken from the portrait of Alexander.[105] Imitating the coins of Lysimachus, Mithridates' coins depict him with the head uplifted, eyes staring into the sky, the hair rising in front in the anastole and falling in luxuriant curls down the sides and back.[106] In other portraits the monarch wears on his head the lion scalp as he tries to portray himself as the reembodiment of Alexander.[107]

The Roman general, Pompey, conquered Mithridates in 66 BCE and, as did his opponent, he tried to imitate Alexander. He assumed the anastole hair style, wrinkled his brow, and would glance up like Alexander.[108] Other Romans, too, assumed the image of Alexander. Aesillas (93-92 BCE), quaestor of Macedonia, Alexander's birthplace, is shown on a coin which magnifies the attributes of Alexander—the thick, exaggerated curls which begin with the anastole rising on the forehead and hair falling along the face and neck—so that no one can miss the resemblance.[109]

From this period is a well-preserved, early Roman head in the Capitoline Museum in Rome.[110] It has the anastole hairstyle with curls descending on the side of the face, the high forehead, wide eyes, ample nose, slightly open lips, long cheeks and strong chin. The turn of the neck and head to the left is also overstated. However, as a whole, the impression is that of detachment and reserve, a thoroughly Roman presentation. As a product of the capital rather than of a Roman province, it reveals the attraction of the Romans for this almost mythical hero whose feats, like those of Heracles, transcended the human into the realm of divinity.

As state after state became subordinate to Rome in the centuries before the turn of the era, and with the death of Cleopatra, the last Hellenistic monarch of Egypt, in 30 BCE, Rome considered itself the rightful heir of Alexander's empire. With this mantle, Rome also adopted Alexander's program to fuse all peoples into one family, all dependents of one rule. Thus, Augustus was acclaimed "friend of Alexander" by Strabo. It was noted that he even had Alexander's image engraved on his signet ring.[111] As Augustus' patron, the Macedonian hero became patron not only of the imperial family but of Rome itself.

The Portrait of Alexander Following the Augustan Period

In the first three centuries CE Alexander's portraits change more rapidly according to fashion. Where shortly before and during the early first century CE the models relied upon the classical works of Phidias and Praxiteles, the Flavian era (69-96 CE) tended to imitate the romantic Hellenistic models. There is a large head which was found in Tarsus, now in the Ny Carlsberg Glyptotek, Copenhagen, which has the familiar anastole hair shape above the forehead, and curly hair framing the face and descending down the sides.[112] The face is broad, and the width of the nose adds to the impressiveness. In the

Roman portraiture the features of the human Alexander become exaggerated in order to display Alexander as a divine protector of the state.

Continuing this movement toward monumentality, a Roman bronze statuette in the Cabinet des Médailles, Bibliothèque Nationale, Paris, depicts a seated Alexander.[113] Also of the Flavian period, it has been restored (the throne is new while the base is ancient), but the restoration is probably correct with the right hand holding a lance and the left a sword and scabbard. The enthroned Alexander is noble, majestic and yet pensive. There is no mistaking the significance of the statuette: Alexander is at once the hero whose might conquered nations and also the ruler of the earth, one to be ranked with Zeus. This statue may be related to a statue of Alexander enthroned as Zeus which Pausanias saw at Olympia.[114]

The Hadrianic period (117-138 CE) sees the resurgence of classicism and a suppression of the sentimental emotionalism of the former age. This is represented in an even more impressive statue, a larger-than-life porphyry head in the Louvre.[115] The hair is less nervous, falling down in controlled waves, the turn of the neck more natural, and the face less organic, made up of planes joined by angular contours. The eyebrows are sharply modeled, the lips isolated from the cheeks with deep grooves, and the whole highly polished. The overall impression is that of cool reserve, of abstraction.

Reflecting the growing cult of Alexander, a gold medallion found at Aboukir, Egypt, depicts Alexander in three-quarters view, wearing a cuirass and carrying a spear and shield.[116] It shows the anastole, straight hair parted at the middle, creases in the forehead, the impressive nose and eyes, full lips and aggressive chin, all typical of the portraits of Alexander. However, this is the image of the Severan Emperor Caracalla, sole ruler from 212 to 217 CE. It is clear that the artist is deliberately identifying Caracalla with Alexander, placing the emperor on the same divine heights as that occupied by his elected ancestor.[117] Another medallion from Tarsus also reveals the growing cult of Alexander. The gold medal was possibly a prize for victory in the Olympian festival of 242-243 CE celebrated in the presence of the emperor Gordian the Third.[118] On it, with hair streaming back and down along the neck and wearing the lion's scalp of Heracles, Alexander exhibits the qualities of grandeur, glory and divinity. His detached, distant stare reinforces these attributes. Other depictions of Alexander are to be found in the time of Gallienus (260-268 CE) and Diocletian (284-305 CE), embossed on silver plate, carved in gemstones, and embroidered on tunics and cloaks. Trebellius Pollio writes in the late third or early fourth century CE, "It is said, that those who wear the likeness of Alexander carved in either gold or silver are aided in all that they do".[119]

In the mid-fourth century Alexander is again invoked as partner in ruling the empire. But this time, it is the Christian emperor Constantine who calls upon the hero to accompany him on a medal. Constantine appears in front, and alongside him is Alexander, wearing the radiate crown of the sun god, Helios.[120] And if one looks closely, the unruly anastole emerges ever so slightly. The rest of the visages, except for the aquiline nose of Alexander, are matched perfectly—large eyes for eyes, prominent eyebrows for eyebrows, full lips for lips, and resolute chin for chin. In nearly everything, they are identical, the Christian ruler and the ancient, pagan hero.

Conclusions

It is now only a small step from the ancient to the modern world when a king as illustrious as Constantine finds in the image of Alexander not just inspiration, but identity. The ancient Alexander-Heracles-Zeus-Ammon-Helios now becomes the "Sun King" Louis the Fourteenth. *Alexander's Entry into Babylon* of the Gobelin tapestry designed by Charles Lebrun and Louis Testelin in 1664, mentioned at the beginning of this article, was not only a grand pretext to depict the ruler in ancient splendor and an impressive presentation of his might and wealth, but it was intended to command reverence, just as if one was actually standing before the godlike Louis himself. The impact of this weaving would not have been possible without the creation by ancient artists of a portrait that not only bore certain attributes which enabled it to be recognized easily, but which also communicated the ideas of a noble prince and an heroic general whose ancestry, deeds and impact were nothing less than divine.

The steps by which the portrait of Alexander evolved from the image of the young son of a minor ruler in northern Greece to the majestic depictions in nearly all of the artistic media after Alexander's time can be thus reconstructed: the portrait early acquired luxurious, heroic hair worn like a crown, a bulging forehead and large eyes revealing surpassing intelligence and communication with heaven, a wide nose, full lips and strong chin expressing resolve and boldness, and superhuman strength encased in timeless youth. To these were added the familiar attributes of divinity—the lion's scalp reflecting Alexander's heritage from Heracles, the ram's horns from Zeus-Ammon, the elephant's scalp from Dionysus and the radiant crown of Helios. And, finally, came pathos and monumentalty. These attributes constituted an iconographical "vocabulary" which the ancient artists combined to create a portrait which, once firmly established, propelled the image of Alexander into a trajectory which continues to inspire legends and portraits today. "Alexander's Revenge" indeed!

Notes:

1   Catalogues of works depicting Alexander are to be found in Katerina
    Rhomiopoulou, et al., *The Search for Alexander: An Exhibition* (Boston, MA,
    1980) (hereafter cited as *Search*), and, Andrew Stewart, *Faces of Power:
    Alexander's Image and Hellenistic Politics* (Berkeley, CA, 1993).

2   Nicholas Yalouris, "Alexander and His Heritage," in *Search*, p. 19.

3   *Alexander in Submarine*, illumination from a fourteenth-century French
    manuscript of *The Romance of Alexander*, Bodleian Library, Oxford University,
    Ms. No. 264, folio 50a, ibid., fig. 5.

4   *The Ascent of Alexander*, woodcut by Hans Schäufelein (ca. 1480-1539), in the
    Royal Library at Windsor Castle, ibid., fig. 4.

5   Gold medallion of Pope Paul the Third, ibid., fig. 8. Alexander's dismounting and
    bowing before the Jewish High Priest is described in *The Chronicle of George the
    Monk* 1.19, in *Legends of Alexander the Great*, trans. and ed. Richard Stoneman
    (London, 1994), pp. 25-28.

6   This seems to be a reference to the South American Inca rulers who were
    identified by these three plumes.

7   *Alexander's Entry into Babylon*, painting by Francesco Fontebasso, in Bourg-en-
    Bresse, Musée de l'Ain, ibid., fig. 7.

8   *Alexander's Entry into Babylon*, Gobelin tapestry designed by Charles Lebrun and
    Louis Testelin, 1664, at the Mobilier National, Paris, ibid., fig. 6.

9   For example, Stewart, *Faces of Power*.

10 The dangers in the identification and dating of Alexander's images is reviewed in
    Stewart, *Faces of Power*, chapter 2.

11 Arrian, *The Campaigns of Alexander* 7.28, trans. Aubrey de Sélincourt (London,
    1971).

12 Plutarch, *Alexander* 7.4 in *The Age of Alexander. Nine Greek Lives by Plutarch*, trans.
    Ian Scott-Kilvert with an Introduction by G. T. Griffith (London, 1973), p. 255.

13 Quintus Curtius Rufus, *History of Alexander* 7.9 in *The History of Alexander*,
    trans. John Yardley (London, 1984), p. 168.

14 John Onians, *Art and Thought in the Hellenistic Age: The Greek World View 350-
    50 BC* (London, 1979), pp. 40 ff.

15 Otto Mørkholm, *Early Hellenistic Coinage from the Accession of Alexander to the
    Peace of Apamea (336-186 B.C.)* (Cambridge, England, 1991), pp. 41 ff.

16 Philip the Second, Medallion from Tarsus, Margarete Bieber, *Alexander*, fig. 1;
    Margarete Bieber, *The Portraits of Alexander the Great*, Proceedings of the
    American Philosophical Society 93/5 (1949), fig. 1; G. M. A. Richter, *The
    Portraits of the Greeks*, abridged and revised ed. R. R. R. Smith (Ithaca, NY, 1984),
    fig. 184, p. 224; M. B. Sakellariou, ed., *Macedonia. 4000 Years of Greek History
    and Civilization* (Athens, 1988), fig. 74.

17 Ivory of Philip the Second from Vergina, Rhomiopoulou, *Search*, color plate 32,
    catalogue no. 170; Sakellariou, *Macedonia*, fig. 79; Manolis Andronikos, *The
    Royal Graves at Vergina* (Athens, 1978), figs. 16a-b, 20; Richter, *Portraits*, p. 224.

Richter adds a question mark after her entry concerning this ivory head indicating some uncertainty as to the identification of the tomb's occupant. Stewart, *Faces of Power*, pp. 45-46, dates this and the two following ivory portraits of Olympias and Alexander to half a generation later.

[18] Manolis Andronikos, "The Royal Tombs at Vergina: A Brief Account of the Excavations," in *Search*, p. 34.

[19] Pausanias, *Greece* 1.9.4 in *Guide to Greece*, trans. Peter Levi (London, 1971); Richter, *Portraits*, p. 224.

[20] Pausanias, *Greece* 5.20.10; Richter, *Portraits*, p. 224.

[21] Pliny, *Natural History* 34.75; Richter, *Portraits*, p. 224..

[22] Ibid., 34.78; Richter, *Portraits*, p. 224.

[23] Arrian, *Campaigns* 1.17.11; Richter, *Portraits*, p. 224.

[24] Bieber, *Alexander*, p. 19; a mosaic from Baalbek depicting the birth of Alexander shows Philip as a young man dressed in a long-sleeved tunic and chlamys, but this is a late mosaic with limited value in reconstructing the portrait of Philip, Richter, *Portraits*, p. 224.

[25] Bieber, *Alexander*, p. 20._

[26] Gold Medallion from Abukir, dated to the reign of the Severan emperor Caracalla, 212-217 CE; Bieber, *Alexander*, fig. 2; Bieber, *Portraits*, fig. 2.; Richter, *Portraits*, p. 225, fig. 185; Rhomiopoulou, *Search*, color plate 5a, catalogue no. 10.

[27] Bieber, *Alexander*, p. 22.

[28] Ibid., pp. 22-23; Richter, *Portraits*, p. 225.

[29] Ivory of Olympias from Vergina, Andronikos, *Royal Graves*, figs. 18, 20; Sakellariou, *Macedonia*, fig. 77; Richter, *Portraits*, p. 225, omits a reference to the ivory head, probably questioning it as she does the head of Philip. See also note 17.

[30] Alexander and Olympias, Cameo in St. Petersburg, Bieber, *Alexander*, fig. 3; Bieber, *Portraits*, fig. 3. This cameo is dated to the Julio-Claudian period in Stewart, *Faces of Power*, p. 51.

[31] Bieber, *Alexander*, fig. 4; Bieber, *Portraits*, fig. 4.

[32] Pausanias, *Greece* 5.20.10; Richter, *Portraits*, p. 225.

[33] Pausanias, *Greece* 5.17.4; Richter, *Portraits*, p. 225.

[34] *Head of Youthful Alexander*, Acropolis Museum, Athens, Bieber, *Alexander*, p. 25; Bieber, *Portraits*, figs. 5-6; Stewart, *Faces of Power*, color plate 1, fig. 5, pp. 106-12, 421 (bibliography); Jean Charbonneaux, *Hellenistic Art (330-50 B.C.)* (New York, NY, 1973), fig. 219; Kostas Papaioannou, *The Art of Greece* (New York, NY, 1989), fig. 634; Richter, *Portraits*, no. 188, p. 226.

[35] *Alexander Rondanini*, Munich, probably by Leochares; Bieber, *Alexander*, pp. 25-26., fig. 8; Bieber, *Portraits*, figs. 9-11; Stewart, *Faces of Power*, figs. 10, 12, pp. 113-17, 429 (bibliography).

[36] *Eubuleus*, unfinished bust found in the Agora of Athens, Bieber, *Alexander*, fig. 10a-b; Stewart, *Faces of Power*, pp. 114, 117, figs. 13, 20; Charbonneaux, *Hellenistic Art*, fig. 212.

[37] The alternative direction of the turn of the head apparently means little according to Bieber, *Alexander*, p. 9.

[38] *Alexander as Crown Prince*, probably third century BCE, Louvre catalogue no. Ma 3499 (on deposit from the Musée Guimet, Paris), Bieber, *Alexander*, fig. 11a-b; Bieber, *Portraits*, figs. 7-8; Richter, *Portraits*, pp. 226-27, fig. 191; Stewart, *Faces of Power*, pp. 251-52, 426 (bibliography), fig. 85.

[39] Coin of Lysimachus, minted in Magnesia on the Maeander, ca. 300 BCE, Newell Collection, Bieber, *Alexander*, fig. 45; Bieber, *Portraits*, fig. 41; Margarete Bieber, *The Sculpture of the Hellenistic Age* (New York, NY, 1961), fig. 415.

[40] *Ivory head of Alexander the Great*, Archaeological Museum of Thessaloniki, Andronikos, *Royal Graves*, figs. 17a-b, 20; Sakellariou, *Macedonia*, fig. 78; Rhomiopoulou, *Search*, color plate no. 34a, catalogue no. 171. On dating see note 17.

[41] *Marble Herm Portrait of Alexander the Great* from Tivoli, now in the Louvre, catalogue no. Ma 436; Bieber, *Alexander*, figs. 13-17; Bieber, *Portraits*, figs. 13-17; Stewart, *Faces of Power*, pp. 165-71, 423 (bibliography), figs. 45-46; Charbonneaux, *Hellenistic Art*, fig. 232; Jirí Frel, *The Getty Bronze* (Malibu, CA, 1982), fig. 52; Sakellariou, *Macedonia*, fig. 87; Rhomiopoulou, *Search*, fig. 3; Richter, *Portraits*, pp. 225-26, fig. 186.

[42] *Battle of Alexander and Darius*, after Philoxenos, Mosaic found in Casa del Fauno, now in the Naples Museum, Bieber, *Alexander*, fig. 28; Bieber, *Portraits*, figs. 27-28; Stewart, *Faces of Power*, pp. 130-150, 431, color plates 4-5a; Charbonneaux, *Hellenistic Art*, figs. 115, 117; Richter, *Portraits*, p. 226, fig. 187.

[43] Ibid., pp. 40-42.

[44] Philipp Fehl, *The Classical Monument. Reflections on the connection between Morality and Art in Greek and Roman Sculpture* (New York, NY, 1972), p. 40.

[45] See note 41 above.

[46] See note 41; Bieber, *Alexander*, pp. 32-33.

[47] Plutarch, *Alexander* 4.1, p. 255; Bieber, *Alexander,* pp. 32-33.

[48] Bieber *Alexander*, p. 34.

[49] Epigram by Archelaus or Asclepiades in *The Greek Anthology*, trans. W. R. Paton (Cambridge, MA, 1918), 16.120, p. 227.

[50] *Fouquet Alexander*, statuette, Louvre, probably *Alexander with the Lance* by Lysippus; Bieber, *Alexander*, fig. 18; Bieber, *Portraits*, fig. 18; Stewart, *Faces of Power*, pp. 163-71, 422 (bibliography), fig. 32; Charbonneaux, *Hellenistic Art*, fig. 233; Frel, *Getty Bronze*, fig. 51; *Search*, fig. 41.

[51] J. Paul Getty Villa, Malibu, CA, catalogue no. 73.AA.117; Frel, *Getty Bronze*, fig. 76.

[52] *Alexander on Bucephalus* is probably from a group by Lysippus, representing the Battle on the River Granicus, Naples. Bieber, *Alexander*, figs. 19-21; Bieber, *Portraits*, figs. 22-24; Stewart, *Faces of Power*, pp. 127-30, fig. 21.

[53] Bieber, *Alexander,* p. 36.

[54] *Alexander Riding*, bronze found in Begram, Afghanistan, Musée Guimet, Paris; ibid., fig. 23; Stewart, *Faces of Power*, pp. 172-73, 423 (bibliography), fig. 52.

[55] Bieber, *Alexander*, p. 37.

[56] *Alexander as Zeus, with Eagle, Thunderbolt and Aegis*, Neison Gem, St.

Petersburg, ibid., fig. 25; Bieber, *Portraits*, fig. 26; Stewart *Faces of Power*, p. 436 (bibliography), fig. 67.

[57] Plutarch, *De Iside et Osiride* 24, p. 360D; Bieber, *Alexander*, p. 37.

[58] Ibid., p. 38.

[59] Pliny, *Natural History* 7.125, Apuleius, *Florida* 7; Bieber, *Alexander*, p. 38.

[60] Plutarch, *Alexander* 27, pp. 283-84.

[61] For example, the coin of Lysimachus as king of Thrace, 306-281 BCE; Bieber, *Alexander*, fig. 32; Stewart, *Faces of Power*, fig. 117; or, the silver tetradrachm also by Lysimachus, minted at Lampsakos in Mysia, Thrace, 300-298 BCE, *Search*, fig. 17; Mørkholm, *Hellenistic Coinage*, figs. 179, 180.

[62] R. R. R. Smith, "Three Hellenistic Rulers at the Getty," *The J. Paul Getty Museum Journal* 14 (1986), 62-63, notes 5-8; see, for example, the silver tetradrachm of Demetrius Poliorcetes, minted in Amphipolis, in Mørkholm, *Hellenistic Coinage*, no. 173.

[63] Ibid., note 9.

[64] Ibid., notes 8, 13.

[65] J. R. Ellis, "Zenith and End of the Macedonian Kingdom: Political History," in *Macedonia: 4000 Years of Greek History and Civilization*, ed. M. B. Sakellariou (Athens, 1988), pp. 126, 130.

[66] Plutarch, *Alexander*, pp. 312-13, n. 1.

[67] Ellis, "Zenith," pp. 131-33.

[68] Peter Green, *Alexander of Macedon, 356-323 B.C. A Historical Biography* (Berkeley, CA, 1991), pp. 5, 40, etc.; Arrian, *Campaigns* 3.3.

[69] Green, *Alexander*, p. 5; Mørkholm, *Hellenistic Coinage*, p. 43; see also Stewart, *Faces of Power*, fig. 30.

[70] Bieber, *Alexander*, fig. 31.

[71] Mørkholm, *Coinage*, pp. 81 ff.

[72] *Alexander Sarcophagus*, found in Sidon, made for King Abdalonymus of Sidon, now in Istanbul; Bieber, *Alexander*, fig. 34a; Bieber *Portraits*, fig. 29; Stewart, *Portraits of Power*, pp. 294-306, 422-23 (bibliography), figs. 101-103, 105-106; Charbonneaux, *Hellenistic Art*, figs. 48-50; Sakellariou, *Macedonia*, fig. 89.

[73] Bieber, *Alexander*, fig. 32; Stewart, *Faces of Power*, sarcophagus, fig. 103, coin, fig. 104.

[74] Bieber, *Alexander*, figs. 39a-b; *Greek and Roman Portraits 470 B.C.-A.D. 500*, Boston Museum of Fine Arts (Boston, MA, 1972), fig. 11; Stewart, *Faces of Power*, p. 282, fig. 71, rejects this portrait since it comes from Sparta, a city opposed to Alexander.

[75] Rhomiopoulou, *Search*, fig. 29.

[76] Green, *Alexander*, p. 380.

[77] Bieber, *Alexander*, fig. 41; Bieber, *Portraits*, figs. 34, 36; Stewart, *Faces of Power*, pp. 231-43, 434-35 (bibliography), color plate 8c, figs. 76-79.

[78] Bieber, *Alexander*, fig. 43, also p. 34; Stewart, *Faces of Power*, pp. 283-84, 318-23, 433-34 (bibliography), color plate 8b, fig. 117; see also the coins of Lysimachus

struck at Magnesia on the Maeander, Asia Minor, 286-281 BCE, *Greek and Roman Portraits*, fig. 12; Bieber, *Portraits*, fig. 37.

79 Bieber, *Alexander*, p. 54.

80 Bieber, *Alexander*, fig. 47; Bieber, *Portraits*, figs. 38-40; Bieber, *Hellenistic Age*, figs. 412-14; Stewart, *Faces of Power*, pp. 334, 335, 427 (bibliography), figs. 134, 135. Stewart dates this statuette to about 160 BCE.

81 Bieber, *Alexander*, p. 55.

82 Rufus, *History of Alexander* 10.20; Green, *Alexander*, p. 478.

83 Bieber, *Alexander*, figs. 50-52; Bieber, *Portraits*, figs. 42-44; Stewart, *Faces of Power*, p. 163.

84 Bieber, *Alexander*, fig. 53; Bieber, *Portraits*, fig. 46; Stewart, *Faces of Power*, pp. 331, 424 (bibliography), fig. 124, dated ca. 350 BCE; R. P. Hinks, *Greek and Roman Portrait Sculpture* (London, 1935), fig. 16; Susan Walker and Andrew Burnett, *The Image of Augustus* (London, 1981), fig. 3.

85 Bieber, *Alexander*, fig. 55; Bieber, *Portraits*, figs. 47-48.

86 Bieber, *Alexander*, p. 59.

87 Bieber, *Alexander*, fig. 61; Bieber, *Portraits*, fig. 55.

88 Bieber, *Alexander*, fig. 62; Bieber, *Portraits*, fig. 56.

89 Bieber, *Alexander*, fig. 63; Bieber, *Portraits*, fig. 57.

90 Bieber, *Alexander*, fig. 69; Bieber, *Portraits*, fig. 20; Stewart, *Faces of Power*, pp. 246, 422 (bibliography), fig. 83; Walker and Burnett, *Augustus*, fig. 1.

91 Bieber, *Alexander*, fig. 70; Bieber, *Portraits*, fig. 21; Stewart, *Faces of Power*, p. 422 (bibliography).

92 F. W. Walbank, "Zenith and End of the Macedonian Kingdom: Political, Social and Economic Institutions," in *Macedonia. 4000 Years of Greek History and Civilization*, pp. 154-58.

93 Bieber, *Alexander*, figs. 71-72a,b; Bieber, *Portraits*, figs. 57-58; Bieber, *Hellenistic Age*, fig. 455; Stewart, *Faces of Power*, pp. 332-33, 428 (bibliography), figs. 128, 129; Charbonneaux, *Hellenistic Art*, fig. 318; Fehl, *Classical Monument*, plate 32.

94 *Alexander with the Thunderbolt*, Bieber, *Alexander*, fig. 77; Bieber, *Portraits*, fig. 19; cf. Stewart, *Faces of Power*, pp. 51-52, 208-209, fig. 70, a Roman bronze statuette formerly in the Los Angeles market.

95 Bieber, *Alexander*, figs. 80-85; Stewart, *Faces of Power*, pp. 334-35, 427 (bibliography), fig. 132.

96 Stewart, *Faces of Power*, pp. 286-87, 428 (bibliography), fig. 99; Rhomiopoulou, *Search*, color plate 25, catalogue no. 153.

97 Stewart, *Faces of Power*, pp. 286-87.

98 Rhomiopoulou, *Search*, color plate 4, catalogue no. 9; Stewart, *Faces of Power*, p. 429.

99 Rhomiopoulou, *Search*, color plate 4, catalogue no. 7.

100 Ibid., catalogue no. 155; Stewart, *Faces of Power*, pp. 284-86, 430-31 (bibliography), fig. 97.

101 J. Paul Getty Villa, Malibu, CA, catalogue no. 73.AA.27; Stewart, *Faces of Power*, pp. 116-21, 209-14, 438-39 (bibliography), figs. 16, 146-49; Rhomiopoulou, *Search*, color plate 2, catalogue no. 6.

102 J. Paul Getty Villa, Malilbu, CA, catalogue no. 73.AA.28; Stewart, *Faces of Power*, pp. 439-40 (bibliography), figs. 150-153; Rhomiopoulou, *Search*, color plate 2, catalogue no. 13.

103 J. Paul Getty Villa, Malibu, CA, catalogue no. 73.11.29; Stewart, *Faces of Power*, p. 440 (bibliography), figs. 154-157.

104 Stewart, *Faces of Power*, pp. 440-51 (bibliography), figs. 154-187.

105 Bieber, *Hellenistic Age*, figs. 482-483, p. 122; Walker and Burnett, *Augustus*, fig. 5.

106 Mørkholm, *Hellenistic Coinage*, fig. 625; Stewart, *Faces of Power*, pp. 235, 285, 337, fig. 139.

107 Bieber, *Alexander*, pp. 68-69; Stewart, *Faces of Power*, pp. 284-285.

108 Bieber, *Alexander*, p. 69.

109 Ibid., fig. 87, located on page following p. 88; Mørkholm, *Hellenistic Coinage*, fig. 605; Stewart, *Faces of Power*, pp. 328-30, 432 (bibliography), fig. 123.

110 Bieber, *Alexander*, fig. 90; Bieber, *Portraits*, figs. 70-71.

111 Strabo, *Geogr.* 13.594; Suetonius, *Augustus* 50; Bieber, *Alexander*, p. 72.

112 Bieber, *Alexander*, fig. 93; Stewart, *Faces of Power*, pp. 337-338, 430 (bibliography), fig. 140.

113 Bieber, *Alexander*, fig. 96; Bieber, *Portraits*, fig. 72.

114 Pausanias, *Greece* 5.25.1; Bieber, *Alexander*, p. 74.

115 Bieber, *Alexander*, figs. 97-98; Bieber, *Portraits*, figs. 74-75.

116 Now in the Walters Gallery, Baltimore; Rhomiopoulou, *Search*, color plate no 5, catalogue no. 11; Bieber, *Alexander*, fig. 114; Bieber, *Portraits*, fig. 59; Stewart, *Faces of Power*, pp. 50-51, 274-275, 332-333, fig. 130.

117 Rhomiopoulou, *Search*, p. 103; Stewart, *Faces of Power*, pp. 50-51.

118 Bieber, *Alexander*, p. 80, fig. 115; Bieber, *Portraits*, fig. 87.

119 *Triginta Tyranni* 14.6, quoted in Bieber, *Alexander*, p. 80.

120 Medal of Constantine and Alexander, Cabinet des Médailles, Bibliothèque Nationale, Paris; André Grabar, *Early Christian Art* (New York, NY, 1968), fig. 11.

Richard A. Zionts

SERPENTS AND HERETICS:
THE IMPACT OF HELLENISTIC POETRY ON A
FOURTH-CENTURY CHURCH FATHER

Introduction

Late Antiquity was a time of transformation and re-integration. As Peter Brown has demonstrated, the period between 200 and 500 CE was a time of transformation and re-integration rather than downfall, destruction and disintegration.[1] It was a time which served as a bridge between classical antiquity and the Middle Ages; a time of adaptation of older classical models from the Hellenistic-Roman world into a new, emerging, evolving cultural political and religious life in which Christianity and Islam would hold sway with significant Jewish minorities in their midst.

With the arrival of Alexander the Great and onward, the Greek-Hellenistic cultural heritage took root in the Middle Eastern world and continued its ongoing influence, including the development of rabbinic Judaism and early Christianity.

As has been ably demonstrated by such contemporary scholars as Ellis Rivkin and Henry Fischel, Pharisaic Judaism is impossible to imagine without certain concepts and ideas which were part of the Hellenistic world. The rabbinic sages were well-acquainted with classical Greek models of hermeneutics and philosophy and assimilated these models successfully into Pharisaic or later rabbinic Judaism.[2]

The same phenomenon occurred around three to four centuries later within early Christian ranks. Many of the early patristic writers were well-grounded in the classical tradition. This includes Irenaeus of Lyons, writing in the late second century CE. In his work, the *Adversus haereses*, Irenaeus refers to the writings of various Greek and Hellenistic authors, in particular, to those doxographical collections or handbooks available at the time as well as from the sources of his own rhetorical training.[3]

Nicander of Colophon and Epiphanius of Salamis

The same transformation of earlier Hellenistic literature was employed by Epiphanius, bishop of Salamis or Constantia in Cyprus, writing in the late fourth century CE. It was Epiphanius who adapted an earlier didactic work by Nicander of Colophon, a Hellenistic Greek poet writing in Alexandria in second century BCE five centuries earlier. Nicander of Colophon's two works, still extant, consist of the *Theriaca,* a didactic poetic treatise on the recognition of poisonous reptiles, insects, and other creatures and how to avoid them or get rid of them. His other work, the *Alexipharmaca,* is another didactic poetic treatment written in Greek hexameter on remedies one might use in healing the bites of such poisonous creatures.

Epiphanius of Salamis was familiar with Nicander's works, especially Nicander's *Theriaca,* and borrowed much of Nicander's imagery and descriptions of poisonous serpents, lizards, scorpions and other venomous creatures as well as methods of expelling such poisonous reptiles, especially serpents. Numerous examples of this may be found throughout Epiphanius' magnum opus known as the *Panarion,* a Greek loan-word from the Latin word *panarium,* meaning simply a „bread basket" or any small, easily carried receptacle for holding things. For Epiphanius, the word *Panarion* applied to his work is rendered as a "medicine chest," containing information on how to recognize poisonous heretical groups and once recognized, how to deal with their venom. Throughout Epiphanius' works, he continuously draws comparisons between the various heresies he attacks and the various poisonous creatures enumerated by Nicander of Colophon.

Epiphanius demonstrates his indebtedness to Nicander of Colophon in Proem II, Chapter 1, of his work titled "The Heresiology of Epiphanius, Bishop, Entitled *Panarion,* where he writes: „Nicander, too, the investigator of beasts and reptiles, imparted the knowledge of their natures. And others, who studied roots and plants, [described] what they were made of— Dioscurides the Wood-Cutter, Pamphilus, King Mithridates, Callisthenes, Philo, Iolaus of Bithynia, Heraclidas of Taranto, Cretenus the Root-Collector, Andrew, Bassus the Tulian, Niceratus, Petronius, Niger, Diodotus, and certain others. And no more than they do I, in my similar attempt to reveal the roots and origins of the sects, [describe them] to harm those who care to read (my description)".[4]

Epiphanius continues: "Those authors made a diligent effort, not to point evil out, but to frighten men and ensure their safety, so that they would recognize the dreadful, dangerous beasts and be secure, and escape them, by God's power, by taking care not to engage with such deadly creatures if they encountered them, and were menaced by their breath or bite, or the sight of them. And [meanwhile], from the same concern, these authors prescribed medicines made from roots and plants, to cure the illness caused by these serpents".[5]

Thus, at the very outset of his work, Epiphanius adapts the work of ancient Hellenistic didactic writers and declares his intention to further adapt their approach in creating a Christian heresiological work. Taking poisonous reptiles and serpents in a metaphorical sense, Epiphanius states that he will provide arguments which will serve as "antidotes" to counteract the "poison" of these heretical sects and their false teachings. These antidotes will serve to help anyone who has fallen, either willingly or unwillingly, into the "snake-like teachings" of these sects.[6]

Epiphanius' association of the serpent or snake with groups he considers to be "heretical" may be traced back to Genesis 3.14-18, where the source of the idea of eternal enmity or conflict between humanity and the serpent is set forth. It is here that we read of the beguiling of Eve by the serpent who purposely misleads her, enticing her and Adam to eat of the forbidden fruit of the tree of knowledge. This act, initiated by the beguiling serpent, is what led to Adam and Eve's transgression and expulsion from the Garden of Eden. Thus, the serpent is the symbol of those forces which seek to mislead people and undermine their "true beliefs". A later Jewish writer, in the Wisdom of Solomon found in the Apocrypha, states: "For God created us for incorruption, and made us in the image of His own eternity; but through Satan's envy death entered the world and those who belong to his company experience it" (trans. RSV). In later Jewish pseudepigraphical and midrashic sources, we find references stating that the serpent was actually the *Satan* or Samael in disguise.[7] This idea is carried forth into early Christian theological writings, including the New Testament where Satan is identified as the serpent. One example of this is found in II Corinthians 11.3 where it states: "... as the serpent deceived Eve by its cunning, your thoughts will be led astray from a sincere and pure devotion to Christ" (trans. RSV). Thus, the symbol of the serpent as a deceiver becomes a most appropriate metaphor for Epiphanius in his work against the so-called "heretics" of the late fourth century CE.

Epiphanius' introduction is modeled after the opening lines of Nicander in Nicander's *Theriaca* which he begins by stating: „Readily, dear Hermesianax, most honoured of my many kinsmen, and in due order will I expound the forms of savage creatures and their deadly injuries which smite one unforeseen, and the countering remedy for their harm. And the toiling ploughman, the herdsman, and the woodcutter, whenever in forest or at the plough one of them fastens its deadly fang upon him, shall respect you for your learning in such means for averting sickness".[8]

It should be mentioned at this point that Epiphanius was certainly not the first early Christian church writer to refute "heresies". His work contains elements of previous heresiological writers, Justin Martyr, Irenaeus of Lyons and Hippolytus as well as arguments from Scripture, theological principles, and Christian tradition. Epiphanius also utilizes the Hellenistic rhetorical skill of the *psogos* or invective, designed to vilify and defame one's opponents. As Robert Wilken points out, Christian writers, trained in the same [Hellenistic rhetorical] tradition, put the technique of the *psogos* to use not to deal with political foes or personal enemies, though on occasion they did this as well, but to assail religious opponents, chiefly heretics and Jews, but also pagans. Christians became as adept as the pagan sophists at heaping abuse on their foes ...".[9]

The originality of Epiphanius' *Panarion* is not his invective as it is his analogizing the leader of the heresy and his followers to dangerous serpents or some other venomous creature. Thus, unlike his predecessors (Justin Martyr, Irenaeus, and Hippolytus), Epiphanius adds his own original touch by analogizing each heresy or heretical group with a particular type of serpent. Epiphanius' use of serpents, the need to recognize them, caution in dealing with them and remedies for their expulsion indicates that he followed an older Hellenistic work on serpent recognition and remedies. His is an adaptation of an older Hellenistic and later, Roman genre of didactic poetry, transformed by him into a Christian didactic work.

We will now see how Epiphanius set about accomplishing this adaptation and transformation as we explore his work, the *Panarion*. The first twenty of the eighty books of the *Panarion* deal with those groups which preceded the advent of Jesus. These groups include: Barbarism, Scythianism, Hellenism, Judaism, and Samaritanism as well as what Epiphanius terms "the outgrowth of Hellenism"[10] which are: Pythagoreans or Peripatetics, Platonists, Stoics, and Epicureans. Next, he includes four groups which came from Samaritanism: Gorothenes, Sebuaeans, Essenes and Dositheans. Then, seven sects derived from Judaism: Scribes, Pharisees, Sadducees, Hemerobaptists, Ossaeans, Nasareans, and Herodians. In all of his discourses against these twenty "heresies," Epiphanius does not employ any poisonous serpent or reptile imagery or derogatory comparisons between poisonous creatures and these twenty groups. It is interesting to speculate as to why. Perhaps it is because these first twenty of his eighty „heresies" were on the scene long before the advent of Jesus. Another reason might be found in the fact that Christianity is based upon Judaism and shares in many aspects of Hellenistic culture such as Stoicism and Neo-Platonism. Therefore, invidious derogation of Judaism and Hellenistic culture would undermine important foundations of Christian doctrine and teaching.

Epiphanius begins his references to poisonous serpents in Book 21 of the *Panarion*. Book 21 is titled „Against Simonians," i.e., the teachings of Simon Magus and those who were his followers. It is, however, in Book 26 of the *Panarion* that we find the very first parallel between Epiphanius' work and that of Nicander of Colophon—in the context of an attack against Gnostics or Borborites. Epiphanius, in keeping with his practice of ending his refutations with an analogy of the heretical group or leader to a species of serpents or other poisonous reptiles, compares the licentiousness of the Borborites to a snake which he terms „the viper with no pangs" [i.e., pain of giving birth].[11] Epiphanius writes: „So, we are told, when the viper with no pangs grew amorous, female for male and male for female, they would twine together, and the male would thrust his head in the jaws of the gaping female. But she would bite the male's head off, in passion, and so swallow the poison that dripped from its mouth, and conceive a similar pair of snakes, a male and a female, within her. When this pair had come to maturity in her belly and had no way to be born, they would lacerate their mother's side to come to birth— so that both their father and mother perished".[12]

Nicander writes, in his 2nd-century BCE work, the *Theriaca*: "Beware of meeting at the crossroads the dusky male viper when he has escaped from her bite and is maddened by the blow of the smoke-hued Female, in the season when, as the Male covers her, the lustful Female fastens upon him, tearing him with her foul fang, and cuts off the head of her mate; but forthwith in the act of birth the young vipers avenge their sire's destruction, since they gnaw through their mother's thin flank and thereby are born motherless".[13] The same Greek words for male and female viper are used by both Epiphanius and Nicander: *Echidneis* and *Echidna*. Also, the cannibalistic act is described in both the *Panarion* and *Theriaca* as well as the piercing of the female's side in the act of birth. It is highly probable, then, that Epiphanius borrowed this account of the male and female viper's act of reproduction, adapting it for a Christian religious purpose.

The numerous references and parallels between Nicander and Epiphanius may be seen on a chart which I have created for our perusal (see appendix). I would like to elaborate on just a few of these which I think are of particular historic, literary, and theological interest.

In his *Panarion*, written to refute a Jewish-Christian sect known as the Ebionites, Epiphanius writes: "But why should I spend any further time on tidal beaches by the sea, which are flooded here and dry there, and fish are often stranded on some of them and injure people's feet when they cross their high parts? (For some of the fish are poisonous, I mean sting-rays, sea-snakes, sharks and sea-eels, as I have just now said)".[14] These sea creatures, mentioned by Epiphanius (with the exception of the shark) may all be found in Nicander's

Theriaca: „Furthermore, I have knowledge of all the creatures that sea whirls in its briny surges, and the horror of the *smuraineis* (murry or sea-eel), since many a time has it sprung up from the fish-box and striking them with panic has hurled toiling fishermen from their boat to seek refuge in the sea ... . Again, from the death-dealing *trugona* (sting-ray) and the ravening *drakonta* (sea-snake) I can protect you. The sting-ray causes trouble when it strikes with its sting the toiler labouring at his hauled drag-nets ...".[15]

These sea creatures are common throughout the Mediterranean waters and were, no doubt, as familiar to Epiphanius as they were to Nicander. Nicander was a resident of the eastern Mediterranean and, as far as historians can determine, lived in cities near the sea, including Colophon and Alexandria. Epiphanius was bishop at Salamis or Constantia, a seaport center on the eastern shore of the island of Cyprus. Epiphanius' reference to tidal pools and beaches with sea creatures left stranded on the dry land would reflect the observations of both men of such a familiar scene. Nicander's description of these sea creatures, however, takes place within the context of actual fishing experience while Epiphanius' adaptation is on dry land, depicting the creatures as stranded on tidal beaches, causing possible injury to the feet of passers-by. Epiphanius' adaptation is an apt one. These Ebionites, this Jewish-Christian sect evidently still in existence in Epiphanius' time, is, in his judgment, out of the living waters of mainstream catholic Christianity, stranded in the backwaters of time and history, yet still able to cause injury to anyone who stumbles over them.

Another interesting parallel and adaptation of Nicander by Epiphanius is found in Epiphanius' *Panarion* 51, written „Against the sect which does not accept he Gospel according to John and his Revelation." Epiphanius writes: "Following these sects ... another sect sprang up. It is like a snake without much strength, which cannot stand the odor of dittany—that is, storax—or of frankincense or southernwood, or the smell of pitch, incense, lignite or hartshorn. For those who are familiar with them say that these substances have the effect of driving poisonous snakes away".[16]

Epiphanius' adaptation of Nicander is seen in Nicander's *Theriaca* where he makes mention of three of the same anti-snake repellents found in Epiphanius: *libanotis* or frankincense, *abrotonon* or wormwood, and *asphaltos* or bitumen, often referred to as pitch. In line 850 of his work, Nicander mentions several remedies for poisonous creatures including „the fruit-bearing rosemary frankincense" *(kachruforo libanotidi)*. Nicander also refers to wormwood as a snake repellent in his *Theriaca* as he writes: "But if these things (i.e., poisonous serpents) bring trouble, and night brings bed-time near, and you are longing for rest when your work is done ... you should cut and strew beneath you ... wormwood *(abrotonoio)* which grows wild upon the hills in some chalky glen".[17] He also includes two other references to wormwood as a snake repellent. Finally, the use of pitch or bitumen *(asphaltos)* is mentioned by Nicander in his *Theriaca* where he writes: "Burn also a portion no less heavy of the strong-smelling black cummin, or else of sulphur, or again of bitumen" *(asphaltoio).*[18]

It is significant to note that Epiphanius' adaptation of Nicander includes what is, for him, an important scriptural and theological interpretation. In referring to the church's ability to destroy the would-be attempts of „the snake-like heretics," Epiphanius writes: „But they will not prevail in the ark [i.e., the symbol of the church and its teachings]. The holy Noah is ordered by God's direction to make the ark secure (here Epiphanius uses the Greek verb *epasphalisasthai*), as God says to him, 'Thou shalt pitch *(asphaltoseis)* within and without' (Genesis 6.14)—to prefigure God's holy church, which has the power of pitch *(asphaltou)*, which drives the horrid, baneful, snake-like teachings away. For where pitch is burned, no snake can remain. The holy storax incense stuns them, and they avoid its sweet odor. And the power of southernwood or frankincense drives them away if it grows down over the serpent itself and sprouts above its den".[19]

Conclusion

Thus, we can see that the magnum opus of Epiphanius, his *Panarion* or "Medicine Chest," together with its parallels to the *Theriaca* of Nicander of Colophon, a second-century BCE Hellenistic Greek didactic poem, clearly shows the continuing influence of Hellenistic culture into the time of Late Antiquity. It also demonstrates that many of the elements of classical culture were appropriated and adapted by the early Christian church just as they were by rabbinic Judaism several centuries earlier. It also points to the fact that Epiphanius of Salamis had received some form of education in or exposure to the classical works of antiquity. According to Sozomen, writing in the fifth century CE, Epiphanius spent his youth in Egypt, receiving his education from well-known monastics.[20] From Epiphanius' writings, it is obvious that he had access to a range of biblical and early Christian texts, especially the works of Eusebius. While in Egypt, Epiphanius may have spent time in Alexandria. Perhaps it was in that great center of Hellenistic culture, that Epiphanius encountered the work of Nicander. Whatever the possible reasons, Epiphanius' use of Nicander reveals the continuing influence of an otherwise obscure Hellenistic epic in the fourth century CE. In this regard, Epiphanius takes his place with such writers as Eusebius and Jerome, whose breadth of classical learning shows forth in their work as well.

Appendix

Parallels and Correspondences between Epiphanius of Salamis' *Panarion* and Nicander of Colophon's *Theriaca and Alexipharmaca:*

Nicander

Epiphanius

Theriaca 128-135:
Reference to the Female Viper, *echidneis,*
whose young gnaw through their
their mother's side, thus, born
without pangs of birth.

Panarion 26.19.3-5:
The Female Viper, *echidna,*
with no pangs of birth,
(young lacerate their
mother's side to
come to birth).

Theriaca 320-334:
... the *sepedon* ... its color, like
that of a [red] carpet, is spread
over a rough surface.

Panarion 28.8.4:
The Rot Viper ... [whose]
whole body is covered with
long red hair ... (*sepedon*).

Theriaca 738-740:
An aggressive foe, the one men
call the [small] wasp-spider
(*sfeikeion*).

Panarion 29.9.5:
Like an insect that is small,
yet still causes pain with its
poison (*sfeikion*).

Theriaca 821-830:
... the horror of the murry
[see-eel] (*smuraineis*) ...
the death-dealing sting-ray (*trugona*)
... the ravening sea-snake (*drakonta*).

Panarion 30.34.7:
Some of the fish are
are poisonous ... sting rays
(*trugonas*), sea snakes
(*drakainas*), sharks
(*charcharias*) and sea-eels
[murrys] (*smurainas*).

Theriaca 334-339:
... the dispas ... from its bite the
heart is inflamed utterly, and in the
fever the dry lips shrivel with
parching thirst (*dipseis*).

Panarion 34.22.3-4:
... if the *dispas* strikes
someone, the pain from
its particularly hot
poison will make him thirsty
(*dipseis*) and want a drink, and will
impel him to keep coming up and
drinking.

Theriaca 373-383:
After him you shall learn of the
amphisbaena ... two-headed, ever
dull the of eye.

Panarion 35.3.9:
... or crush him quickly like
a head cut off from
Two-headed viper, the
amphisbaena.

Alexipharmaca 335-347:
Do not let the agonizing drink of
the hateful *buprestis* escape
your knowledge ... .

Panarion 38.8.6:
After exposing the opinion—
like exposing poisonous
dung-beetles ... (*buprestis
kantharis*).

Theriaca 805-807:

As for those of the *bembix* from
the hills.

Panarion 41.3.4:

Like a *bembix* or wasp-flying
Insects with stings.

and

Alaxipharmaca 183-184:
... and buzzers (*bembikes*) from
the hills fall upon the grapes and
feast their fill of sweetness.

Theriaca 811:
... the deadly wasp (*sfeix*).

Panarion 44.7.2:
... a smarting wasp (*sfeix*).

Theriaca 283-308:
... the blood-letting snake
(*haemoroou*).

Panarion 48.15.6:
... the viper of hemorrhage
(*haemorria*).

Theriaca 484-488:
There, too, are the bites of the
Gecko (*askalabou*), hateful,
Though he is of no account

Panarion 49.3.4:
... a toothless, witless
serpent, like a gecko ...
(*aphrosuneis, emempleion
askalabotou*).

Theriaca 850:
[Anti-Snake Repellents]
... fruit-bearing rosemary
frankincense (*kachruforo libanotidi*)

Panarion 51.2.1-3:
[Repelling Poisonous Snakes]

Theriaca 34-35:
… you may expel the … doom
that snakes bring if you char
the tines horn of a stag
(*keira kapneion elaphoio*) or else
set fire to dry lignite (*engagida
petrein*) … or take the heated root
of the frankincense-tree … or again
of bitumen (*asphaltoio*)

Frankincense (*libanitidos*)
Wormwood (*abrotonous*)
Pitch [Bitumen] (*asphaltou*)
For where pitch is burned,
no snake can remain … and
the power of wormwood or
frankincense [drives them
away]

Theriaca 61-67, 574:
Wormwood (abrotonoio).

[Cf. also, Epiphanius, *Panarion*
51.2.1., hartshorn
(*keratos teis elaphou*)].

Theriaca 438ff.:
… the green and dark-blue dragon
… Wormwood (*abrotonou*).

Panarion 57.10.8:
… like the so-called agate
dragon (*drakonta*).

Theriaca 397-399:
Consider too the King of Snakes
(*herpeiston basileia*).

Panarion 59.13.4:
Let us toss this sect [the
Cathari] aside like the face of a
basilisk … which … has
a very grand title [i.e., royal]
(*basilikos*).

Theriaca 488-492:
[Harmless Snakes]
Harmless reptiles also there are …
and men call these: *elopas, libuas,*
and curling mouse-hunters (*muagros*),
the quick darters (*akontiai*), moluroi,
and blind-eyes, too (*tuphlopes*) which
are reported innocuous.

Panarion 61.8.5:
[Harmless Snakes]
Like the quick-darting snake
(*akontios*), the blind-snake
(*tuphlopos*) or the mouser
(*muagrou*)

and

Panarion 62.8.5:
Like a *libys* or an *elops* or
molurus … can do no harm with
their bites.

Alexipharmaca 567-576:
If a man imbibe a draught from the
sun-loving toad (*phrunoio*) …
and the spleen of the deadly toad
(*phruneis*).

Panarion 64.72.3:
… spit out the oil of the
toad's poison (*to iou tou
phrunou*), and the harm
that has been done by the
noxious creatur.

Theriaca 412-420:
Learn now the doom inflicted
by the dryinas (*druinao*), which
others call chelydrus. It makes its
home in oaks (*en drusein oikia
teuxas*) or maybe Valonia oaks … .

Panarion 65.9.4:
For there is a viper called
the dryinas (*druinas*) … .
Its den is very often near
grass, or also, oaks (*druas*).
This is why it is called a
dryinas—from its preference
for [oak] trees.

Theriaca 463-467:
… you will find the long monster
cenchrines (*kenchrineo*), which men
call the spangled lion … .

Panarion 66.88.2:
… the cenchritis
(*kenchritidos*) which has
coils of many illustrations
for the deception of those who
see it.

Theriaca 811-812:
Yes, and I know, too, the devices
of the woodlouse (*ioulos*) … and
of the two-headed centipede
(*skolopendra*) … .

Panarion 75.54.31:
… as though I had stamped
on the serpent called the
many-footed millipede
(*polypoun skolopendran*) or woodlouse (*ioulon*) with
the foot of the truth … .[21]

Notes:

[1] Cf. Peter Brown, *The World of Late Antiquity* (London, 1971), pp. 7-9.

[2] Cf. especially Ellis Rivkin, *A Hidden Revolution* (Nashville, TN, 1978). One should observe, in particular, the list of Greco-Roman analogues incorporated into Pharisaic and later, Rabbinic Judaism, esp., pp. 242-44. These include: a scholar class, special teacher-disciple relationship, concept of oral or unwritten laws, and the use of proof-texting. See also Henry A. Fischel, *Rabbinic Literature and Greco-Roman Philosophy: Study of Epicurea and Rhetorica in Early Midrashic Writings* (Leiden, 1973).

[3] Cf. Robert M. Grant, *After the New Testament* (Philadelphia, PA, 1967), esp. pp. 158-69. Grant points out that doxiographical collections were used widely by early Christian writers and included quotes from the works of Plato, Pseudo-Plutarch, Pseudo-Democritus, Strabo, and others.

[4] *Panarion*, Proem II: 3.1-2. All references to the *Panarion* are taken from *The Panarion of Epiphanius of Salamis, Book I (Sects 1-46)*, Nag Hammadi Studies 35 and *The Panarion of Epiphanius of Salamis, Books II and III (Sects 47-80, De fide)*, Nag Hammadi and Manichaean Studies 36, trans. Frank Williams (Leiden, 1989 and 1994).

[5] *Panarion* , Proem II: 3.2-3.

[6] *Panarion* 2.4-5.

[7] Jews of later post-Exilic times elaborated on the story of Eve and the serpent and some later writers went so far as to equate the serpent with Samael, the major name of the Satan or the "Adversary" in Judaism from the Amoraic period onward (ca. 200-500 CE). In these later midrashim, Samael becomes the tempter and seducer of humanity.

[8] *Theriaca*, lns. 1-7. All references to the *Theriaca* and *Alexipharmaca* are taken from *Nicander: The Poems and Poetical Fragments*, trans. A. S. F. Gow and A. F. Scholfield (Cambridge, 1953).

[9] Cf. Robert Wilken, *John Chrysostom and the Jews: Rhetoric and Reality in the Late 4th Century* (Berkeley, CA, 1983), p. 115.

[10] *Panarion* 2.3.

[11] Ibid., 26.19.2

[12] Ibid., 26.19.3.

[13] *Theriaca*, lns. 128-135.

[14] *Panarion* 30.34.7.

[15] *Theriaca*, lns. 821-830.

[16] *Panarion* 51.2.1-3.

[17] *Theriaca*, lns. 61-67.

[18] Ibid., lns. 43-45.

[19] *Panarion* 51.2.1-3.

[20] Sozomen, *Historia ecclesiastica* 6.32.

[21] Translations of Gow and Scholfield, *Nicander*, and Williams, *Epiphanius*.

Nancy van Deusen

ARISTOTLE'S ADVICE TO ALEXANDER AND THE ISSUE OF RULERSHIP
(The *Physics* Exemplified in the Thirteenth Century)

Introduction

Alexander had propped himself up on his pillow. The blood was drained from his face. His hair lay flattened against his perspiring forehead, and his eyes looked enormous, fathomless, each wreathed in a black shadow. His lips were dry and white as a sheet.

He tried to talk but couldn't, and he laid his hand on the edge of the bed and nodded as each soldier walked past him and bent down mutely to kiss it. Out in the corridor as the soldiers filed out, they broke into sobs.

It was the thirteenth day of June. Toward nightfall Alexander closed his eyes and never opened them again.

So concludes Nikos Kazantzakis' novel, *Alexander the Great*.[1] The work is one of hundreds of volumes on the topic of this figure's meteoric rise to power, an almost miraculous career based on one victory after the other, suddenly, irrevocably, coming to an end one day in June, well over two millenia ago. The finality of his end was as striking as the rise, event by event, and the brilliance of his career. What continues to fascinate us so about the figure of Alexander the Great?[2]

The figure of Alexander gripped, in noteworthy ways, a thirteenth-century literate public as well. Teachers, administrators, and students of the thirteenth-century university were—so many years after the fact—utterly captivated by Alexander. What accounts for this interest in a Macedonian emperor from the distant past? It is probably safe to say that students at the University of Paris in the thirteenth century had as few specific notions about Macedonia as most undergraduate students today. How was this figure understood to have more than biographical interest? More specifically, and to the point of this study, how is Alexander presented by a trio of thirteenth century intellectuals, actually, in these cases, academic professionals within the newly-formed university system? It is the concept of *ductus-tractus-conductus*, and issues of desire and choice that intrigue and involve Philip the Chancellor, Robert Grosseteste, and Roger Bacon, in an ongoing discussion that spanned the entire century of the founding and growth of the Universities of Paris and Oxford. Our discussion also revolves around both of these universities, since all three, in all probability, had association, one way or another, with each other—in the cases of Grosseteste and Bacon, of course, the association can be proven, since Bacon acknowledges some of his intellectual debts to Grosseteste. But a shared preoccupation just with the issue at hand, that is, with the nature of *ductus* and its contingent issue of free will is the relationship that unites these three writers.

Plutarch, for what it is worth, tells us that Alexander was furious when he learned that Aristotle had published his teaching—the private tutoring that had commenced when Alexander was thirteen years old.[3] The philosopher, however, mollified his former pupil by assuring him that no one would be able to understand the written works without his own oral explications. Aristotle, if he did indeed say anything of the sort, was absolutely right, and the transmission of his principal writings into Latin-speaking intellectual culture proved this. The *Physics*, for example, was only gradually assimilated, with a considerable lag between its earliest translations during the course of the second half of the twelfth century and a thorough-going discussion of the principles it contained throughout the thirteenth—a discussion that lasted for at least three centuries. Moreover, the *Physics* with its many obscurities, produced a flood of commentaries, so many that most of them are still unidentified, much less edited, today.[4] So we are at the beginning of an understanding, fleshed out by the texts themselves, of how a work such as the Latin *Physics* was regarded and understood, as well as changes in its reception during the course of the thirteenth to the fifteenth centuries, in taking on these three seminal writers, Philip the Chancellor, Robert Grosseteste, and Roger Bacon. In other words, we are at the source of this flood of commentary literature, as the *translatio vetus*, cited, for example, by Adelard of Bath and Thierry of Chartres before the middle of the twelfth century, is challenged and exchanged for new translations.[5] These new late-twelfth and early thirteenth-century translations would usher in, and instigate a serious program, at first centered in Paris, to understand just exactly what the issues presented in the *Physics* were. As an indication of the interest in this work, by the end of the twelfth century, the *Physics* had been translated into Latin at least four times, three times from the Greek itself, once from the Arabic. In the first decades of the thirteenth century, Philip the Chancellor quotes it, refers regularly to it; in the second and third generations of the thirteenth century, Robert Grosseteste and Roger Bacon wrote two of the first commentaries on the *Physics*.[6]

But interest alone does not necessarily make for understanding; the *Physics* is not easy to comprehend—in Greek, Latin, or for that matter, English. In comparing multiple versions of all three languages, one arrives at the conclusion that the concepts and directions of arguments contained in the *Physics* are shaped, to an astonishing extent, by their linguistic carriers. *Words* themselves are the real problem with the *Physics*.[7] Greek terms, made into richly-larded multivalent concepts as they are used and explained by Aristotle, had, in fact, no direct Latin equivalents. The Latin term *motus*, or the English *motion*, for example, did not contain the spectrum of contingent qualities that the Greek term that has influenced the English expression kinetics contains, and the English *motion* also falls short of the mark as well.

Medieval intellectuals of the early thirteenth century certainly realized this too. The more abstract questions are, the more important the role their linguistic presentation plays. Substantives are a case in point. When one can easily conceptualize the "thing," its designation is secondary. Cat is fairly straightforward in any language; *ductus*, however, for which there are no direct English equivalents is not. It is interesting that *ductus*, *conductus*, for example, are explained by examples within contexts in which they occur, in principal Latin dictionaries used today, rather than in terms of direct English equivalents. Since so many Greek philosophical terms were simply absorbed into the Latin language with no attempt at all at finding Latin equivalents, it is a measure of the perceived importance of the Latin term *ductus*, that late twelfth-early thirteenth-century translators made sure that the concept would be presented in the Latin language, not simply retained as a transliterated Greek term. They hit upon many other Latin equivalents as well, such as *tractus, dirigo/directum, conductus*. *Ductus* for a multivalent concept of motion said, by Aristotle himself, to be difficult to understand, actually lent itself well to designation within the Latin language. But having words for it was only one step in the direction of truly understanding this concept—a concept so abstract that exemplification was, as thirteenth century intellectuals discovered, absolutely necessary.[8]

The *Physics* Exemplified

The *Physics* sets forth, and brings into discussion, topics that are almost impossible to imagine. As Roger Bacon, in the third generation of the thirteenth century, in his *Opus tertium* wrote, "these things, that is, continuity and motion of measured time, although comprehensible to the intellect, no matter how great one's intellectual power is, can only be imagined with the greatest difficulty. One needs a special illumination".[9] For example, it is nearly impossible to conjure up in one's mind, the concept of the "nature of motion," although, as Aristotle states, the *motions of natures*, and the diversities of these motions that distinguish the natures that place them in motion—such as an ant, a cat, or an elephant—are not so difficult to imagine. Another example of the difficulty one has with the imagination of themes and concepts presented in the *Physics*, is the problem of, as the Latin translation has it, *ductus*, or incremental, measured motion, beginning decisively, and leading by directed, forward thrust, to an undisputed goal, a termination. This is Aristotle's concept of *theoria*, presented in the *Physics* as especially difficult to understand. It is a remarkable paradox of intellectual history— actually, a cruel joke—that Alexander himself—his *figura*, and the life he led—became, in the reception of one of Aristotle's most elusive ideas, during the course of the thirteenth century, the very example that Aristotle apparently had assured Alexander would be needed in order to understand his most esoteric, quintessentially abstract, teaching.

Ductus, conductus, as a Latin concept, which, on account of its conceptual content as well as the frequency with which it is used and explained, is the translation of Aristotle's multifaceted concept of incremental, measured motion. The concept, the Greek *theoria*, epitomized and drew together crucial components of Aristotle's discussion of the nature of motions, as well as the possibility that directed motion could be measured and divided for the purpose of measurement into ever smaller self-contained increments. It was possible, using this construct of directed, incrementally-divided motion, to chart the progress, from one increment to the next, or from one part of a continuum to the next park eventually leading, in the case of a directed motion, to a *terminatio*, or final end. All of the increments are related by their place within the continuity, their order or *ordo*; all have to do both with the nature of the directed motion, and, at the same time, demonstrate this nature. Furthermore, as Aristotle stated, a directed motion could be divided into self-contained increments indefinitely. Tremor, or sporadic, undirected back and forth motion, could not be measured, because its parts could not be separated into increments and ordered, both actually, as well as logically. Tremor, therefore was essentially useless for artistic and scientific purposes, a distinction, of course, that Aristotle does not make, since his method is to present a basic principle such as *ductus* in the *Physics*, with exemplifications of this principle in his other works, such as the *Nichomachean Ethics*, or the *Poetics*. Motion, as an abstraction, was explained in the *Metaphysica*, as a component of the artistic process—or the plot of a play—in the *Poetica*, and it was compared to the continuum of a regimen or of life's conduct in the *Ethics*. All of these *countenances* or faces of motion were useful for an understanding of its total nature, and by the end of the thirteenth century, anyone who had attended the university of Paris, would have had an introductory course in the *Metaphysics*, as well as a course of study that systematized the exemplification of the basic principles contained therein in terms of the mathematical disciplines, namely arithmetic, geometry, astronomy or physics and music. But we are dealing here with the earlier, less systematic stage of this progress, as the *Physics* causes a great deal of excitement, and concurrent consternation, in terms of attempts to truly understand the principles it contains.

Alexander's story of incremental progress, leading along, incident by ordered incident, a trajectory of meteor-like directionality, culminating, with no possible uncertainty, in a termination, exemplified in terms that one could readily imagine—even if one knew very little about Alexander himself—exactly what it would seem that Aristotle had in mind as as he worked over concepts crucial to the *Physics*. In a sense Alexander, with the broad outlines of his persona and life, functioned as a delineatory myth, in which a broad structure was available, with details that could be negotiated, and varied from one telling to another. Alexander himself provided the case in point for the construct of *ductus*. This was not lost on a thirteenth-century Latin-reading audience.

What we have here looks like a veritable Alexander fever. The problem of *ductus*, the central problem of the *Physics*, could be exemplified by the imagined Alexander-figure within the continuity of a context afforded by event after event of Alexander's life. Marker provided by *figura*, indicating individual increment, contained within a continuum could all be explicated by directing one's attention to this particular character. And attention is exactly what was given. On the abstract level, the problem of figure within *course* (*figura* within *modus*) brought together the four quadrival arts, as, for example, arithmetic's integer number within numerical order indicated by the *figurae* of number. The construct also focused upon and brought together a complex of problems and designations, namely, those of steadfastness, procession, reversion, limitation, infinitude, participation, and power.

But just why was this principle of motion, the subject of the *Physics* so problematic? It would seem that motion, as a concept, would be quite straightforward. Aristotle, however, does not use a simple motion concept that could have been easily translated into the Latin *motus*. One notices this at the onset of the commentary on the *Physics* by Robert Grosseteste, written in the mid-thirties of the thirteendh century, as the result of his own study, and prompted by his own intellectual interest in the subject; and the commentary, also on the *Physics*, by Roger Bacon, written thirty years later no doubt as a textbook for his students at the University of Paris.

Robert Grosseteste begins by presenting concepts of internal, innate *via* or track by which a line of investigation is followed from beginning to end, the formation and material of movement (*passio*), and sets forth the intention to investigate what is meant by the mobile:

> *Via* autem *innata* nobis ad *perveniendum* ...
> et iterum ad noticiam passionum forme et materie pervenitur
> et intencione huius nominis mobili.[10]

To paraphrase Grosseteste's Latin text: The nature of mobility is according to the *partes* into which movement is divided, which are integrated within this movement. This is true, generally, as well, for the so-called *via cognicionis* or *line* of investigation, in which parts or components are defined within a totality, with each discretion determined by intellective cognition.[11] Each of the *partes* are described according to their nature, and indicated again by motion—of the hand—as each part is indicated and delineated by means of a figure.[12] And so by the motion of the hand, property accorded to each individual component within an entire line of investigation can be delineated, just as has been exemplified in music, in which highness or lowness of sound are both indicated by figures that delineate differences.

Figures made by motions of the hand, within a context, is the construct immediately set forth by Grosseteste in the opening to his commentary on the *Physics*. All of this before Grosseteste quotes Aristotle at all. In his succinct, no-nonsense style, Grosseteste, right at the onset of his commentary, presents the crux of the matter, and the manner in which Aristotle's concept of motion differs from what one, in the early thirteenth century could have expected for *motus*, that is, a directed, goal-oriented course that is unified in its directionality and is composed of individual, ascertainable increments, all themselves indicated by delineatory motions, or figures. This can be exemplified in music, as we very well know from Boethius, writes Grosseteste. What is perceptible to the senses, in terms of highness or lowness is also delineated by a differentiated figures.

Grosseteste clearly makes an issue of the *partes*, as well as the *figurae* that track and describe the very nature of these *partes*. Further on, he will make an issue, as well, of the fact that this trajectory course or *ductus* is on a surface, or plane. Finally, course results in change. All are crucial points, and all are essential for an understanding of Aristotle's *Physics*. Although all of these aspects had been worked over within the late-antiquity Greek commentary tradition, from approximately 200-600 CE, especially by Proclus; none of the concepts mentioned were completely familiar, not thoroughly explicated, and the entire *complex* of these concepts altogether, was not easy for them—or for us for that matter—to understand. Furthermore, although the concept of a *course* divided into *increments* had been suggested several times by the

Apostle Paul,[13] and by Augustine, especially in the *City of God*,[14] none of the writers, with whom a thirteenth-century reading public would have been familiar, had presented such a complete explanation of this set of physical principles. And in spite of the fact that Roger Bacon's commentary is extensive, the edge of excitement appears to be blunted in his commentary on the *Physics*, written some thirty years later. He begins matter-of-factly, writing that the subject of his book is the mobile body.[15] Aristotle's term for increment within a series that is trajectory in nature, is *proton*: an energized module. Bacon gives evidence both of his excellent command of Greek, as well as his knowledge of Aristotle's *De anima*, by beginning with a concept of "ensouled body" as the crucial point of the opening discourse.[16] But the difference in emphasis between Grosseteste and Bacon is apparent immediately, in that Grosseteste, as we have seen concentrates at once on the linear aspect of the construct—on continuity—Bacon, rather, on the individual, self-contained, identifiable increment.

Suffice it to say that the *Physics* was a minefield of intellectual problems. Furthermore, one of the greatest difficulties for the reader lay in the danger of accepting the *sound* of words without realizing that the exact nuance of meaning, therefore the entire point of the argument, had totally eluded him; that familiar terms made up for, and in fact, obscured a lack of genuine understanding. This, of course, frequently occurs in translation. Familiar words within one language, deliberately chosen in order to be meaningful to a readership, obscure the fact that an entirely new concept has actually been introduced. In addition to advising their students to learn Greek, this tendency to substitute comfortable, well-known, words for difficult, new, multivalent linguistic engines was what both Grosseteste and Bacon—and many other commentators on the *Physics* through the fourteenth century—put themselves to a great deal of trouble to avoid.[17]

The *Physics* obviously both deserved and necessitated exemplification. All three writers, Philip the Chancellor, Robert Grosseteste, and Roger Bacon, right at the beginning of three centuries of doing battle with, and attempting to understand, the *Physics*, supplied examples each writer—and personality—carefully chose. Let us look at these, as well as what each type of exemplification makes out of the multivalent concept of motion explained in the *Physics*. An immediate indication of the importance of the concept of *ductus* is the sheer frequency of use of this term in all of their written works, with ocher synonomous expressions, as well. There is constant recourse on the parts of Philip the Chancellor, Robert Grosseteste, and Roger Bacon to expressions of motion, propulsion, pushing and pulling, direction, training, discipline as a directed, reflective motion, persistence in a chosen direction, as well as ambulatory progress, in the use of terms such as *ductus, ducit, trahit, tractus, dirigunt, ambulavit*.[18] For all three authors, the *ductus* principle, a term substituted because it was closer than the straight-forward Latin *motus* to the Greek terms used, is taken from the common source of the *Physics*, therefore, is the same; each writer, however, finds a different exemplication that is justified by the discipline in which he is writing (that is, in some cases, theology), an ax he wishes to grind, as well as his own personal predilection. In reading all three authors in juxtaposition, one realizes that the later, more often than not, appears to point to differences between the authors. Each of three examples, from Robert Grosseteste, Roger Bacon, and, finally from Philip the Chancellor will be included in order to provide a multi-faceted view of this concept as it was understood during the course of the thirteenth century. Interestingly enough, all three examples from all three writers will be taken from sources other than the *Physics* itself. And this is entirely to be expected, since the *Physics* itself contains very few examples, emphasizing, rather, as Aristotle indicates in this work, basic principles.

Firstly, Robert Grosseteste discussed *ductus*, as a motion concept, in his *De generatione sonorum, Concerning the generation of sounds*, written, no doubt, in the 1220's.[19] His comments that make use of, or explicate the concept of *ductus* in his commentary on the *Physics* itself would fill a separate paper, so essential is this concept to his explications. The example of the use Grosseteste makes of the concept that I have chosen is, rather from his treatise on the Ten Commandments, in which he directs its application to an understanding that is ultimately theological. He repeatedly uses the verb *ducit,* in the context of *direction* toward a goal, as for example, *que nos per hanc peregrinacionem sine errore ducit ad patriam*:

> who leads us (directed motion) through this pilgrimage (increments dividing course) without errors (no deviation from course) to the fatherland (final goal).

The use of *ducit* in this short passage, exposes the directional force and consistent motivational power which is attributed to God, who is simultaneously King, righteous Judge, and Priest. Further on in his argument, this concept of ongoing, focused directionality is made more specific when contrasted with the lack of focus, diffusion, and deflection, of a plurality of false gods:

> Et dicit pluraliter *deos alienos,*
> quia ad totum humanum genus *dirigitur* hoc preceptum,
> in quo diversi diversa variis erroribus delusi pro Deo coluerunt,
> et etiam idem aliqui plures deos habuerunt.[20]

The entire human race is *directed* according to this precept, that they are deluded by various and diverse errors because they have a plurality of gods. So much, for the time being, for Grosseteste, and his exemplification.

Roger Bacon's use and explication of the concept of *ductus* in his commentary on the *Physics* forms an underlying conceptual basis, since it does so in the Aristotelian text. Prepared for this by his own commentary on the *Physics*, Bacon also seized upon the figure of Alexander, as well as the *course* of Alexander's life. Bacon also obviously thought that Alexander provided an exemplification for a fuller understanding of Aristotle's other works, such as the *Physics*, in what was considered to be Aristotle's *Secret of Secrets*, or *Concerning the Reigns of Princes, Kings, and. Lords*, perceived, in the thirteenth century, to be the most esoteric of Aristotle's teaching. Surely the reason why Roger Bacon edited and emended *The Secret of Secrets* was because he thought, as did most, that this work contained direct applications of Aristotle's most important principles. Known in two Latin translations from the Arabic, one made during the course of the twelfth century, the other in the early thirteenth, the *Secret* was presented anew, with commentary and prologue by Roger Bacon.[21] The *Secret* certainly discusses motion in detail— the motions of eating, of digestion, the motions to be kept in mind and followed in preparing one's evening meal with regard to getting a good night's sleep, motions of excercise, for example, and the divisions of motions, such as divisions or kinds of wine, as well as medicines. There are motions and divisions for every conceivable situation, ordering the *ductus* of daily life, into manageable increments, leading, hopefully, as the prologue states, to long life. It is the *regimine sanitatis*. The secrets of nature, as Bacon states, are exposed.

Foods, wines, sleep patterns, the qualities of animals, and tempers, are all discussed in the first three parts of this relatively lengthy treatise. One can get waylaid by such nuggets as: "Desire lasting benefits, avoid animal pleasures, think of the future and be temperate". I was especially drawn into: "Music is the solace of the king" which was followed by a recital of the effects of music, as well as the "secret of knowing the minds of your familiars".[22]

Finally, in chapter nine, well into the treatise (that is, part three of four parts), the *Secret of Secrets* brings up counsel, the counsel of kings or of rulership in which the secrets of the heart are made manifest (notice the number of times course, and connection concepts are used):[23]

> de consiliariis regis et modo consilii,
> et quod non manifestet alicui secretum quod est in corde suo,
> et quod attendat in quo omnes et sapientes conveniunt,
> et quod non ostendat eis vel alicui in quo mens sua quiescit

donec progrediatur in actum et experienciam,
et quod equalis honor debet fieri omnibus suis consiliariis.

That is: concerning the counsel of kings and the mode of counsel, and what of any secret thing is not manifested that is in the heart, and what concerns the convening of wisdom in all, and what is not readily apparent but which is demonstrated in the progression of action and in experience, that is, becomes revealed through motion and time.

The section brings together the major themes of the Aristotelian corpus of works, more or less, in a nut shell, that is, motion, divided motion leading to a goal, encapsulated increment linked to increment, by which the outcome is justified logically by each individual event that has formed the progression to this outcome. All of these aspects are clearly related to the goal of the *Metaphysics*, that is, wisdom,[24] and furthermore, are related to a situation that could be imagined, namely, the counsel of the king. By means of this counsel, which the writer of the *Secret* indicates should be sought, the king ultimately *chooses*, decision by decision, event by event, to shape his destiny.

Consensus has been for some time that Aristotle did not write the *Secret of Secrets*. This decision—one of the rare times in which scholars in fact agree—was based primarily on the fact that no Greek version of the treatise has ever been found. I also do not believe that Aristotle wrote it, but more for internal reasons. There are too many examples, too many narratives that illustrate, often in engaging ways, his point. These stories, of course, contribute to the immense interest in the *Secret* for so many years to come, well into the mid-sixteenth century. Examples, in the thirteenth century, of exactly what Aristotle had in mind were difficult to come by, and absolutely necessary.

Ductus, when it came down to its outworking with respect to life, was primarily a matter of choice. The ruler, that is, Alexander, was to take counsel, which, presumably would be rational, weigh his own inclinations, his volition, and arrive at a decision. This, according to many medieval writers, from Augustine to Philip the Chancellor, constituted free will, *liberum arbitrium*. On the basis, then, of individual choices that formed particular events, the entire motion of one's life as a process was formed. Philip the Chancellor's large-scale *Summa de bono*[25] brings together the entire medieval corpus of writing on this particular subject, from Augustine to Peter the Lombard, indicating as well, by means of quotations, his knowledge of, and appreciation for, Aristotle's *Physics*. Again, the subject of free will was given new dynamism, as well as new intellectual tools by the reception of the *Physics*.

But I would like to return to a subsidiary, though oft-mentioned theme, that of example itself. Examples, in the thirteenth century, were important first because Aristotle himself divides his discussion of basic principles from their exemplification. The Philosopher discusses *ductus, tractus* as directed motion that could be divided into self-contained segments, and thus measured, as physical motion. This discussion became the foundation of the discipline of physics as this discipline was established in order to understand the implications of the principle of the nature of motion. The principle was also explained as an artistic principle—the plot of a theater piece with its characters indicated by consistent figures within that plot—in the *Poetics*, and as the underlying principle within moral action in the *Nicomachean Ethics*. There was, however, another source of *exempla*, which from Augustine to Roger Bacon, had formed a bridge between the physical world and life itself, as well, ultimately, theology. This bridge was music, and upon this function music's place within the mathematical arts was based.

Forming a bridge himself between the ecclesiastical milieu of the episcopal see of Notre-dame, and the theology faculty of the University of Paris in the first generation of the thirteenth century—a liaison that at times could not have been easy to effect, Philip the Chancellor knew what any undergraduate at that time would have known, that music by its very nature, composed of one note after the other, exemplifies increment or self-contained *part* within *ductus*, particular event, or tone, within the ongoing continuity that constitutes melodic motion. His songs exemplify *ductus*, are referred to by a unique title, *conductus*, a title that was in use only during the period of the most intense attempts to understand the new concept, that is, from around 1220 to approximately 1260. An example from many *conducti* that we can be reasonably certain that he wrote calls to mind the structure of *event* organized within integrated *motion*, *leads*, increment by increment, to a *termination*. Each event is based upon choice. Choice forms the substance of the text. (This example, a *conductus*, is taken from a manuscript associated with the Notre-dame-university milieu of cat. 1235, now in the Florentine Laurentiana library.)[26]

> Just as flavour flows down
> In the fount's stream,
> And just as scent imbues the vessel
> As it is poured in,
> So the life of a ruler
> Teaches his people,
> And so does his wares
> Approve or censure the potter.

The learned abuses
The rules of his learning,
Whose discipline
is stained by a blot,
For by a defect is sunk
The sailor's craft;
When the head suffers,
So do the spearate members.

Ambition is the root of all evil;
It flows from the sin
Of the Roman Curia,
Where by privilege
Daughters corrupted,
By their mother's contagion
Strive today.

Reason wholly falls
Under the power of the senses,
And contempt
Leads on to riches;
From Christ's manor
The buffoon is enriched,
And one deserving of great punishment
Is granted rewards.

But hold! when the judge comes,
And when he winnows
The grain on the threshing floor,
The vine which makes not fruit
Will be cut down
From the keeper's vineyard.
The scars of Christ's wounds,
The cries of the poor,
The filth of the works which we have not cleansed
All accuse;
The first and the last
Farthing will be required.

The *conductus* itself, with a melodic line, or course, broken, or divided, by single notes and syllables, exemplifies *ductus*. This was the reason for music's inclusion within the quadrivial arts, as the science that provided exemplification for basic concepts.

Conclusion

To summarize these conclusions, first, as is always the case, translation includes and is based upon interpretation. In this case, what is otherwise known about motion from the entire *Physics* is in a sense crammed into the Latin concept *ductus*, which has reinforcing and enhancing synonyms, such as *via, tractus, regnum. dirigo*, and others as well. Although *ductus* is an ordinary Latin word, it is used with new meaning, new contexts, new frequency, during this period of greatest intensity of the reception of the *Physics*. Commentators spanning the thirteenth century, such as Robert Grosseteste and Roger Bacon, as well as *Summa* writers such as Philip the Chancellor, needless to say, show their priorites by their choice of passages to comment upon; and this is very interesting, since their choices from the *Physics* emphasize all of the component tenets of this new concept of motion. These components, one by one, were not entirely new, since, aspects such as motion upon a surface or plane, for example, would have been transmitted by Simplicius, Plotinus, Porphyry, and Proclus, all through Boethius and Johannes Scottus Eriugena, by the commentary on Plato's *Timaeus* by Chalcidius, and by translations into Latin of Plato's *Parmenides, Meno,* and *Phaedo* in the mid-twelfth century. But Aristotle brings together all of these components of a complete concept of the nature of motion—and Philip the Chancellor, Robert Grosseteste, and Roger Bacon all knew it.

Furthermore, categories such as "Aristotelian," "Platonic," and "neo-Platonic" all select one emphasis over other, equally important emphases. Perhaps this is a way of avoiding a great deal of fine-tuned reading. The concept and discussion of the "prime mover" for example, with respect to Aristotle was not especially a medieval priority, nor does it seem to be *Aristotle's* priority. These three thirteenth-century writers, whose prolific and important work has been given the barest smattering of an introduction in this study seem to be more balanced in bringing out Aristotle's own priorities, rather than a construct superimposed upon his major physical work. In this century, the epistemological concentration on the "prime mover" as the major question or problem for what is known as "Aristotelianism" corresponds to an unquestioned research direction of a search for origins as the object of the historical discipline. Clearly, this epistemological orientation also accommodates the evolutionary hypothesis very well indeed. But the selections of, and concentration on, the question of "prime mover" and the axiom, "all that moves is moved by another"—actually a misquotation and misunderstanding of Aristotle—totally ignore what he himself delineated as "extremely important and difficult to understand." His concentration was on the nature of motion which could be incrementally measured within, and using the material of time. Philip the Chancellor, Robert Grosseteste, and Roger Bacon, each in his own way, apparently, with the enthusiasm the newly-translated *Physics* generated, took Aristotle at his word.

The figure of Alexander illustrated this new concept of *ductus*. With an auspicious beginning, each significant event, choice by choice, by differentiation and distinction, as well as internal motions, measured out segments of the course of the Macedonian Conqueror's life. Each segment or choice was also logically, rationally, related to the next. Both *course*, that is *via, ductus*, and the individual events, *partes*, formed two axes for measuring time, material, and motion itself, granting ways for conceptualizing abstractions that are, though constantly used, largely taken for granted today. And so the great mystery of change could be accounted for, the before and the after, why it was that Alexander, in all of his glory, one day simply died.

Notes:

[1] Nicos Kazantzakis, *Alexander the Great. A Novel*, trans. Theodora Vasils (Athens, OH, 1982).

[2] It is noteworthy in this context, and in partial answer to this question, that even today a major university research library, such as at the University of California, Los Angeles, lists over 725 items that have directly to do with Alexander the Great. Alexander's life was also approached as a challenge to political and historical writing during what would be known as the Hellenistic Age, without, curiously, motivating a new genre of biographical writing. See A. Momigliano, *Studies in Historiography*, 2 Vols. (London, 1966), and *Essays In Ancient and Modern Historiography* (Oxford, 1977); as well as a useful summary of both the problems of coherently dealing historiographically with Alexander's life, as well as bibliography in *The Oxford History of the Classical World*, ed. John Boardman, Jasper Griffin, and Oswyn Murray (Oxford, 1986), pp. 198-203.

[3] Plutarch of Chaeronea (c. 46-120 CE) *Lives*, relates that "Alexander was instructed by his teacher not only in the principles of ethics and politics, but also in those secret and more esoteric studies which philosophers do not impart to the run of the mill student, but only by word of mouth to a select circle of the initiated". When he learned that Aristotle had published some treatises dealing with these esoteric matters, he wrote him this letter: "Alexander to Aristotle, greetings. You have not done well to write down and publish those doctrines you taught me by word of mouth. What advantage shall I have over other men if these theories in which I have been trained are to be made common property? I would rather excell the rest of mankind in my knowledge of what is best than in the extent of my power. Farewell". (Plutarch, *Alexander*, in *The Age of Alexander. Nine Greek Lives*, trans. and annotated by Ian Scott-Kilvert with an Introduction by G. T. Griffith [London, 1973], p. 259); cf. Richard Dales' introduction to his edition of Robert Grosseteste's *Commentary on the* Physic*s of Aristotle, Roberti Grosseteste Episcopi Lincolaiensis. Commentarius in VIII Libros Physicorum Aristotelis*, ed. Richard C. Dales, Studies and Texts in Medieval Thought (Boulder, CO, 1963), p. vi.

[4] Cf. Albert Zimmermann, *Verzeichnis Ungedruckter Kommentare zur Metaphysik und Physik Aristoteles aus der Zeit von etwa 1250-1350*, Vol. 1 (Leiden & Köln, 1971).

[5] See Bernard G. Dod, "Aristoteles latinus," in *The Cambridge History of Later Medieval Philosophy. From the Rediscovery of Aristotle to the Disintegration of Scholasticism, 1100-1600*, ed. Norman Kretzmann, Anthony Kenny, and Jan Pinborg with Eleonore Stump (Cambridge, 1982), pp. 45-79, esp. pp. 46-51.

[6] Dales suggests that Grosseteste's Commentary on the *Physics*, cited above, was written 1228-1229. Bacon's Commentary, edited by Ferdinand M. Delorme, OFM, with Robert Steele (*Ouestiones supra Libros Octo Physicorum Aristotelis*, Opera hactenus inedita Rogeri Baconi, Fasc. XIII [Oxford & London, 1935]), before 1267.

[7] The *Physics* was the most commented upon work of Aristotle's natural

philosophical works through the first half of the fourteenth century. Cf. John E. Murdoch, "Infinity and Continuity," in the *Cambridge History of Later Medieval Philosophy*, p. 565.

[8]   The crucial concept here, to be discussed and exemplified below, is *theoria*, which, according to Georg Wieland was first understood by Thomas Aquinas. Cf. "Aristotle's Epics: Reception and Interpretation," in the *Cambridge History of Later Medieval Philosophy*, p. 662. Wieland views *theoria* as an ethical concept, while I will argue that it is a fundamental concept explained by Aristotle as central to a concept of motion in the *Physics*, and because of its importance to this work, was discussed from the earliest reception of that work on.

[9]   *Opus tertium*, ed. J. S. Brewer, Rerum Britannicarum Medii Aevi Scriptores (1859; repr. Wiesbaden, 1965), pp. 191f.: "Omni intellectus noster est, cum continuo et tempore quia sicut eadem mensura temporalis mensurat esse; sed tunc quantum est de potestate intellectus nostri, sine speciali illuminatione non possumus intelligere hujusmodi ...".

[10]   Grosseteste, *Commentary on the* Physics *of Aristotle*, (ed. Dales), p. 1. The entire context: "Cum scire et intelligere adquirantur ex principiis, ut *sciantur et intelligantur naturalia*, primo determinanda sunt naturalium principia. *Via autem innata nobis ad perveniendum* in principiorum cognicionem est ex intencionibus universalibus ad ipsa principia et *ex totis* que constant ex ipsis principiis. In noticiam namque prime materie et prime forme perveniuntur ex hiis universalibus intencionibus materia et forma, que sunt communes ad omnem materiam et ad omnem formam; et iterum ad noticiam *passionum* forme et materie pervenitur ex intencione huius nominis *mobile*. Primo namque accipitur intencio huius nominis confuse, accipitur enim solummodo primo quid est quod dicitur per vocabulum. Deinde *per divisionem pervenitur in partes integrantes ipsam, materiam scilicet et formam*, et ex earum noticia adquisita reditur *ad perfectam noticiam mobilis ex suis principiis*". (I have emphasized the vocabulary that has and will play an important role in the discussion that follows.)

[11]   It is true that *via* is a perfectly normal Latin word. Instances of Grosseteste's use in many other contexts, and the fact that the *Physics* primarily concerns a new, loaded interpretation of a concept of divided continuity, places *via* into a nexus of Latin equivalents for loaded expressions in the Greek text. As I have indicated above, it was not easy to find such expressions, not because they did not exist in the Latin language, but, much more, that their very normalcy seemed to exclude them from a philosophical environment. Use in translation turned them into loaded expressions or terms, as, I believe, is the case here.

[12]   Grosseteste, *Physica,* p. 4: "Partes tamen sunt descripte in ipsa natura proprinquius ipsi nature et sic sunt nociores nature; id est, in ipsa natura prinpinquius descripte, utpote in motu manus scribentis est figura litttere scribende, et expressior est in ipso motu manus tota figuracio littere quam parciales figuraciones. Ipse tamen parciales figuraciones motui manus ipsi sunt proprinquiores. Racio huius, quod sensus comprehendant confuse, est in capitulo quinto prime musice, ubi dicit Boecius quod armonia est facultas differencias acutorum et gravium sonorum

sensu aut racione perpendens. Sensus enim et racio quasi quedam facultatis armonice instrumenta sunt. Sensus namque confusum quidem est ac proximum tali quale ipsum est, idem quod sentit, advertit". Again, the reference to Boethius's treatise on music was one that everyone who could read would have regarded as a commonplace, yet, the conjunction of topics, allusions, and example is significant.

[13]   *Course* (continuity composed of increments): cf. 2 Timothy 4. 7.

[14]   Continuity in terms of "perseverance" or "conduct," cf. Augustine, *City of God*, (An Abridged Version from the Translation by Gerald G. Walsh, SJ, Demetrius B. Zema, SJ., Grace Monahan, OSU, and Daniel J. Honan, with Original Foreward by Etienne Gilson [New York, NY, 1958]), p. 221: "These saints, however, although certain of their reward if they persevere, can never be sure of their perseverance. For, no man can be sure that he will continue to the end to act and advance in grace unless this fact is revealed to him by God. In His just and secret counsel, God, although He never deceives anyone, gives but few assurances in this matter". p. 279: "Thus, from a bad use of free choice, a sequence of misfortunes conducts the whole human race, excepting those redeemed by the grace of God, from the original canker in its root to the devastation of a second and endless death". Both passages—and many others as well—present a construct to be imagined and reflected upon of continuity measured by individual, incremental events.

[15]   *Physica*, p. 1: "*Ouoniam intelligere et scire circa omnes scientias accidit* etc. Iste liber, cujus subjectum est corpus mobile". Bacon continues with the question, what is nature; answering, nature is the principle of motion and status. ("Quod corpus mobile sit subjectum, non videtur quia est subjectum in libro *Physicorum*. Preterea, nature est principium motus et status ...".)

[16]   Translational fortunes of both the *Physics* and *De anima* were, in the late twelfth, early thirteenth centuries, similar, that is, both works were translated, and generated discussion at around the same time; their subject matter was, as Bacon, and many others, noticed, intertwined.

[17]   Roger Bacon's *Opus maius* contains a lengthy discussion on the uses, and necessity, of learning languages other than Latin, including as he mentions, the fact that false interpretation is almost unavoidable, and forms a significant cause of error, even when the text itself is "absolutely correct," that is, without orthographical mistakes. Cf. *Opus maius*, 2 Vols, trans. Robert Belle Burke (London, 1928), I: 93.

[18]   Roger Bacon also makes a point of the opposite of all of the above, that is, the eratic and unstable, as in the following passage (*Opus maius*, I: 35, quoting Jerome's commentary on the book of Isaiah): "The multitude after learning the truth easily changes its mind ... for although the throng is rather prone to evil, and since it too frequently finds a leader weak, yet unless the leader hinders, it is quite easily directed to imperfect good; *because of its own nature it is unstable, and once set in motion cannot preserve a due measure*, and for this reason as far as it is concerned *easily turns to the opposite view* ...".

[19]   *De generatione sonorum*, ed. L. Baur, *Die Philosophischen Werke Grossetestes*,

Bischofs von Lincoln (Münster, 1912), pp. 7-10, cf. pp. 58*ff, in which Baur draws attention to the parallelism of Grosseteste's *Commentary on the Posterior Analytics*, his treatise on the liberal arts, and that on the generation of sound, with respect to just the subject at hand, that of contiguous, identifiable *partes* within a longitudinal transversal motion. Baur's priority in pointing this out is the influence of Boethius on the three parallel passages; I would rather suggest that Grosseteste used known conceptual material, recognizable to any of his readership, in order to emphasize an important point that had, at the time of his writing, a new dimension. Grosseteste contrasts tremor with longitudinal, directed, motion, as does Aristotle in the *Physics*.

[20]   Robert Grosseteste, *De decem mandatis*, ed. Richard C. Dales and Edward B. King, Auctores Britannici Medii Aevi X (Oxford, 1987), pp. 11f. The entire context: "Non igitur coram Deo nostro deos alienos habeamus, aut aliud ab ipso summum bonum credendo, aut aliud summe amando, aut cultura soli Deo debita aliud colendo. Et dicit pluraliter *deos alienos*, quia ad totum humanum genus dirigitur hoc preceptum, in quo diversi diversa variis erroibus delusi pro Deo coluerunt, et etiam idem aliqui pluses deos habuerunt. Et quia quidam coluerunt pro Deo opera creacionis, quidam figmenta false ymaginacionis, quidam vero figuras et formas quas figuravit et fabricavit manus artificis; hos autem omnes bene dicit alienos, quia alienus est qui natus est alicubi perductus alio ubi nil adhuc iuris, vel iuste possessionis, nec permanentem mansionem, inter indigenas adquisivit". I have chosen the passage for its concept of diverse gods leading in all sorts of various directions, which is just the opposite of the concept of *ductus*.

[21]   Cf. "Introduction" to Roger Bacon, *Secretum secretorum cum glossis et notulis*, ed. Robert Steele, Opera hactenus inedita Rogeri Baconi, Fasc. V (Oxford, 1920), pp. ix-xxii.

[22]   Bacon, *Secretum secretorum*, (ed. Steele), pp. 51f.

[23]   Bacon, *Secretum secretorum*, (ed. Steele), p. 33, pp. 135ff.

[24]   The clarion-call of the opening phrase of Aristotle's *Metaphysics* indicates this agenda: All men by nature desire to know.

[25]   Philip the Chancellor (d. 1236), *Summa de bono*, 2 Vols, ed. Nicolaus Wicki, Corpus philosophorum medii aevi. Opera philosophica mediae aetatis selects II (Bern, 1985). The question of choice, and the place of will recurs in The Chancellor's work, cf. esp., pp. 227ff. An extensive discussion of Philip the Chancellor's *ductus*-concept and its relationship to the *Physics* is forthcoming.

[26]   Florence, Biblioteca Laurentiana Pluteus 1.29, f. 418f (see example). Gordon A. Anderson's translation (abridged) of the Latin text has been included here. For both Latin text and translation, see Gordon A. Anderson, *Notre-Dame and Related Conductus*, Opera Omina X: One-Part Conductus Transmitted in Fascicuole X of the Florence Manuscript (Henryville, PA, 1981), pp. XIIIf.

James Otté

THE ENDURING HELLENISTIC GIFT:
THE INVISIBLE AND INDIVISIBLE ATOM

Introduction

Strictly speaking, the atomic theory was a Hellenic, not a Hellenistic idea. But of its first proponent, Leucippus (fifth century BCE), almost nothing is known, and the writings of his student, Democritus (460-370 BCE), have survived only in fragments. Our knowledge of atomism is, therefore, substantially based on two authors of the Hellenistic era, Epicurus (341-270 BCE) and his Roman disciple Titus Carus Lucretius (c. 97-55 BCE), whose long poem *De rerum natura* constitutes the most complete and mature exposition of the atomic theory.

Atomism was the answer to the question: "What is the material composition of the world?" The Presocratics had suggested a variety of answers. To Thales (640-546 BCE) it was "water," to Anaximenes (570-500 BCE) it was "air," and to Heraclitus of Ephesus (535-475 BCE) it was "fire". Empedocles (495-435 BCE), however, provided the classical answer, the one generally accepted in Antiquity and in the Middle Ages, when he suggested the archetypal four elements: earth, water, air, and fire. As the agents of change he added "love and strife: the twelfth century *amicitia et lis*". The atomists rejected the explanations of their predecessors, i.e., both their definitions of the basic elements as well as the process by which these changed into another.

According to Diogenes Laertius, Democritus taught that the universe consists of:

> [A]toms and empty space; everything else is merely thought to exist. The worlds are unlimited; they come into being and perish. Nothing can come into being from that which is not nor pass away into that which is not. Further the atoms are unlimited in size and number, and they are borne along the whole universe in a vortex, and thereby generate all composite things—fire, water, air, earth; for even these are conglomerations of given atoms. And it is because of their solidity that these atoms are impassive and unalterable. The sun and the moon have

been composed of such smooth and spherical masses, i.e., atoms, and so also the soul, which is identical with reason. We see by virtue of the impact of images upon our eyes. All things happen by virtue of necessity, the vortex being the cause of the creation of all things.[1]

Democritus' primary interests seem to have lain with explaining the physical structure of the universe. But a sufficiently large number of the surviving fragments of his writings also demonstrate his concern for a life guided by noble ethical standards. Here are some examples:[2]

> If anyone harken with understanding to these words of mine many a deed worthy of a good man shall he perform and many a foolish deed be spared.

> 'Tis not in strength of the body nor in gold that men find happiness, but in uprightness and in fullness of character.

> Not from fear but from a sense of duty refrain from your sins.

> He who does wrong is more unhappy than he who suffers wrong.

> Strength in body is nobility in beasts of burden, strength of character is nobility in men.

> Those who have a well-ordered character lead also a well-ordered life.

> Men achieve tranquillity through moderation in pleasure and through symmetry of life ... .

Apparently aware that his teachings were either misunderstood or misrepresented, perhaps both, Democritus added:[3]

> The end of action is tranquillity, which is not identical with pleasure, as some by false interpretation have understood, but a state in which the soul continues calm and strong, undisturbed by any fear or superstition or any other emotion.

These are indeed lofty and noble ideals! Why then was the ethical component of Democritus, like atomism upon which it rested, rejected by most ancient authors? Why were the opponents so vehement in their attacks? I shall try to answer these questions below, but let us first examine Aristotle's response to atomism.

The Issue of Atomism

Aristotle rejected the atomism of Leucippus and Democritus on philosophical grounds, as he formulated his own conception of the world. His objections to atomism, more often wrong than correct, are too numerous to be discussed within the confines of this paper, but here are just a few examples: Thus spake Democritus, "Atoms and empty space [exist]; everything else is merely thought to exist". To Aristotle, in contrast, empty space is an impossibility. Democritus said, "It is because of their solidity that atoms are impassive and unalterable". Aristotle replies, "... there are no indivisible magnitudes, such as the atoms of Leucippus and Democritus" (316a. 14). To Democritus the atom has no other properties than size and shape, to which Aristotle responds by observing that "it is strange that no property except shape should attach itself to the indivisible" (326a. 13). To Democritus: There are unlimited worlds; they come into being and perish. In contrast, Aristotle maintained that there is only one finite world with the earth in its center.

Aristotle's objections to atomism were ignored by another Greek, Epicurus. Asserting that the principal goal of philosophy was *hedone*, i.e., happiness, or serenity of the mind, Epicurus endeavored to set the mind free from anxiety and fear. Convinced that ignorance of nature's laws, fear of death, and belief in the often capricious gods caused irrational anxiety, Epicurus turned to the study of nature. Only a means to an end, his examination of nature taught him that solstices, eclipses, rises and settings of heavenly bodies occur without the ministration or ordering of gods, and he maintained that the regularity of phenomena in the sky is due to the arrangement of atoms and not to god.[4]

Epicurus also modified the atomism of Democritus. To the initial properties of the atom, namely: size and shape, he added a third one, namely: weight. He also modified the view held by Leucippus and Democritus, namely, that the atoms eternally move in all directions to one in which the atoms move 'downwards' in space, and "since in a void speed does not vary with weight, heavy and light atoms all fall 'as quick as thought'". But, as his critics pointed out, atoms in their parallel fall could not collide. Epicurus extracted himself from that impasse by imparting upon the atoms a property he called the 'swerve,' an occasional deviation from their 'downward' movement. To a baseball aficionado, a 'swerving atom' resembles a knuckle ball. The concept of the "swerve" served yet another function. G. E. R. Lloyd speculates:

> Although the evidence is incomplete and in part unclear, Epicurus apparently applied the doctrine of the swerve to his account of the soul,

to rescue his moral philosophy from determinism. Already in antiquity this doctrine was the subject of ridicule. Yet the moral argument is not so crass as has often been made out. As a materialist, Epicurus explained mental events in terms of physical interactions of soul-atoms, and his problem was to say what moral responsibility could mean in such a system. It has commonly been supposed that his solution was to postulate a swerve in the soul-atoms for every "free" action. Yet there is no direct evidence that this was his view, and indeed to account for *choice* by assuming the intervention of an *uncaused* event at the moment of decision is bizarre.[5]

But is his explanation indeed any more bizarre than the attempts at reconciliation of free will and moral responsibility with Predestination? In a more recent interpretation by D. J. Furley, cited by Lloyd, the "swerve" as an agent allowing free will gains in plausibility.

> It is more likely that Epicurus' account of responsibility, like Aristotle's, depends rather on his notion of character, and that the function of the swerve is merely to introduce a discontinuity at *some* point in the motions of the soul-atoms in order to make room for the possibility of free choice. The swerve need not, indeed should not, take place at the moment of choice: all that is necessary is that a swerve occurs at some stage in the soul-atoms to provide an exception to the rule that their interactions are fully determined.[6]

Epicurus and his followers pursued atomism to its logical conclusion: the eternal atoms shatter at death to become part of someone or something else. In other words, the substance, i.e., the atoms persist, while their reordering into a new collective configuration provides individuality to something new. Is that not also the logical origin and destination of "ashes to ashes, and dust to dust?" Their physics based on free falling atoms in a void, the Epicureans concluded that fear of the gods and the afterlife was unfounded. The gods, if they existed, would not concern themselves with the mundane affairs of men. Moreover, if there were gods, they too would be composed of atoms. The soul, too, is nothing but a temporary collection of atoms which ceases with death. Their teaching imbued with materialism and tinged with atheism, the Epicureans gathered enemies. Their opponents misrepresented *hedone* as sensual pleasure and unbridled debauchery. One now finds that an Epicurean is synonymous with a gourmet, and our term hedonism still reflects the negative, and one must say, false connotation that some ancient writers conferred upon it. Few, if any, detractors seemed to be aware of the admonition Democritus had spelled out, "The end of action is tranquillity, which is not identical with pleasure" (see above).

Rejected for the most part in Greece, Epicureanism, not surprisingly, fared even worse in tradition-minded Rome.

> The Epicurean gospel was spread by zealous missionaries throughout the Greek world, and a century or so after the Master's death it was preached within the walls of all-conquering Rome (175 BCE). The Roman aristocracy whose system was founded on authority and tradition, expelled these first apostles as dangerously subversive.[7]

Unable to lose its stigma, Epicureanism gained few converts in Rome. Rejection in the imperial city whose Latin tongue dominated the West, would doom Epicureanism, and with it the atomic theory upon which it was founded, for more than a millennium. There was one great exception.

The first century Roman writer Titus Lucretius Carus (c. 97-55 BCE), endorsed the atomism of Epicurus and preached its materialism with enthusiasm. In his *Laudatio* (III, 3) he honored Epicurus and called him "an ornament of the Greek race" (*Graeciae gentis decus*". And like his master, he advocated a philosophy that promised to set men free from their worst anxiety: fear of the gods and fear of death. Even those who rejected his message adored his poetry. In Virgil he gained an admirer, if not a disciple.[8]

Horace cited him some 148 times. But, in the words of Michael Grant, "Lucretius' poem made little mark in ancient times, and it was far from fashionable among medieval churchman".[9]

Lucretius' long poem, *De rerum natura*, constitutes the most complete and mature exposition of atomic theory. It preserved in one body the most complete account of ancient atomism. Indeed, without this long poem our knowledge of atomism would be far less complete, especially if we contemplate the fact that beyond *De rerum natura*, there are only the fragments of the atomists and overwhelmingly unsympathetic references by their detractors. Moreover, *De rerum natura* provided a direct and complete link of atomism to the Middle Ages and the Renaissance. While not an original thinker, Lucretius codified what he had inherited from the Greek atomists. Marshall Clagett assesses Lucretius' poem as follows:

> Although not a work of science, it was to have great influence on scientists, not so much on medieval scientists—on whom its influence, if any, was indirect–as on the scientists of the early modern period, who in seeking to abandon Aristotelian philosophy turned to atomism.

> The principal source of the content of the poem was the teaching of the Greek atomist Epicurus. But the ethical aspects of Epicureanism are planed down, and the result is a treatise on physical theory written in ringing poetic cadences; we must touch these difficult topics, Lucretius tells us, 'with the Muses' delicious-honey'.[10]

Lucretius' beautiful poetry found admirers, as we have seen. But while his readers indulged in the honey-covered verses of his poem, they found his message bitter and distressing.

If one Roman helped save atomism from oblivion, another Roman, Marcus Tullius Cicero (106-43 BCE), who outlived Lucretius by about twelve years, attacked atomism on account of its physics and its ethics. The icon of the Republic, Cicero was also Lucretius' first critic. "In a letter to his brother Quintus (Feb, 54 BCE) [Cicero commented that De rerum natura] 'was written with many high-lights of genius, *but* with much art'".[11] The phrase: 'with much art,' appears to mean contrived. Preferring Stoic ethics, Cicero attacked what he perceived as a lack of ethics in the teachings of the Epicureans.[12] An academic skeptic, Cicero favored the Stoics, particularly on ethical issues, with which he attacked the Epicureans. According to Cicero, "Strato taught that everything which is or which is made is the result of weights and movements," to which Cicero added, this "frees God from his great work and me from fear".[13] In contrast, atomism envisioned a cosmos—perhaps we should call it a chaos—in which atoms fly about at random, and where in the absence of a creator-god or divine overseer, accident triumphs over purpose. It also pitted Epicureanism against Stoicism, which was well established in Rome by the time of the last century before the Christian era.

Like Cicero, most Roman writers of the late Republic objected to a gospel that reduced individuals, the soul, even the gods, to temporary configurations of atoms. They also refused to distinguish between the physics of a materialistic theory and its implications for religion. So they rejected both. To resort to a common modern phrase: "The [Romans] threw out the baby with the bath water".

Cicero concerned himself with atomism in all of the following of his works: *Academici libri, Tusculanae disputationes, De finibus bonorum et malorum, De fato* and *De natura deorum*. Of these treatises, *De natura deorum* (ed. 44-43 BCE) had a strong influence upon Lactantius (c. 250-c. 325) and St. Augustine (d. 430), while among twelfth century atomists at least Adelard of Bath, (early 12th century) was familiar with the original.[14] Ironically, Cicero's extensive attack on Epicurean physics did much to preserve it. His *De natura deorum* is a virtual gold mine of matters atomic.

For the most part, Antiquity and the early Middle Ages rejected atomism.

If Aristotle had opposed it for "scientific" reasons, he and many others also rejected it on philosophical grounds. Some of these preconceptions were not laid to rest until the advent of modern science. In an equally concise and perceptive paragraph, E. J. Dijksterhuis explains why atomism met with so much resistance and hostility:

> However important the place occupied in Antiquity by the aesthetical and teleological conception of nature may have been, there was one school of thought which always rejected it explicitly: in the world of Atomism beauty finds no place and the concept of purpose is without force. Here nature does proceed [aimlessly] in everything, and achieves its effects only at the expense of immense waste. It is therefore not surprising that Atomism had so few adherents in Antiquity: anyone with a Platonic, Aristotelian, Stoical, or Neo-Platonic turn of mind was bound to shrink from it instinctively with an aversion based on the essence of his world-view and springing from aesthetical as well as ethical motives. The achievements of Atomism in the explanation of natural phenomena had not yet reached such a level that scholars could feel obliged to overcome this aversion on account of an evident element of truth in the theory. [15]

Failing to meet the interests of the prevailing *Weltanschauung*, atomism, and its ethical component, Epicureanism, also lacked what the cynic might label "the opiate of the masses".

With the advent of Christianity, aesthetic and teleological conceptions of nature gained additional impetus. Who knew not of the lilies of the field which were more beautifully arrayed than Solomon in all his glory (Mt. 6.28)? Who could fail to grasp the divine purpose in a world in which its creator was aware of every bird before it took to its wings? The materialistic and atheistic atomism of Epicurus had no chance of acceptance in such a deliberately religious environment. And so, the impact of Lucretius on both Roman and medieval authors was almost nil.[16]

The medieval rejection of Lucretius is echoed by Margaret Osler who concluded: "There is virtually no evidence that Lucretius was read at all (only four ninth century manuscripts survive) ... ".[17] That is not surprising. For, in addition to the reasons discussed above, Lucretius' majestic poem must have had a very limited readership in Antiquity because: "From the collapse of classical civilization, only one battered manuscript of the poem was preserved to form the basis of all existing copies".[18]

Bernhard Pabst, a recent student of *Atomtheorien* in the Middle Ages, is much more specific. He writes:

Although the impact of Lucretius in the Middle Ages remains an important and difficult question for medieval philology, on the basis of present research it can be stated that the poem achieved only very limited acquaintance.[19]

Pabst points out that the evidence for direct knowledge of Lucretius is confined to a short period of time. Two important manuscripts of Lucretius' work originated in the ninth century—one at Saint-Bertin near Saint-Omer, the other at the monastery of St. Martin at Mainz. There is some evidence that Hrabanus Maurus as well as Walafried Strabo may have consulted the latter manuscript, but its influence was limited to poetic reminiscences. Neither one of these authors was receptive toward the cosmic view of the Roman poet. Lucretius' text was also available in the following centuries. It is listed in the catalogs for the libraries at Bobbio in the 10th century, at Corbie in the 12th century, and at Murbach. But so far there is no evidence that Lucretius was cited by any writer of the time. We must therefore conclude that Lucretius was not accessible for medieval atomists.[20]

The same holds true for the secondary transmission of Lucretius. The Church Fathers Arnobius (4th century) and Lactantius (c. 240-320) frequently cite Lucretius, but usually as confederates engaged in a struggle against idolatry and polytheism. To them Lucretius is at best the object of attack. Citations from Lucretius in the grammarians, so Pabst, are taken so much out of context that one could not conclude that Lucretius was an atomist, least of all, could one garner from them any hint of the ancient atomism.[21]

That all changed in the twelfth century. In his significant study entitled, *Atomtheorien des lateinischen Mittelalters*, Bernhard Pabst has demonstrated that between 1100 and 1380 no fewer than eighteen scholars taught a corpuscular structure of bodies, and that during the twelfth century alone the atomic theory enjoyed greater acceptance than at any time in Antiquity.[22] The Renaissance of the twelfth century was also a renaissance of atomism. Pabst shows how in the first half of that century the atomic theory experienced its greatest dissemination, and how during the ensuing three centuries it produced a most ingenious diversity of explanations. No longer a single theory, from the twelfth century on the label *Atomtheorien* is most appropriate.

This renaissance of atomic theories, as the author shows, rested on the fact that ancient and early medieval sources contained enough substance to formulate an atomic system.[23] Such a system however, while potentially present earlier, depended on intellectual expansion and on increased interest in natural philosophy to attain actualization. The scholars from the Schools of Chartres and Salerno provided the new thought with its greatest impulses. When completed, so Pabst, "the scholars of the twelfth century conceptualized a world system which resembles that of modern natural philosophical thought more closely than that of any subsequent medieval periods".[24] William of Conches was one of its finest representatives. William assumed a limited number of basic elements and predicated upon each element a certain type of atom. In this regard, Pabst maintains, "William's position agrees with that of [John] Dalton who in the nineteenth century laid the foundation of the modern atomic theory".[25] William of Conches was a most pivotal and germinal thinker in the evolution of medieval atomic theories. His impact is perhaps best judged by the fact that no fewer than 150 medieval manuscripts containing his corpuscular theory have survived.[26]

Between the twelfth century Renaissance and John Dalton (1766-1844), founder of the modern atomic theory, lay that other Renaissance. It rediscovered Lucretius the poet, but its contributions to atomism are minuscule. Like a relic in the realm of religion, Lucretius touched the humanists, as these curious anecdotes reveal:

> Poggio Bracciolini wrote to a friend in 1418 of a manuscript discovered in a 'distant and unfrequented place,' and it was printed in 1473 at Brescia. Botticelli's Venus, in his *Primavera*, was suggested to him by Politian [i.e., Angelo Poliziano, *juvenis Homerus*], who had in mind Lucretius' Invocation to Venus.[27]

Grant wryly adds: "The Renaissance rejected Lucretius' philosophy but revered his poetry".[28]

In the seventeenth century the French priest Pierre Gassendi (1592-1655) elevated the atomic theory of Democritus and Epicurus to the status of Christian acceptability and respectability. Dijksterhuis explains Gassendi's role in these words:

> A Catholic priest of great scientific reputation and unsuspected orthodoxy was fascinated by [the atomic theory] and regarded it his life-work to introduce it into Western thought in a theologically acceptable form. He succeeded in this and consequently this theory, which in the twenties of the [seventeenth] century had still been looked upon as a mischief bordering on heresy, rose in a short time to the rank of a respectable theory, of which no Christian scientist need to be ashamed.[29]

Conclusion

Thus the religious stigma was removed. In the succeeding centuries chemists and physicists increasingly endorsed atomism because it, better than any other theory, explained the nature of matter. They demonstrated that the original four elements could be reduced to a combination of elements, e.g., water consists of two atoms of hydrogen and one atom of oxygen. Then in 1905 Albert Einstein concluded that in theory energy is equal to a small amount of mass multiplied by the speed of light squared, or: $E = mc^2$. In this equation the atomic theory of the ancient Greeks had culminated into a formula that could divide, indeed, destroy the atom itself. Conventional wisdom declares: "Ideas are stronger than swords". Of all the gifts Hellas bestowed upon Western Civilization—upon all Civilization—the atomic theory was perhaps the most profound, the most enigmatic, and the most paradoxical. It has transformed the world. Applied to technology it illuminates cities and it powers nuclear submarines. Beaten into a sword, it has the potential to destroy civilization, the world itself. In the fifth century BCE, Aristophanes asked, "Oh! democracy! whither, oh! wither are you leading us?" Were the playwright to return, would he now ask, "Oh! atomism! whither, oh! wither are you leading us?" If the answer were annihilation of the human race as punishment for the *hybris* it displayed in handling the atom, even a vengeful Alexander would be moved to tears.

Notes:

[1] Diogenes Laertius, *Democritus* IX.44-45 in *Diogenes Laertius: Lives of Eminent Philosophers*, trans. R. D. Hicks, 2 vols. (Cambridge, MA, 1925), II: 453-55.

[2] C. M. Bakewell, *Sourcebook of Ancient Philosophy* (New York, NY, 1907), fragments 35, 37, 40, 41, 45, 57, 61, 191.

[3] Diogenes Laertius, *Democritus* 9.45 (trans. Hicks), II:455.

[4] See G. E. R. Lloyd, *Greek Science after Aristotle* (New York, NY, 1973), p. 21.

[5] Ibid., p. 23.

[6] Ibid., p. 24; see D. J. Furley, *Two Studies in the Greek Atomists* (Princeton, NJ, 1967).

[7] So Lucretius, in Ronald Latham, ed. and trans., *Lucretius: On the Nature of the Universe* (Baltimore, MD, 1970), p. 8.

[8] In another paper given at The Claremont Consortium for Medieval and Early Modern Studies I attempted to show that Virgil actually was a secret atomist. James Otte, "Virgil, Atoms and the Void: Was the Roman Poet a Victim of Misinterpretation or a Secret Atomist?" (Colloquium in Honor of Richard C. Dales, Claremont, CA, March 1996).

[9] Michael Grant, *Latin Literature: An Anthology* (London, 1978), p. 63.

[10] M. Clagett, *Greek Science in Antiquity* (Princeton, N.J., 1988), p. 130.

[11] Latham, *Lucretius*, p. 9.

[12] Margaret Osler, ed., *Atoms, Pneuma, and Tranquility* (Cambridge, 1991), p. 4.

[13] Cited in Clagett, *Greek Science*, p. 90.

[14] Bernhard Pabst, *Atomtheorien des lateinischen Mittelalters* (Darmstadt, 1994), pp. 23-24.

[15] E. J. Dijksterhuis, *The Mechanization of the World Picture*, trans. C. Dikshoorn (New York, NY, 1969), p. 77.

[16] Cf. the assessments of Grant and Claglett cited above, "Apart from its extensive influence on Virgil, [Lucretius'] poem made little mark in ancient times; and it was far from fashionable among medieval churchmen. But its essential hopefulness was an inspiration to the humanists," *Latin Literature*, p. 63; "His poem, *On the Nature of Things*, whose principal source of content was the teaching of the Greek atomist Epicurus, was to have great influence on scientists, however, its influence upon medieval scientists, if any, was indirect," *Greek Science*, p. 130.

[17] Osler, *Atoms*, p. 4.

[18] Latham, *Lucretius*, p. 9.

[19] Pabst, *Atomtheorien*, p. 22.

[20] Ibid., pp. 22-23.

[21] Ibid., pp. 22-23.

[22] Ibid., p. 22.

[23] Ibid., 319.

[24] Ibid., pp. 85ff, 320.

[25] Ibid., pp. 131-32.

[26] Ibid., p. 132.

[27] Grant, *Latin Literature*, p. 63.
[28] Ibid.
[29] Dijksterhuis, *Mechanization*, p. 425.

Claudia Rapp

A MEDIEVAL COSMOPOLIS: CONSTANTINOPLE AND ITS FOREIGN INHABITANTS

Introduction

The concept of "cosmopolitanism" has a fascinating history.[1] The Stoic philosophers of the Roman Empire held the positive view that the man of true wisdom looks beyond the confines of the polity into which he was born, and considers himself a citizen, a "polites," of the whole world and, beyond that, of the "kosmos". This wider notion of citizenship was first propagated in the English language by the great English geographer Hakluyt who outlined this ideal in 1598: "to finde himselfe Cosmopolites, a citizen and member of the whole and only one mysticall citie universall, and so consequently to meditate of Comopoliticall government thereof".[2] It is thus considered beneficial and praiseworthy for individuals to think of themselves in global terms, to use a modern expression.

But when it is adopted by larger civic bodies, this cosmopolitan mind-set does not necessarily bestow the same benefits. When the noun "cosmopolis" and the adjective "cosmopolitan" came into use at the beginning of this century as referring to cities and societies, their application was colored by the distinct desire to protect the integrity and cohesiveness of society from extraneous influences. George Bernard Shaw spoke in 1907 of "cosmopolitan riffraff".[3] Only since the 1950s has cosmopolitanism acquired an unquestioned positive meaning, not only for individuals, but also for societies. It is in this sense of describing a city where the whole world is at home, that I have chosen the title of this presentation.

Would a Byzantine inhabitant of Constantinople have agreed with my characterization of the city as a cosmopolis? Yes and no. Yes, he would take great pride in the fact that his capital city attracted people from all over the world, from England to China and from Scandinavia to Ethiopia. Yet, it was more than obvious that those who visited the capital of the Byzantine Empire for a limited period of time, usually as merchants or diplomats, were not normally made to feel "at home," but constantly were reminded of their status as outsiders and guests. But if foreigners, attracted by the economic opportunities of this center of politics, trade and commerce, took up residence in Constantinople, they were gladly accommodated and granted a surprising degree of social and cultural autonomy and religious tolerance.

The reason for this openness is that Byzantium was, in modern parlance, a multi-ethnic society. What constituted a person's identity was his or her religion and place of origin or residence. In the eyes of the central government, what constituted a person's citizenship in the Empire was his recognition of the Emperor as highest authority, payment of taxes, and adherence to Orthodox Christianity. But religious belief was treated with some flexibility: The Empire included minorities of Christian dissenters, particularly Nestorians and Monophysites (most prominent here are the Armenians), as well as non-Christians, especially Jews.[4]

It is important to be aware of the inadequacies in our terminology. If we called our inhabitant of Constantinople a "Byzantine," he would respond with a blank stare: The term is anachronistic. It was coined by seventeenth century scholars to denote the Empire whose capital of Constantinople was the re-foundation by the Emperor Constantine the Great (324-337) of an ancient city by the name of "Byzantion". If we called him a "Greek," his hand would move in a threatening motion towards his dagger: "Graeci" was the denigrating term so favored by Latin diplomats in their dealings with the Empire in the East. In their own definition, the Byzantines were "Rhomaioi," the only true heirs and continuators of the Roman Empire after its collapse in the West as a result of the Germanic invasions of the 4th and 5th centuries. If, finally, we called him a "Hellene," he would probably become very angry and draw that dagger: The word "Hellene" had since the fourth century acquired the sense "pagan"—the ultimate insult to any Christian. No, our friend would simply identify himself as John Doe, of Constantinople, an orthodox Christian, whose parents or ancestors had come from such and such a city in Asia Minor, Syria, or Greece.

If regional origin along with religious belief constituted a person's identity in the Byzantine Empire, then Constantinople with its diverse population and many foreign inhabitants cannot be taken as representative of the conditions of the provinces of the Empire. As the Empire's capital, however, the city is representative of how the central government wished to present itself to its own people and to the rest of the world.

Constantinople and Its Foreign Inhabitants

For over a millennium, Constantinople was the cultural, political, economic and religious center of the Eastern Mediterranean. Its location at the intersection of important trade routes by land and by sea gave the city a privileged position as an international marketplace. The palace was not only the residence of the Emperor and his court, but also the seat of government and the focal point for encounters with foreign ambassadors. All of Orthodox Christendom looked to Constantinople as the seat of the Patriarch of Constantinople, highest in rank among the Patriarchs, and the location of important Church Councils. And her prestigious institutions of higher learning and her libraries attracted the most brilliant minds. From the provinces, people would flock to the capital, in the hope of finding employment in the imperial administration, to obtain an education, to conduct business, to visit relatives, to pursue a legal case at the highest court of appeals or to petition the Emperor. Extended visits of bishops from the provinces were taken for granted. They formed the "synodos endemousa" (the endemic synod) which served as an advisory body for the Patriarch.

And the city was designed as a veritable showcase to impress all of them: Constantine the Great had planned it as his capital in the East. He enlarged the ancient city of Byzantion and gave it a palace for the emperor, government buildings, a hippodrome for public entertainment, and churches. Under the reign of Justinian in the sixth century, the city reached its first peak of beauty and ostentatiousness. By then, it had been enlarged, under Theodosius II (408-450), by the famous landwalls which were virtually impenetrable for over 1000 years until they crumbled in 1453 under the fire of Ottoman cannons. Justinian was known to his contemporaries as a "lithomaniac," and his church of Saint Sophia bears witness to his ambition even up to the present day. In the 10th century, the city experienced another revival under Constantine VII Porphyrogennetos and his successors. The well-documented visits of an Italian diplomat, and of Russian traders fall in this period, as do the first attestations of a Muslim community in the city, all of which I will discuss shortly. Since the late eleventh century, the desperate need for political allies and military support against the Normans in the West and the Seljuq Turks in the East forced Byzantium to grant ever-increasing concessions to the maritime republics of Italy—most prominent among them Venice, Genoa and Pisa—culminating in the Venetian pillaging expedition also known as the Fourth Crusade and the establishment of a Latin Empire in Constantinople between 1204 and 1261. Constantinople never fully recovered from the ransacking and pillaging by the Crusading armies. In its heyday, it probably had a population of half a million—and that is a conservative estimate, which also excludes the suburbs. After Michael VIII Palaeologos (1258-1282) had wrested the capital from the Crusaders in 1261, he made every effort to revive the economy and to infuse the city with new life, but his resources were limited. Over the next centuries, the city and especially its old center went downhill. The imperial palace complex fell into disrepair and the court took up residence in a more modest dwelling on the northwestern fringe of the city. Some neighborhoods and especially a few monasteries were still thriving. The Italians were taking up permanent residence in the city and in the suburbs and put up their own churches and convents. But the outcome was inevitable: In the final battle for the city and the Empire in 1453, there were hardly enough men to defend the walls, and those who put up valiant resistance included Scots, Catalans and Castilians, Genoese, Venetians, and Anconitans. When Mehmet the Conqueror entered Constantinople, he found the city a patchwork of inhabited quarters and deserted areas with dilapidated buildings and some parts that had over time been turned into gardens.

In this fateful and changing history of Constantinople, there is only one constant factor: Not the fact that it was the residence of Emperor and Patriarch—for they were in exile in Nicaea during the interlude of Crusader rule (1204-1261)—but the continued presence of foreigners in the city. They came from near and far and marveled at what they saw. The earliest descriptions of Constantinople by foreigners date from the 7th century. The first one, by the Gallic bishop Arculf, is very brief and of little interest,[5] but the second one comes from a Chinese traveler, whose report was incorporated into the Annals of the T'ang Dynasty. He is an acute observer who pays special attention to the workings of government and to technical know-how. Here is what he has to say about the capital of the empire of "Fu-lin," as he calls it:

> Their kings are not people of duration. The most worthy is selected and seated on the throne. If in the empire a misfortune or something unusual occurs or if wind and rain do not come at the right time of year, the king is immediately deposed and another one instated on the throne. The crown of this king has the form of a bird with outstretched wings. The crown and necklaces are all fitted with pearls and precious stones. He sits on a bench with golden ornaments. ... Approaching the royal palace from outside, there are three gates, one behind the other, fitted with rare and precious adornments and carvings. A large golden scale is suspended above the second gate. The crossbar of the scale is in a horizontal position and has twelve golden balls. This indicates the twelve double-hours of the day. A golden figure was made, of the size of a man, and placed at the side. Every two hours, a ball falls down and makes a clear and resounding sound. Thus they mark the time of day, and this happens without a mistake. ... When at the height of summer the people are suffering from too much heat, water is diverted and flows over the buildings. The contraption for this is cleverly hidden, so that others cannot recognize it. The inhabitants hear only the sound of

water on the roof and then suddenly see water spraying down from the eaves on all four sides. The suspended waves become a waterfall, the moist draft brings a cool breeze. This is a marvelous effect.[6]

The Chinese traveler was not untypical in his reaction. He focused his attention on the figure of the emperor and his surroundings and on various technical gimmicks. Three hundred years after him, an Italian diplomat would find similar features worthy of note. He was Liudprand of Cremona, and he made the trip from Italy to Constantinople twice.[7] His experience on both occasions was vastly different. Liudprand made his first journey when he was in his late 20s, and stayed in Constantinople from fall 949 to spring 950. He came from a family distinguished through their political service and this venture, in which he was to represent Berengar, the Lombard King of Northern Italy, to the court of Constantine VII Porphyrogennetos (913-959), was considered an educational experience for him. Liudprand had happy memories of this stay which he described later in his *Antapodosis*. This work contains the famous description of the reception hall in the imperial palace, complete with the "automata," or moving objects, in the form of statues of lions that roar and thrush their tails, birds that chirp and a hydraulic device that lifts the Emperor's throne while the ambassador lays flat on the ground in prostration before the Emperor. About twenty years after this first mission, Liudprand, who had in the meantime become bishop of Cremona and an important figure at the court of the German King Otto I, was again dispatched to Constantinople. He recorded this visit in his *Relatio de legatione Constantinopolitana*, not long before his death. This time, his experience was much different.

Instead of the cultured bonhomme Constantine VII Porphyrogennetos, he was dealing with the military-minded Nicephorus Phocas (963-969), and he was representing not a minor Italian King who was trying to be polite, but a recently crowned *Imperator Romanorum* who was in the process of attacking Byzantine territory in southern Italy and who had the audacity to ask for the hand of an imperial princess in marriage. The contrast in the treatment of Liudprand on these two occasions by the Byzantine authorities is especially illuminating and in many ways typical: The reception of foreigners in Constantinople, whether diplomats, traders, or prisoners of war, depended on the general political climate. The Byzantines have a word for this kind of adjustment of a theoretical principle to concrete circumstances: "oikonomia," which literally means "household management".

In Liudprand's case, this meant the most humiliating treatment. Arriving at one of the city gates, he was left to wait in the pouring rain until nightfall; only then—once imperial permission had been obtained—was he allowed to proceed to his assigned lodgings, not on horseback, as his status would demand, but on foot. He and his 25 attendants were assigned what he decried as a dilapidated building "with no air conditioning," at a considerable distance from the palace. The building was usually guarded by at least four armed soldiers[8] who were under orders not to admit any visitors.[9] Liudprand recognized this arrangement for what it was, calling his lodging a "prison".[10] To make things worse, he was assigned a personal attendant, an exceedingly grumpy and unhelpful character, who served double duty as Liudprand's shadow, observing his every move.[11] In short, the foreign diplomat was treated like a spy, and this was quite intentional, as the emperor would not fail to point out on the occasion of their first encounter.[12]

Even despite such obstacles, Liudprand was successful in making contacts and procuring information. He mentions that he received "secret messages" from South Italian envoys who also happened to be in the city.[13] More interesting still are those little asides where Liudprand betrays the existence of a socially stratified community of Westerners in the Capital of the East: "One of his friends" sent him a basket of fruit, which was promptly destroyed by the guards; "some poor Latin-speaking people" came to his house to beg for alms and were beaten up by the soldiers; his own Greek-speaking servant seems to have used his trips to the market for the gathering not just of food, but also of useful information, until the authorities put an end to this and insisted that he sent his ignorant cook instead,[14] and when he mingled with the crowds on a high feast day, Liudprand managed to speak to "some persons" unobserved.[15]

The imperial administration clearly placed great value on control and intimidation of foreign diplomats, but no less did it emphasize indoctrination. Great care was taken to ensure Liudprand's presence at public and ceremonial occasions. He was invited to private and public banquets, imperial processions, and the celebration of the liturgy on high feast days. But even those occasions could turn sour. At one such banquet, Liudprand felt slighted when a savage-looking Bulgarian envoy, who—Liudprand notes with condescension—had only recently converted to Christianity, was given precedence of seating; he left the table in outrage, only to be held back by imperial officials who informed him that he would now continue his meal in the company of the Emperor's servants at an inn. It was only thanks to the Emperor's personal intervention that this incident did not escalate. Anxious to pacify the Italian visitor, Nicephorus sent him a gift of "a fat goat, of which he himself had eaten, elegantly stuffed with garlic, onions and leeks, dripping with fish sauce".[16]

Liudprand's overall unhappy experience must be attributed to the fact that he came as the representative of a hostile power at the height of a political crisis, following the imperial coronation of Otto I in Rome that made him a rival to the Byzantine Emperor in claiming the inheritance of the *Imperium Romanum*. In fact, the fear that Liudprand would take some vital information home with him may well be the reason why the Emperor repeatedly denied his requests for permission to return home. Other groups of foreigners were not treated much better: The same kind of strict surveillance of outside visitors as potential spies experienced by the diplomat from Italy was also applied to merchants. Their treatment is set down in the *Book of the Eparch*, a tenth century handbook of rules for the 22 guilds in Constantinople, which operated under the supervision of the Eparch, the mayor, of the City. A special official, the *legatarius*, was responsible for the foreign merchants in the city. They were lodged in hostels, presumably at public expense, for a maximum of three months. They had to transact their business under the ever watchful eye of Byzantine officials and in observance of strict rules prescribing the availability, quantity, quality and price of specified goods. Transgressions could be punished with confiscation of goods and flogging.[17]

We are particularly well informed about the treatment of the Russian traveling merchants who came to Constantinople once a year, in the spring. They offered furs, wax and honey for sale, and returned with their purchases of oil, wine and walnuts, and luxury items such as silks and glass. By the tenth century, these visits had become a regular feature and it became necessary to regularize them in the form of trade agreements.[18]

The text of the trade agreements of the years of 907, 911, and 944 is preserved in the Russian Primary Chronicle, which was compiled in the early 12th century.[19] This source also describes the usual pattern of the sojourn of Russian merchants in Constantinople: Immediately upon their arrival, a Byzantine official verified their authorization by the Prince of Kiev[20] and took down their names (and presumably also an account of their merchandise). They were assigned a hostel outside the city, in the quarter of S. Mamas. They were only allowed to enter the capital through one specific gate (where their names were probably checked against a list), in groups of fifty, without their weapons, and accompanied by a "guide," i.e. a Byzantine official who must have kept a close eye on them. The Empire assumed responsibility for their upkeep and comfort. For a maximum of six months,[21] they received a monthly allowance of grain, bread, wine, meat, fish and fruit. They could take as many baths as they pleased—an important fringe benefit for a people who began the tradition of the Scandinavian sauna. Finally, in preparation for their return journey, ample provisions were made available as well as everything they required for their ships.[22]

The treaties as they are preserved in the Russian Primary Chronicle distinguish between Russian "agents," i.e. diplomats, and actual "merchants," the diplomats being of higher status: Their authorization by the Prince of Kiev (up until the third treaty of 945) was in the form of a gold seal, while that of the merchants was in silver. Once in Constantinople, the "agents" receive provisions of better quality and in larger amounts than the "merchants".

Here we observe a similarly close connection between diplomacy, trade and espionage as in the case of Luidprand. The Russian diplomats shared with the traders the dangers of the journey, they were assigned to the same hostel in Constantinople, and both groups were treated as potential spies. An additional concern was, of course, the protection of the imperial monopoly for the production of manufactured silk products and especially of purple-dyed silks, purple being the color reserved for the emperor alone. This monopoly was jealously guarded: When Liudprand was about to depart from Constantinople, a thorough search of his baggage by imperial officers (who had obviously been alerted to this fact) produced five garments of this "forbidden" kind. He was ordered to leave them behind, but not without reimbursement for this loss. Luidprand was clearly embarrassed to have been caught red-handed with these highly desirable luxury items, but brushed this aside by the dismissive remark that "back home" it is the "third rate whores and parasites" who wear clothes of such bright color.[23]

Among the visitors to Constantinople we have so far encountered are traders such as the Russians and diplomats (and potential spies) such as Luidprand of Cremona. A further group who resided in the capital for a limited period of time were the prisoners of war. Because they are neglected in modern scholarship, I would simply like to propose some of my own observations on the role and status of Arab prisoners of war in Constantinople, which I hope to elaborate in the future elsewhere. *High-ranking* prisoners of war, I am inclined to think, were treated in much the same way as the hostages that were often exchanged to confirm a treaty. Their status resembled that of diplomats rather than of prisoners. Their sojourn in the capital was limited in time; eventually, hostages returned to their countries and prisoners of war were ransomed or exchanged. Their presence offered a unique opportunity for the government to impress future foreign leaders, whether they ended up as allies or enemies, with the cultural and political superiority of Byzantium.[24] By the same token, it allowed these foreigners to acquire an intimate knowledge of Byzantine government, and to experience for themselves the life and lores of its people.

This oscillating aspect of the status of diplomats and prisoners of war is borne out by the structure of the imperial administration. The portfolio of the foreign minister of the Byzantine Empire, the *logothetes tou dromou* (Logothete of the Course) extended to both visiting diplomats as well as captured enemies. Within the foreign ministry, there was one officer called the "barbaros". The seals of some of these officials in the 9th century have survived. Although our sources do not provide detailed information about this office, we may safely surmise that the duties of the "barbaros" included defraying the expenses of visiting ambassadors from foreign countries, and the monitoring of all foreigners in the capital.[25]

Our most important source for the treatment of high-ranking foreign prisoners is the *Book of Ceremonies*, a tenth century compilation of the protocol observed by the Emperor and his court on specific occasions, both contemporary and of earlier date. Many passages show that the Logothete of the Course played an important role both at the solemn reception of foreigners in the imperial palace, as well as at the ceremonial display of captured enemies.[26] One striking example is provided by the descriptions of the victory celebrations which included the public humiliation of "Saracen," i.e. Arab, prisoners of war in the Forum of Constantine. The highlight of this display was the moment when the Arab leader[27] prostrated himself on the ground before the Emperor, who then placed his right foot on the captive's head and his sword on his neck as a gesture of victory. At the same instant as the Arab leader was symbolically crushed, the other Arab captives also fell to the ground, the Byzantine soldiers who were carrying the Arab weapons now turned them upside down, pointing them to the ground, and a choir erupted in singing "What God is great as our God?". In this carefully choreographed public ritual, the Logothete of the Course played the important ceremonial role of assisting the Emperor.[28]

Although the situation of these and other Muslim prisoners of war in Constantinople is not very well documented,[29] some scattered references both in Byzantine and in Arabic sources allow us to draw a thumbnail sketch. The passage from the *Book of Ceremonies* just cited is followed by the protocol to be observed when recent prisoners of war are paraded in the hippodrome. Although the origin of these men is not specified, the context allows us to identify them as Arabs. On this occasion, the ritual of the humiliation of the captured soldiers remained the same as before, but the venue was changed: It was now staged in front of the crowds who had gathered in the hippodrome to watch the public entertainment—all part of the victory celebrations. Contrary to our expectations, these captives were not removed as soon as they had fulfilled their role as ritual victims. Instead, with the Emperor's permission, the prisoners were able to remain in the hippodrome and to watch the chariot-races. For this purpose, they were assigned places either in a separate location, by themselves, or together with previous prisoners of war.[30]

This is truly remarkable. Prisoners of war, both those who had ended up in the capital after a previous campaign and those who had just suffered ritual humiliation were allowed to be present at the chariot races in the hippodrome. After all, the hippodrome was the focal point of the political life of the capital.

It was here that the emperor showed himself to the population. It was here, on the occasion of the chariot races, that he received acclamations by content citizens, or was subjected to derisory and critical chants by an angry mob. These were the occasions where the Byzantine polity constituted and celebrated itself, and to allow the presence of Muslim prisoners of war at these moments means to accord them a place, however marginal, in the "democratic process," as we would perhaps call it nowadays.[31]

There is further evidence for the privileged treatment of Arab prisoners of war in the *Book of Ceremonies*:[32] The guest list for the Easter banquet in the imperial palace included among the imperial officials of lesser rank, "18 of the Agarene [i.e. Arab] prisoners in the great Praetorium". Their inferior status was expressed by their costume: they were wearing simple white cloaks, without a belt, and they were bound in fetters.[33] Still, they enjoyed the privilege of being invited to join the imperial household on the highest feast day of the Orthodox Church.

The Praetorium where they were imprisoned was located in the vicinity of the imperial palace.[34] The earliest attestation for this Muslim prison comes from the reign of Leo VI (886-912), who persuaded one of its inmates to send a false message to Syria. The prisoners were certainly not treated as criminals: Not only could they watch the chariot races and were invited to banquets in the palace, as we have already seen, but their facility also included a mosque. By the mid tenth century, a legend was circulated by both Byzantine and Arab authors, according to which the foundation of this mosque went back to a request made by the Arab general Maslama during his year-long siege of Constantinople of 717-718.[35]

This mosque was not only used by the prisoners of war in the city. Muslim traders and diplomats must have also frequented it.[36] The tenth century Arab geographer al-Muqaddasī explains the importance of including a description of Constantinople in his work: "... because the Muslims have a mosque there, where they gather and worship freely. ... It is necessary to describe the routes to Constantinople because it is of use to the Muslims for the ransom of prisoners, for embassies, for warfare, and for trade".[37] In the subsequent centuries, the mosque sometimes became an object of negotiation with Muslim rulers. Byzantine Emperors would promise them that their names be mentioned in Friday prayers and demanded in return certain favors for the Christian population under Muslim rule.[38] This first mosque was destroyed in 1201 in a riot, but another one was erected soon thereafter. The second mosque, we are told, was located in the quarter of the Muslim merchants, not far from the Church of St. Irene of Perama. This is, incidentally, the first time we hear of a Muslim quarter in Constantinople. The second mosque was destroyed by Pisan and Venetian Crusaders in 1204, despite the joint resistance of Byzantines and Muslims.[39] A Muslim quarter continued to exist after the reconquest of the capital by Michael VIII Palaeologus in 1261, when it was apparently moved to the western part of the city. It had some long-term residents. One of them, 'Abd Allāh b. Muhammad, a merchant from Sinjar, lived for twelve years in Constantinople, until, in 1293, he came to Damascus and shared his experience with the father of the Arab historian al-Jazarī, who preserves a record of this conversation: 'Abd Allāh described a quarter especially for Muslims that was as large as two thirds of Damascus. It was located next to the Jewish quarter, was surrounded by a wall, and had a gate that was closed at night, at the same time as the city gates.[40] A century after al-Jazarī, the Muslim quarter had gained even further prominence. In 1398 the Emperor Manuel II Palaeologus had to enter into negotiations with the Ottoman sultan Bayezit I who was besieging Constantinople. Bayezit demanded greater legal autonomy for the Muslims who were laborers in the harbors of Constantinople or who had come to the city to conduct business. The Emperor was asked to cede his judicial authority and to allow the appointment of a Kadi to administer justice to the Muslims who would thus be living under their own law.[41]

Since the early tenth century, Muslims are thus attested as a permanent presence in the capital. They are recognized as such by the construction of a mosque and the assignment of a particular quarter of residence, which is attested since the end of the 12th century. We know very little about their daily lives, but it is clear that the Byzantine authorities showed a surprising degree of respect for their religion, and for the high-ranking prisoners of war who were treated rather like foreign diplomats and were invited to join in the social and political life of the city and of the palace.

The case of the Italian diplomat, the Russian traders, and the Muslim prisoners of war illustrate the way in which the treatment of foreigners who were present in Constantinople for a limited time was dictated by political and economic considerations. But what about outsiders who did not represent a foreign power? Who were outsiders because of their religion, but otherwise had no country to call their own, and who were long-term residents of the capital? Here, of course, I am talking about the Jews, who were part of the population of Constantinople throughout its history.[42] They are an excellent test case to scrutinize and fine-tune our views of what it meant to be a Byzantine "citizen". We have seen above that Muslim prisoners were allowed to participate in the "democratic process" by attending the races in the hippodrome. The Jews of Constantinople certainly did that and much else: they participated in riots and they helped to defend the city walls during enemy sieges. They were permanent residents of the capital and owned property—another important privilege of citizenship. Whether they were subject to a special tax, and if so, during which periods of the Byzantine Empire, remains a debated question.[43] Quite a few of Constantinople's Jews held prominent positions as court interpreters or as the Emperor's personal physicians. This tradition would be continued by the Ottoman Emperors: Mehmet the Conqueror had a Jewish physician, just like his father. There are even some cases of intermarriage (which was prohibited by canon law) between Jews and Christians in Byzantium, but the bulk of evidence for that comes, to my knowledge, from documents in the Cairo Genizah and pertains to the Jews of Thessalonike.[44] Their worship was respected and protected. The destruction of synagogues was prohibited by law (but also the erection of new ones was forbidden) and Jews could not be cited before a legal court on the Sabbath.

But this positive impression is only part of the picture. At various moments in the history of the Byzantium, Emperors ordered the forced conversion of Jews. It must be added, though, that such measures often met with resistance from Christian ecclesiastics who argued that the administration of involuntary baptism was a perversion of this institution. Jews were barred from the army, from the civil service and from teaching at universities, and a great economic handicap was imposed on them in the prohibition to own or trade in Christian slaves. Also, they did not enjoy the same legal status as Christians: if a Christian was the victim of theft, the thief would make restitution in the value of 3 to 4 times his damages, while a Jewish victim would only receive two times the value. And a Christian who was accused before a court of law was free to reject a Jewish witness.[45]

However, it is impossible to say how long these restrictions were valid and how strictly they were enforced. If some generalization should be attempted, it seems that since the thirteenth century, the Jews of Byzantium enjoyed greater security and stability than ever before. The growing economic potential of the Jewish communities had become difficult to overlook, and the Byzantine Emperors took recourse to the principle of "oikonomia" which allowed them to harmonize practical exigencies with more abstract concepts. Another factor played a role in this: From the late elventh century, Byzantine society became much more permeable by outsiders. This was the period when the Empire was in desperate need for military help against the Normans in the West and the Turks in the East and thus was forced to look for allies among the maritime republics of Italy; the price for such assistance was an ever greater influx of Italian capital and manpower into the Empire. Improving the lot of the Byzantine Jews, who represented an important economic force, went some way to redress the balance.

The history of the Jewish community in Constantinople confirms the extent to which their fate depended on imperial decisions and was intertwined with the general political situation. On the whole, the community was rather wealthy. Most of its members engaged in business, and many specialized in working with textiles or leather. Some owned houses in the city, where they lived with their families or which they rented out. In the mid fifth century, a synagogue was constructed in the quarter of the coppersmiths, the Chalkoprateia, in the immediate vicinity of the palace and other public areas. This happened in 442, while the emperor Theodosius II was absent on campaign.[46] On his return in the following year, he ordered that the building be converted into a church. There are no further references specifically to a synagogue, but it is safe to assume that where there was a community of Jews, such places of worship also existed. We have to wait for half a millennium until the next attestation of a Jewish quarter in Constantinople. In the tenth century, the so-called "Judaica" is located on the northern shore of the peninsula, in the same general area with access to harbor facilities as the colonies of Italian traders from Venice, Amalfi, Pisa and Genoa. But not long thereafter, and certainly before the 1160s, when the Spanish Jew Benjamin of Tudela visited these parts (and commented on the absence of Jews from the city proper), the Jews had been moved outside the city of Constantinople, across the Golden Horn, into the quarter of Galata, or Pera, as it was then known, where they also had a cemetery. This community seems to have been dispersed for good in the upheavals of the capture of Constantinople by the Fourth Crusade in 1204. In the year 1267, not long after the re-establishment of Byzantine rule, the whole area of Pera was given to the Genoese and the Jews disappear from the record in this suburb until the fourteenth century, when the new settlers that arrived there from various areas of the Byzantine Empire, especially from those under Genoese control such as Trebizond and the Crimea, also included Jews.

Constantinople after the Crusaders

After Michael VIII Palaeologus wrested Constantinople from the Crusaders in 1261, he made every effort to revitalize the city. It is very likely that the Jews of Constantinople were also included in this strategy and that they were at that time assigned their area of residence in the Vlanga quarter, on the Propontis. The Arab merchant from Sinjar who provided al-Jazarī with information about the Muslim quarter of Constantinople in the 1280s, also indicates the existence of a Jewish settlement in its vicinity.[47] This Jewish quarter of Vlanga continued to exist until the Fall of the City to the Ottomans in 1453. According to the account of this tragic event by the Italian Nicolo Barbaro, it was in this area that the Ottomans first gained entry into the city. They descended on the "Zudeca, per poder meio robar, per esser li assai richeza in caxa de queli Zudei a masima de zoie (Jewish quarter, in order to make greater booty, for there were significant riches in the houses of these Jews and a large amount of silks[?])".[48] After he had taken over the city, the new ruler, Mehmet the Conqueror, pursued a deliberate policy of openness and repopulation. He attracted a massive influx of Jews to Constantinople, so that by the time of the census of 1477, there were 1500 Jewish houses inside the city; that is to say, they made up an estimated 10% of the population.[49]

Under Byzantine rule in the twelfth century, by contrast, it seems that the Jews constituted about 2% of the population of Constantinople.[50] Still, on his visit to the capital in the 1160s, the Jewish merchant from Spain Benjamin of Tudela was impressed to encounter in the suburb of Pera the largest Jewish community outside Baghdad.[51] According to his account, this community consisted of 80% of Rabbanite Jews, but also had a substantial group of Karaite Jews, numbering 500 (presumably) households, who were separated from the former by a fence.[52] They specialized in the preparation of leather goods. This occupation was particularly loathsome because of the smell of the chemicals it involved. Benjamin writes:

> ... there is much hatred against them, which is fostered by the tanners, who throw out their dirty water in the streets before the doors of the Jewish houses and defile the Jews' quarter. So the Greeks hate the Jews, good and bad alike, and subject them to great oppression, and beat them in the streets, and in every way treat them with rigor. Yet the Jews are rich and good, kindly and charitable, and bear their lot with cheerfulness.[53]

Competition over the business of tanning and preparing skins brought about a very interesting incident that involved Jews and resulted in a veritable diplomatic crisis between Byzantium and Venice. This incident also throws some light on the definition of Jewish versus Byzantine or—in this case— Venetian "'dentity," and finally, it illustrates the mental flexibility of Venice in its overseas possessions. The events occurred in 1319 and 1320.[54] By that time, the Venetians had lived in the area immediately adjacent to the Jewish quarter of Vlanga for a good 50 years.[55] A treaty in 1277 had granted the *bailo* of the Venetian community the right to bestow Venetian status at his will. This process usually involved two witnesses to vouch for the worthiness of the applicant, and the payment of fees to various Venetian officials. Now the Venetians enjoyed considerable economic privileges, not least the far-reaching exemption from most tax obligations to the Empire, including customs duties. Little wonder, then, that Venetian status was eagerly sought after and provided a convenient way for the Venetian community to increase its numbers.

This is where the Jews come in. Back in Italy during this time, Venice pursued a very restrictive policy with regard to the Jews. They were not allowed as permanent residents in the city (until the establishment of the Ghetto in 1516), but those who lived on the Terraferma could obtain a "condotto" that permitted them to engage in specific business for a stated amount of time. In Constantinople, however, the rules were much more relaxed. The Venetian quarter soon housed a large number of Jews. Obviously, these cannot have been "native" Venetians, but were Romaniote Jews from the Byzantine Empire who had successfully petitioned for Venetian status. Another illustration of the flexibility of the Venetians abroad is the fact that from 1397, Jews who entered Venice were stigmatized by the requirement to wear a yellow badge, but the Jews of Venetian status in Constantinople were not subjected to such treatment.[56] Unlike their Byzantine counterparts, the Jews of Venetian status were, however, subject to higher taxation than non-Jews within the Venetian community: On certain days of the year, prescribed sums had to be paid to certain Venetian officials (these were used to finance the celebration of Christian festivals), and boots and brooms of a certain value had to be delivered to the *bailo's* palace on particular occasions.

A number of these Jews of Venetian status lived, not in the Venetian quarter, but side by side with Byzantine Jews in the Vlanga quarter. Those who worked in the leather business had come to an agreement: The Venetian Jews would prepare the skins, and the Byzantine Jews would do the tanning. This kind of team-work, of course, was an open path to defraud the Imperial fisc: The work of Byzantine Jews could be passed off as that of Venetians and therefore claimed as tax-exempt. To eliminate this problem, the Emperor Andronikos II (1282-1328) simply prohibited all Byzantine Jews from engaging in the tanning business.[57] The Venetian Jews in the Vlanga seized this opportunity to take up by themselves the tanning job previously done by the Byzantine Jews. Andronikos retaliated by demanding of the Venetian *bailo*, Marco Minotto, that the Venetian Jews depart from "imperial territory" in the Vlanga quarter and take up residence with the other Venetians. The *bailo* protested against this request, pointing out that under the current agreement (concluded in 1285 and renewed in 1310 for 12 years), anyone of Venetian status was at liberty to take up any profession of his choice and to settle wherever he chose, as long as he paid the required land tax.

The next step for the Byzantine Emperor was to make himself the spokesman of 'his' Byzantine Jews. He replied that the inhabitants of the Jewish quarter of Vlanga no longer wished to rent out their houses to Venetians. Venice in turn referred to the original agreement which allowed the presence of Venetian Jews in the Vlanga. The imperial displeasure at these developments soon took on a more concrete form: The *bailo's* report to the doge in Venice of March 1320 reveals the extent of the hostilities: He complained about arbitrary confiscations (skins had been burned or thrown into the sea), the imposition of taxes on furs brought by Venetians to Constantinople, and attempts to hinder the Venetians to go about their profession or to enter their houses. In short, the Venetian community had been hit where it hurt: Their profit margin was under assault. In response to these offenses, Venice made two requests: restitution of damages, which was granted in 1324, and the demand that the Venetian quarter be protected by a wall.[58]

This incident is revealing in many ways: It shows the tendency of Jews to live and work together, regardless of their official status as Byzantine or Venetian. In Constantinople, Byzantine Jews were accepted members of the community as tax-payers, participants in public life, and property owners. The only difference that truly set them apart was their religion. But, as the initiative of Andronikos II demonstrates, even that did not prevent the Emperor to take up their cause when the situation (and his self-interest) required such action. In short, this episode of the Jewish tanners is further confirmation for the remarkable flexibility and adjustment to change of which the Byzantine Empire was capable when this was required by the circumstances.

Over the thousand-year history of the Byzantine Empire, visitors and settlers from all over the world flocked to its capital in Constantinople in order to enjoy its religious and cultural attractions, to profit from its economic opportunities, or to conduct political negotiations. Only a small segment of these could be discussed here, but their treatment is nonetheless indicative of an imperial policy that took the presence of foreigners, and the character of the capital as a "cosmopolis," for granted. The imperial administration continually sought to devise a variety of strategies to accommodate these visitors and to enable them to pursue the purpose of their presence, while asserting the government's need to exercise control over potentially harmful activities and, before all, the Emperor's desire to dazzle and impress the visitors with the display of power and grandeur. In other words, it was the principle of "oikonomia" that inspired the treatment of Italian diplomats, Russian merchants, Arab prisoners of war and Jewish settlers alike.

Notes:

[1]   Except for the addition of footnotes, this article deliberately retains its character as a lecture presentation in the hope that this format makes the material more accessible. I am grateful to Constantina Scourtis and Jason Moralee for their research assistance.

[2]   R. Hakluyt, *The Principal Navigations, Voyages, Traffiques & Discoveries of the English Nation*, Vol. 1 (1598; repr. Glasgow, 1903), p.15, citing an earlier work, *The Navigation of King Edgar*.

[3]   Shaw's *John Bull's Other Island with a Preface for Politicians* (New York, NY, 1913), p.viii, contains a sneer against "the hybrid cosmopolitans, slum poisoned or square pampered, who call themselves Englishmen today;" in Act I, p.19, an attack is launched against "the modern hybrids that now monopolize England. Hypocrites, humbugs, Germans, Jews, Yankees, foreigners, Park Laners, cosmopolitan riffraff".

[4]   On the issue of ethnic identity, see Cyril Mango, *Byzantium. The Empire of New Rome* (New York, NY, 1980), pp. 13-31.

[5]   J. P. A. van der Vin, *Travellers to Greece and Constantinople. Ancient Monuments and Old Traditions in Medieval Travellers' Tales*, 2 Vols. (Istanbul, 1980), pp. 481-83.

[6]   P. Schreiner, "Eine chinesische Beschreibung Konstantinopels aus dem 7. Jahrhundert," *Istanbuler Mitteilungen* 39 (1989), 493-505, esp. 494-95. Another Chinese document from the early 7th century, P'ei Chü's *Report on the Western Countries*, mentions the trade routes leading to Byzantium, H. Miyakawa und A. Kollautz, "Ein Dokument zum Fernhandel zwischen Byzanz und China zur Zeit Theophylakts," *Byzantinische Zeitschrift* 77 (1984), 6-19.

[7]   For general background, see J. N. Sutherland, *Liudprand of Cremona. Bishop, Diplomat, Historian* (Spoleto, 1988).

[8]   *Relatio de legatione constantinopolitana* 34.7 in *Die Werke Liudprands von Cremona*, ed. J. Becker, 3rd ed. (Hannover & Leipzig, 1915), p.193.

[9]   Ibid., 24.10-11, p.188.

[10]   Ibid., 13. 11, p.183.

[11]   Ibid., 1.2-4, p.176.

[12]   Ibid., 4.6-7, p.178.

[13]   Ibid., 37.18-19, p.194.

[14]   Ibid., 46.6-11, p.200.

[15]   Ibid., 49.27-28, p.201.

[16]   Ibid., 20. 17-19, p.186.

[17]   *Das Eparchenbuch Leons des Weisen*, ed., trans., and annotated by J. Koder (Vienna, 1991), ch.20, pp.132-35.

[18]   The most recent treatment is G. G. Litavrin, "'Die Kiever Rus' und Byzanz im 9. und 10. Jahrhundert'," *Byzantinische Forschungen* 18 (1992), 43-59. For the place of their sojourn, in the suburb of the quarter of S. Mamas, see R. Janin, *Constantinople byzantine. Dévelopement urbain et répertoire topographique* (Paris, 1964), pp. 256-57.

[19] *The Russian Primary Chronicle. Laurentian Text*, trans. S. H. Cross, O. P. Sherbowitz-Wetzor (Cambridge, MA, 1973), for the treaties of the years 904 and 911, pp. 64-69; for that of the year 944, pp. 73-78.

[20] This particular regulation is found in the trade agreement of 944 (p.74) which notes that the previous system of verification through gold seals for agents, silver seals for merchants was now replaced by a written certificate by the Prince attesting to the number of ships that had been sent.

[21] This was a privilege. The usual stay of foreign merchants, prescribed in the *Book of the Eparch*, lasted a maximum of three months, cf. above, note 18.

[22] *Russian Primary Chronicle*, for the years of 904-907 (pp. 64-65).

[23] Liudprand of Cremona, *Relatio de legatione constantinopolitana*, ch.55. 2-3, p. 205.

[24] On this aspect, see H. Hunger, "Der Kaiserpalast zu Konstantinopel. Seine Funktionen in der byzantinischen Außen- und Innenpolitik," *Jahrbuch der Österreichischen Byzantinistik* 36 (1986), 1-11.

[25] J. B. Bury, *The Imperial Administrative System in the Ninth Century. The Kleterologion of Philotheos* (1911; repr. New York, NY, date missing), p. 93.

[26] On this office, see Bury, ibid., pp. 91-93.

[27] The text refers to him as 'Amer,' i.e. 'Amr,' *De ceremoniis aulae byzantinae* 2.19, ed. J. Reiske (Bonn, 1829), p. 610, 17.

[28] Ibid., pp. 609, 18-611, 11.

[29] See the brief remarks by A. Miquel, *La géographie humaine du monde musulman jusqu' au milieu du 11e siècle* (Paris, 1975), pp. 470-72.

[30] *De ceremoniis* 2.20 (Reiske, p. 615, 1-15).

[31] Another possibility would be to interpret their presence as the functional equivalent of the 'indoctrination' of foreign diplomats through grand displays, as we have seen with Liudprand. However, the latter never once mentions the hippodrome.

[32] This event probably took place after the peace with the Bulgarian Tzar Peter in 927, since 'Bulgarian friends' are also named as participants in the celebrations.

[33] *De ceremoniis* 2.52 (Reiske, p.767, 16-768, 12).

[34] The Muslims were probably its only inhabitants. The early 10th-century author Ibn Rosteh mentions a "prison of the Muslims" in the vicinity of the imperial palace: Janin, *Constantinople byzantine,* p.170, quoting the *Kitab al-a'laq al-nafisa*, ed. Goeje, *Bibliotheca geographorum arabicum* VII (Leyden, 1892), pp. 120-21.

[35] Constantine Porphyrogenitus, *De administrando imperio* 21, l.111-114, ed. Gy. Moravcsik, trans. R. J. H. Jenkins, *Dumbarton Oaks Texts* 1, Corpus fontium historiae Byzantinae 1 (Washington, DC, 1967), p. 92. Cf. M. Canard, "Les expéditions des Arabes contre Constantinople," *Journal asiatique* 208 (1926), 61-121, esp. 94-99.

[36] For the presence of Muslims in Constantinople, see Janin, *Constantinople byzantine*, pp. 257-59.

[37] Cited after D. Sturm, "Die Darstellungen der byzantinisch-arabischen Verhältnisse bei den arabischen Geographen des 10. Jahrhunderts," *Byzantinische Forschungen* 18 (1992), 158-59.

[38] See the entries under the relevant years in F. Dölger, *Regesten der Kaiserurkunden des oströmischen Reiches*, Vol.1ff. (Munich & Berlin, 1927ff.), in 987, it was ordered that prayers be said every Friday in the mosque of Constantinople for the Fatimid Kalif of Egypt (this order was renewed in 1027); and in 1050, prayers were promised in the mosque of Constantinople on behalf of Togrul-Beg.

[39] *Nicetae Choniatae Historia* 20-21, ed. J. A. van Dieten, 2 Vols. (Berlin & New York, NY, 1975), p. 525.

[40] M. Izeddin, "Un texte arabe inédit sur Constantinople byzantine," *Journal asiatique* 246 (1958), 453-57, esp. 454-55.

[41] Ducas, *Istoria Turco-Bizantina (1341-1462)*, ed. V. Grecu (Bucarest, 1958), XIII: 5, 20-28, p. 77.

[42] Especially relevant are the monographs by J. Starr, *The Jews in the Byzantine Empire, 641-1204* (Athens, 1939); and Steven B. Bowman, *The Jews of Byzantium, 1204-1453*, Judaic Studies Series (Tuscaloosa, AL, 1985).

[43] Starr, ibid., pp. 11-17; Bowman, ibid., pp. 41-48.

[44] Steven B. Bowman (Paper delivered at the Byzantine Studies Conference, Princeton, NJ, 1993).

[45] Starr, *Jews in the Byzantine Empire*, p. 20.

[46] On this and the following, see D. Jacoby, "Les quartiers juifs de Constantinople à l'époque byzantine," *Byzantion* 37 (1967), 167-227, repr. in his *Societé et démographie à Byzance et en Romanie latine* (London, 1975).

[47] See above, note 46.

[48] Nicolo Barbaro, *Giornale dell'assedio di Costantinopoli*, 1453, ed. E. Cornet (Vienna, 1856), p. 56, quoted in Jacoby, "Quartiers juifs," p. 195, n. 1.

[49] Bowman, *Jews of Byzantium*, p. 194.

[50] A. Sharf, *Byzantine Jewry from Justinian to the Fourth Crusade* (London, 1971), p. 3.

[51] *The Itinerary of Benjamin of Tudela* (Malibu, CA, 1987), pp. 69-72.

[52] See Bowman, *Jews of Byzantium*, p. 107ff.

[53] *The Itinerary of Benjamin of Tudela*, p. 72.

[54] Jacoby, "Quartiers Juifs," pp. 196-205 and idem, "Venice and the Venetian Jews in the Eastern Mediterranean," *Gli Ebrei e Venezia, secoli XIV-XVIII*, ed. G. Cozzi (Milan, 1987). Cf. also Bowman, *Jews of Byzantium*, p. 20ff.

[55] For the topography of the Venetian quarter, see Janin, *Constantinople byzantine*, pp. 247- 49.

[56] By the 14th century, the Venetian Jews in the colonies, such as those in Constantinople, were called 'white Venetians' ('Veneti albi').

[57] There were, however, non-Jewish tanners in the city.

[58] About 20 years after this incident, by 1343, the Venetian Jews lived in a distinct area, called 'Cafacalea' within the Venetian quarter.

Bariša Krekić

VENICE, BYZANTIUM AND THE BALKAN PEOPLES IN THE LATE MIDDLE AGES

Introduction

The eleventh century was in many ways a landmark period of change and of shifts of power in the Mediterranean area. Whether we agree or disagree with older or more recent interpretations of Byzantine internal developments at the time, we can certainly accept the idea of the existence of major changes in relations between the various powers on the northeastern Mediterranean rim. I shall limit myself to a brief consideration of shifts of power, contrasts and ambiguities in relations between three factors in the east central Mediterranean basin: Venice, Byzantium, and the Balkan peoples.

Power, Contrasts, and Ambiguities

One event in particular during the eleventh century brought those contrasts and differences in sharp focus and had the longest-lasting effects of all. That was the Great Schism of 1054. I shall not dwell on those circumstances for they are well known. It must be pointed out, however, that the schism of 1054 deepened ongoing processes, both West and East, which made the contrasts between the two entities ever more intractable: while in Byzantium influence and power shifted increasingly from state to church, in the West the papacy had growing trouble with the newly-emerging, powerful national states. Thus, the ecclesiastical conflict had its very real and concrete political implications and consequences and drove the East and the West further apart.

Venice emerged as the chief intermediary and main beneficiary of this situation. It is important to point out, however, that Venetian policies and attitudes towards the East and the West had nothing to do with ideologies, religious or otherwise. The strength of the Venetian position—then and later—was its pragmatism. Indeed, it was its economic interest, its trade and navigation that dictated Venice's policy towards Byzantium in the East and towards other states in the West. That policy, in turn, enabled Venice to play the great role that it played on the Mediterranean rim and to become the rich and powerful colonial empire later on.

This process was started by the chrysobull issued by Alexius Comnenus (1081-1118) in 1082, a document which, as Donald Nichol says, "was by far the most comprehensive and detailed charter of privileges granted to Venice by a Byzantine Emperor. It was also the most consequential for it became the corner-stone of the Venetian colonial empire in the Eastern Mediterranean". [It] gave the Venetians a foot in the door that led to the wealth of Byzantium".[1] A somewhat different opinion has been expressed by Alexander Kazhdan and Ann Wharton Epstein: "Scholars generally assume that these concessions had a crippling effect on the Byzantine economy, but by so doing they tend to impose on the eleventh and twelfth centuries the economic perspective of the fourteenth century. ... In the eleventh and twelfth centuries the Straits were still under the *imperium's* control ... [and] Italian trade and military assistance was beneficial if not crucial for the Byzantines. ... A significant loss of equilibrium [in the Italo-Byzantine exchange] occurred only under Andronikos I [1183-85]".[2] But even Kazhdan and Epstein do recognize that "the Latin community in Constantinople itself was very sizable" and mention sources which put those numbers into tens of thousands by mid-twelfth century.[3] It seems to me that there can be no doubt that the charter of 1082 laid down the foundations of the Venetian colonial empire in the East. Of course, the culminating point of this process came with the Fourth Crusade, in 1203-1204, by which time the role of Venice as the main intermediary between the Levant and Western Europe was well established. In fact, the Fourth Crusade represented the final confirmation of the shift of wealth and power from East to West in the Mediterranean world, even though Byzantium survived, albeit precariously.

It is important to remember, however, that the Venetian colonial expansion was not accompanied by systematic efforts to impose the Italian language or the Roman Catholic faith on the population of the conquered areas. The Croats in the Dalmatian cities, the Serbs in the cities of the Montenegrin coast, the Albanians further south and the Greeks in Crete and elsewhere in the Venetian domains continued to speak their native languages and to worship in their own churches. In fact, one might say that the Venetians had more trouble with their own "feudatarii" in Crete, than with conquered populations in their colonies.[4] For the Venetians, the important thing was that everybody obey the laws, pay the taxes, perform their duties, make no trouble to Venetian trade and navigation and create no impediment to their role as intermediaries between East and West.

On a more modest scale, a similar role as intermediary gave importance to another city on the Mediterranean rim—Dubrovnik (Ragusa), on the eastern coast of the Adriatic Sea. Much smaller than Venice, Dubrovnik nevertheless developed by the fourteenth century into an increasingly independent city-republic. Its success was founded—like the Venetian one—on a combination of wealth and wisdom, but Dubrovnik was, also, lucky at several points in its development. Thus, in the thirteenth century, when its navigation was restricted by the Venetians, mining began in the Balkan hinterland, and the Ragusans immediately jumped on the occasion and became the main entrepreneurs and exporters of Balkan minerals to the West. Of course, Dubrovnik profited enormously from this trade. One must bear in mind that Balkan mines, in addition to producing copper, lead and iron, produced also substantial quantities of silver.[5] Dubrovnik's role in all of this was very important not just for that city, but also for the Balkan states. Thus, we have there another example of the role of a city on the Mediterranean rim as a link between—one might justifiably say—different worlds. Of course, Dubrovnik itself was also very much and very profitably present on both the Venetian and Byzantine markets. Meanwhile, Byzantium, weakened as it was after the Fourth Crusade, still remained a significant political, commercial and cultural factor in the East. Even after the appearance of the Ottomans on European soil in mid-fourteenth century and their rapid expansion, Byzantium managed to survive for a long time and to resist the new and aggressive conquerors. The Ottoman expansion, however, affected very profoundly the fate of the third element under our consideration—the Balkan peoples.

The Balkan Slavic populations were caught between East and West ever since they settled in the Balkan area, in the early Middle Ages, but the attitudes of the various Balkan Slavic peoples towards the West and the East varied, depending largely on their geographic location. While the Croats very early and very decisively sided with Rome and remained part of the Roman Catholic world after 1054, Bulgaria oscillated several times between Rome and Constantinople during the Photian Schism, in the sixties of the ninth century, until it sided definitely with Constantinople, and stayed that way ever since. It was different in Bosnia and in Serbia. The Bosnian situation—caught between Roman Catholicism coming from Croatia and Hungary in the west, Serbian Orthodoxy coming from the east, and—from late twelfth century until mid fifteenth century—coping with a domestic heretical movement (the "Bogomils" or "Patarenes")—is too complex to be considered here in detail.[6] In addition, the Bosnian political circumstances after the death of its greatest ruler, King Tvrtko I (1353-1391) were not better than the religious ones. Indeed, the Ragusans in the early fifteenth century used to write that "the kingdom of Bosnia is in its usual big discord that the lords and barons have among themselves".[7] This evaluation reflected very accurately the fact that Bosnia was torn by feudal strife among the powerful regional lords and between them and the mostly weak kings. The Serbian situation, however, was different and rather interesting, especially in view of its later developments.

The Serbian Situation

The Serbs were Christianized in mid-ninth century, at a time when the Christian Church was one. After 1054—contrary to the usual assumption that the Serbs sided immediately and totally with Constantinople—they, in fact, hesitated for a long time politically and ecclesiastically between East and West. In the second half of the eleventh century, Michael the new leader of Zeta (c. 1052-1081) before 1055 renewed the treaties with Byzantium, but at the beginning of 1077 Pope Gregory VII (1073-1085) in a letter addressed to him called him "rex Sclauorum". This indicates that Michael had obtained the royal crown either from Gregory, or from an earlier Pope. In addition, from the papal letter it is visible that Michael had asked the Pope to send him the flag of Saint Peter, which means that he was putting himself and his country under papal protection, maybe even vassalage, as King Dmitar Zvonimir of Croatia (1075-1089) had done at the same time.[8] Clearly, the ruler of Zeta found in the ambitious and energetic Pope Gregory VII, who was seeking allies against the German Emperor Henry IV, the person and the authority which enabled Michael to become the first Serbian king.

A hundred years later, in mid-twelfth century, the founder of the unified Serbian state and of the ruling dynasty, Stefan Nemanja (c. 1166-1196) was baptized first in Zeta according to the Roman Catholic ritual, and then, later, in Raška according to the Eastern Orthodox ritual.[9] Nemanja later increasingly gravitated towards the Orthodox spiritual sphere, but maintained good relations with the West and, in 1189, when Frederick Barbarossa traveled through Serbia on his way to Palestine, he and Nemanja met very cordially and Nemanja was ready to become, together with the newly created Serbian state, a vassal of the German Emperor.[10] When the Fourth Crusade, by 1204, practically eliminated Byzantium from Europe, Nemanja's son and successor, the Grand Zhupan Stefan (1196-1228) divorced his Byzantine wife and did not hesitate to marry, maybe in 1207 or 1208, Anna, the granddaughter of the famous Venetian Doge Enrico Dandolo, thus no doubt gaining considerable advantage in his new efforts to establish closer links with the West.[11]

Stefan's calculation proved to be correct: in 1217 he obtained the royal crown for Serbia from Pope Honorius III (1216-1227). The Serbian Grand Zhupan had sent envoys to the Pope, and Stefan's brother Sava had sent one of his pupils to seek the papal blessing for Serbia and the crown for Stefan. The Pope, indeed, sent a legate with the crown to Serbia and he crowned Stefan, who became known as "The First Crowned".[12] Having thus obtained political recognition and independence for his state, Stefan wanted to also have an independent Serbian church. Of course, that was impossible to achieve in dealings with Rome. In the end, the king's brother, the monk Sava—who had already established himself as an able politician and diplomat, as well as an active educator—traveled to Nicaea, and there, from the Patriarch of the Byzantine Church he obtained, in 1219, the autonomy (*autokephalia*) for the Serbian church, whose first archbishop he became.[13]

Thus, it was only in 1219 that the Serbian church took a definitive turn to the East, to the Byzantine religious sphere, but an interesting attempt to change the ecclesiastical orientation of Serbia occurred at the beginning of the fourteenth century. The powerful Serbian king, Milutin (1282-1321) was at the time in direct and open conflict with his older brother Dragutin, who had the support of Catholic Hungary. Milutin, turned to the Pope in an effort to obtain papal support and thus outmaneuver his brother. He first asked Pope Benedict XI (1303-1304) to accept him and his kingdom under papal protection, and repeated this request at the beginning of the pontificate of Clement V (1305-1314). Clement began negotiations concerning the Serbian King's offer to convert with his whole country to Roman Catholicism. In 1308, the Pope sent three legates to Milutin with the task of uniting Serbia with the Roman church and giving to the King the papal flag, as a symbol of papal protection over Serbia.

At the same time, embassies were exchanged between the Serbian ruler and Prince Philip of Taranto, the son of King Charles II of Naples and Sicily (1289-1309), and a formal treaty of alliance between Milutin's envoys and Charles of Valois, the brother of the French King Philip the Fair (1285-1314) was signed at Mellun in March, 1308. There was even talk of marriage of Milutin's daughter and Charles' son. In the end, however, nothing came out of all of this lively diplomatic activity.

As a matter of fact, one can assume with considerable certainty, that Milutin did not seriously intend to fulfill his promises, especially the offer made to the Pope to convert to Catholicism. When he received the papal legates, he told them that he was unable to convert because of internal hostility to such an act. Indeed, the Serbian church and people at large would have, no doubt, opposed very bitterly such a move by their King and Milutin was very well aware of this fact. Finally, one must note that the alliance that Charles of Valois had tried to build had started to disintegrate and Philip of Taranto was losing interest for adventures in the East.[14] Clearly, then, Milutin, who was a master at manipulating people and situations, had concluded that he had gone as far as was beneficial for his purposes. As a result, Serbia remained an Eastern Orthodox country.

There was, however, one more occasion when a Serbian ruler was apparently willing to join the West against the East. That happened half a century later, during the reign of the most successful and most powerful

Serbian medieval ruler, King and Emperor Stefan Dušan (1331-1355, emperor since 1346). Dušan greatly expanded the Serbian state, until it reached from the Adriatic Sea in the west to the river Mesta in the east, and from the Danube in the north to the Gulf of Corinthos in the south. After his coronation as "Emperor of Serbs and Greeks" in April 1346 in Skoplje, his main ambition was to conquer Constantinople and to become the "Emperor and Autocrat" of a Serbo-Byzantine Empire, centered on the Bosphorus.

But it was exactly at this time, in mid-fourteenth century, that a new, far more dangerous enemy, appeared on the horizon—the Ottoman Turks. Having conquered Asia Minor, they crossed into Europe (1352 Tzimpe, 1354 Gallipoli). Dušan was the first European ruler to grasp the magnitude of the new menace and tried to organize a broader European coalition to confront the "infidels". Aware that the papacy was the key to obtaining Western help, he sent in 1354 an embassy to Avignon and proposed to the Pope Innocentius VI (1352-1362) a treaty by which Dušan would recognize the Pope as "Father of Christianity," and the Pope would appoint Dušan as supreme commander of Christian forces against the Ottomans. It must be mentioned that even before this time, Dušan—whose sister Helen, was married to the leading Croatian nobleman, Mladen III Šubić-Bribirski—had shown some interest in the prospects for the union of the Western and Eastern church. Many Roman Catholics lived in his state, especially in coastal cities. There were numerous and large colonies of Catholic Ragusans in Serbian mining centers and some of Dušan's closest political and economic advisers, officials and envoys abroad were Catholics from Dubrovnik and other coastal cities. In response to Serbian ruler's opening, in May 1355, a papal embassy arrived in Serbia and rather laborious negotiations took place, but before any progress could be made, Dušan's sudden death, in December 1355, put an end to all such plans. With that, and with the subsequent disintegration of the Serbian state and its eventual conquest by the Ottoman Turks (1459), the shift of power in the Balkan area meant that Serbia was to remain permanently part of the Eastern Orthodox spiritual sphere.[15]

Contrary to the antagonistic encounter of forces in this portion of the Mediterranean rim, it is worthwhile mentioning another, different encounter, which took place nearby, and where the forces in question found a symbiotic relationship. I have in mind here the Latino-Slavic cultural symbiosis in Dalmatia. This was a mainly urban phenomenon, the result of the encounter of the descendants of the Latin population of the cities on the eastern shore of the Adriatic Sea, closely linked with Italy, with the Slavic, primarily Croatian population coming from the hinterland. This encounter produced a unique blend of the Latin and Slavic cultures and created a specific mentality, open to cultural influences from both sides. The daily contact of the Dalmatian populations with Italy and the constant influx of Slavs from the nearby areas into the cities—not only as simple manpower, but also, in the case of Croatian nobility, as members of the local leadership—contributed to the shaping of a symbiotic relationship. A further contributor to this process was the movement of persons, especially professionals (e.g., doctors, teachers, pharmacists, etc.) from Italy to Dalmatia and the presence of Latin and Italian books in Dalmatian cities. All of this was clearly reflected in the use of language and in the literary works of the Croatian authors in Dalmatia at the time, a fact which was of greatest importance for the development of the Dalmatian Croatian culture in the late Middle Ages and the Renaissance.[16]

Conclusion

I have tried to outline here a fragmentary image of the shifts of power, contrasts, ambiguities and even a symbiotic relationship on the northeastern rim of the Mediterranean. All of this, it seems to me, leads to the conclusion that the Mediterranean was a closely interconnected area, where interdependence and exchanges of influences on its rims and beyond them, linking the sea and the hinterland, were a constant and ubiquitous phenomenon, which lasted for many centuries, resisting numerous turbulent events which marked that region's history.

Notes:

[1] Donald M. Nichol, *Byzantium and Venice: A Study in Diplomatic and Cultural Relations* (Cambridge, MA, 1988), pp. 60, 62.

[2] A. P. Kazhdan and Ann Wharton Epstein, *Change in Byzantine Culture in the Eleventh and Twelfth Centuries* (Berkeley, CA, 1985), pp. 176-77.

[3] Ibid., p. 176. See also G. Ostrogorsky, *History of the Byzantine State* (Oxford, 1968), pp. 356-417.

[4] Fredy Thiriet, *La Romanie vénitienne au moyen âge* (Paris, 1975), pp. 173-74, 209, 232, 260, 271-79.

[5] S. Ćirković, "The Production of Gold, Silver and Copper in the Central Parts of the Balkans from the 13th to the 16th Century," in *Precious Metals in the Age of Expansion,* ed. H. Kellenbenz (Stuttgart, 1981), pp. 41-69. See also B. Krekić, *Dubrovnik in the 14th and 15th Centuries: A City between East and West* (Norman, OK, 1972), pp. 20-22, 50-52.

[6] For discussions and controversies concerning the religious situation in Bosnia, see John V. A. Fine, Jr., *The Bosnian Church: A New Interpretation*, East European Monographs X: East European Quarterly (New York, NY, 1975); S. Ćirković, "Die bosnische Kirche," in *L'Oriente cristiano nella storia della civiltà* (Rome, 1964), pp. 547-75.

[7] Historical Archives in Dubrovnik, *Litterae Levantis,* Vol. VI, f. 35v. For the situation in Bosnia, see S. Ćirković, *Istorija srednjovekovne bosanske države* (Belgrade, 1964), pp. 169-253; P. Živković, *Ekonomsko socijalne promjene u bosanskom društvu u XIV i XV stoljeću* (Tuzla, 1986), pp. 27-35.

[8] N. Klaić, *Povijest Hrvata u ranom srednjem vijeku* (Zagreb, 1971), pp. 386-88; *Istorija srpskog naroda,* ed. S. Ćirkcović, Vol. 1 (Belgrade, 1981), pp. 186-90.

[9] *Ist. srp. nar.,* Vol. 1, p. 208.

[10] Ibid., pp. 255-58; S. Ćirković, *I Serbi nel medioevo* (Milan, 1992), p. 51.

[11] *Ist. srp. nar.,* Vol. 1, p. 299; Ćirković, *I Serbi,* p. 56.

[12] *Ist. srp. nar.,* Vol. 1, p. 300; Ćirković, *I Serbi,* p. 56.

[13] *Ist. srp. nar.,* Vol. l, p. 301; Ćirković, *I Serbi,* p. 59; Ostrogorsky, *Byzantine Sate,* p. 431.

[14] *Ist. srp. nar.,* Vol. 1, pp. 455-57.

[15] Ibid., pp. 550, 554-55; Ćirković, *I Serbi,* p. 162; N. Klaić, *Povijest Hrvata u razvijenom srednjem vijeku* (Zagreb, 1976), pp. 595, 620.

[16] On the Latino-Slavic cultural symbiosis in Dalmatia see, among others, V. Novak, "Slavonic-Latin Symbiosis in Dalmatia During the Middle Ages," *Slavonic and East European Review* 32 (1953), 1-28; the same, "La paleografia latina e i rapporti dell'Italia Meridionale con la Dalmazia," *Archivio storico pugliese* XV/2-4 (1961), 3-16; A. Kadić, "The Croatian Renaissance," in his *From Croatian Renaissance to Yugoslav Socialism* (The Hague, 1969), pp. 9-36; B. Krekić, "On the Latino-Slavic Cultural Symbiosis in Late Medieval and Renaissance Dalmatia and Dubrovnik," *Viator* 26 (1995), 321-32.

Christopher Kleinhenz

TALES OF SHIPS AND SEAS:
THE MEDITERRANEAN IN
THE MEDIEVAL IMAGINATION

Introduction

The early twenty first century is a miraculous age. Computers, CD ROMs and laser discs, special effects cinema, cellular telephones, virtual reality devices. All of these modern technological miracles enable us to see and comprehend the world in new, different, and exciting ways—and, in so doing, they also inspire us to think new and creative thoughts, to reexamine our views and come to understand better the world in which we live—at least to a certain degree for I still can't figure out exactly how radio works, and TV completely baffles me … .

We have in the last quarters of the last century landed men on the moon, sent space probes deep into the mysterious outer reaches of our solar system, launched—and repaired—the orbiting Hubbel telescope that brings us clear and entrancing images of galaxies distant millions of light years. Through the wonders of technology, we have had front-row seats for a number of major cosmic events—the multiple collisions between the comet and Jupiter for one—and, in a more parochial way, we have been treated to many spectacular views of our own planet, glowing with resplendent hues of blue and white against the infinite black backdrop of outer space—earth, our home, our special place in the universe. I begin to sound like Carl Sagan … .

The vision we have today of the planet earth from a vantage point far removed in space is one of vast blue oceans punctuated with brownish landmasses, great swirls of white clouds, and immobile polar icecaps. And this visual impression reminds us that our planetary sphere is, in large part, covered with water, the source and sustainer of life on earth—vegetable, animal, human. We can lose ourselves in contemplation of this miraculous, awe-inspiring sight. I am reminded in this regard of Augustine's monitory words in the *Confessions*:[1] "Men go abroad to wonder at the heights of mountains, the lofty billows of the sea, the long courses of rivers, the vast compass of the ocean, and the circular motions of the stars, and yet pass themselves by ...". In one of his many letters Petrarch tells us that, at a particularly crucial point during his first—and only—adventure in mountain-climbing—his ascent of Mt. Ventoux in southern France, he took his copy of the *Confessions* from his pocket and read these same words.[2] The effect of reading these words was immediate; indeed, they were the occasion of a conversion-type experience. For Augustine and for Petrarch the inner experience, the examination of self were crucial enterprises in their coming to understand their particular place in the cosmos.

We view planet earth today as a special, attractive and welcoming environment—a *locus amoenus*, a pleasant place isolated in the infinite darkness and lonely expanses of the universe. We are, scientifically speaking, light years removed from earlier conceptions of the universe; we no longer hold with Copernicus that the universe is heliocentric, and certainly Ptolemy's view of the earth as the center of the universe should cause us to smile—no matter how great and important we think we are! Nevertheless, we medievalists do not easily give up received ideas. I am still persuaded—all contrary evidence notwithstanding—that the Ptolemaic model of the universe is the only one that makes any sense. After all, if Dante traveled through the heavenly spheres and came back to tell the tale, if he gives it his seal of approval, who are we to dispute it?!

Although the *Divine Comedy* is full of extraordinary moments, one of the most interesting for our topic today concerns the changeover in Dante the Pilgrim's perspective on and understanding of the earth and the material universe as he ascends through the celestial spheres. In *Paradiso* 22, as he moves into the eighth heaven, the Pilgrim looks back toward earth:[3]

> Col viso ritornai per tutte quante
> le sette spere, e vidi questo globo
> tal, ch'io sorrisi del suo vil sembiante.
>
> E tutti e sette mi si dimostraro
> quanto son grandi e quanto son veloci
> e come sono in distante riparo.
>   L'aiuola che ci fa tanto feroci,
> volgendom' io con li etterni Gemelli,
> tutta m'apparve da' colli a le foci (vv. 133-135; 148-153).

[My eyes returned through all the seven spheres / and saw this globe in such a way that I / smiled at its scrawny image. ... And all the seven heavens showed to me / their magnitudes, their speeds, the distances / of each from each. The little threshing floor / that so incites our savagery was all— / from hills to river mouths—revealed to me / while I wheeled with the eternal Gemini.]

The higher the Pilgrim rises, the smaller the planet becomes, and with this diminution in size comes a devaluation of its importance. Indeed, the whole of earth is likened to a small threshing floor, one that despite its insignificant size has the power to incite human beings to extraordinary acts of violence and cruelty: "l'aiuola che ci fa tanto feroci" (*Par.* 22.151). How important can earth and earthly things be if Dante is able to comprehend it all in a single glance?

A second backward glance toward the earth occurs in the Pilgrim's passage from the eighth to the ninth heaven, and here Dante is even more explicit about what his view encompasses:

> Da l'ora ch'ïo avea guardato prima
> i' vidi mosso me per tutto l'arco
> che fa dal mezzo al fine il primo clima;
>   sì ch'io vedea di là da Gade il varco
> folle d'Ulisse, e di qua presso il lito
> nel qual si fece Europa dolce carco.
>   E più mi fora discoverto il sito
> di questa aiuola; ma 'l sol procedea
> sotto i mie' piedi un segno e più partito (*Par.* 27.79-87).

[I saw that, from the time when I looked down / before, I had traversed all of the arc / of the first clime, from its midpoint to end, / so that, beyond Cadiz, I saw Ulysses' / mad course and, to the east, could almost see / that shoreline where Europa was sweet burden. / I should have seen more of this threshing floor / but for the motion of the sun beneath / my feet: it was a sign and more away.]

Dante is able to see the entire Mediterranean basin from the Phoenician coast to Gibraltar, and the same descriptive term—"threshing floor," *aiuola*— is again used to indicate the small and insignificant nature of what mistakenly appears to earth-based, human eyes to be a vast area.

Finally, at the beginning of *Paradiso* 28 Dante reports that he sees an extremely intense point of light surrounded by nine radiant, revolving circles:

> un punto vidi che raggiava lume
> acuto sì, che 'l viso ch'elli affoca
> chiuder conviensi per lo forte acume.
>
> Forse cotanto quanto pare appresso
> alo cigner la luce che 'l dipigne
> quando 'l vapor che 'l porta più è spesso,

distante intorno al punto un cerchio d'igne
si girava sì ratto, ch'avrìa vinto
quel moto che più tosto il mondo cigne;
   e questo era d'un altro circumcinto,
e quel dal terzo, e 'l terzo poi dal quarto,
dal quinto il quarto, e poi dal sesto il quinto (vv. 16-18; 22-30).

[I saw a point that sent forth so acute / a light, that anyone who faced the force / with which it blazed would have to shut his eyes. / ... Around that point a ring of fire wheeled, / a ring perhaps as far from that point as / a halo from the star that colors it / when mist that forms the halo is most thick. / It wheeled so quickly that it would outstrip / the motion that most swiftly girds the world. / That ring was circled by a second ring, / the second by a third, third by a fourth, / fourth by a fifth, and fifth ring by a sixth.]

And Beatrice—always the patient guide and teacher—explains this unusual sight with the following words:

Da quel punto
depende il cielo e tutta la natura (*Par.* 28.41-42).

[On that Point / depend the heavens and the whole of nature.]

The pilgrim has been granted a vision of the spiritual conception of the true, immaterial universe that depends on God for everything: the Triune God is the brilliant point of light surrounded by the nine choirs or orders of angels. The physical universe is nothing but a copy, an essentially imperfect earthly manifestation of this divine order. Indeed, in the Ptolemaic model the position of the earth at the center of the universe should not give human beings any sense of pride or satisfaction, for being at the center of the universe means that we are, at the same time, at the furthest possible remove from the highest heaven, the Empyrean, and from God. Our state of exile—albeit temporary— in this vale of tears is brought home to us clearly and incisively. Dante becomes aware of this fact only near the end of his long pilgrimage, and precisely at this spectacular epiphanic moment. This general prologue has been intended to address questions concerning our knowledge and experience of the "universe," of the "known world," of the conceptions we have of the world and our place in it. In the Middle Ages the Mediterranean was for all practical purposes the extent of their "known world" and this determines their frame of reference. Since the great age of discovery our horizons have been ever expanding, and we have continued "to boldly go"—as Captain Kirk of the Starship Enterprise so ungrammatically put it—"where no man has gone before," through the universe in search of new worlds and new forms of life.

The universe now, the Mediterranean then. These are the coordinates for our voyage together in this essay.

Let us return to the earlier passage in which Dante is able, from his heavenly vantage point, to view the entire Mediterranean basin:

> io vedea di là da Gade il varco
> folle d'Ulisse, e di qua presso il lito
> nel qual si fece Europa dolce carco (*Par.* 27:82-84).

[beyond Cadiz, I saw Ulysses' / mad course and, to the east, could almost see / that shoreline where Europa was sweet burden.]

The boundaries of the sea are clearly marked on the East by the Phoenician coast and, in the West, by the Straits of Gibraltar, the ancient Pillars of Hercules. Dante's manner of description through mythological, legendary and literary references suggests a geography replete with symbolic and allegorical significance, and it is precisely this ambiguous quality, this double nature—both real and metaphorical, literal and allegorical–that makes the *Divine Comedy* the compelling work that it is.

Dante and his contemporaries continued to call the Mediterranean by the name the Romans had given it: *Mare Nostrum*, "our sea". According to the view of the time, the Mediterranean was located in the midst of the three great land masses—the continents of Europe, Asia and Africa—and this geographical configuration was represented cartographically in the form of the T-O *mappae mundi*: Asia on the top half to the East, Europe in the lower left quadrant (Northwest) and Africa in the lower right (Southwest). The T is formed by the Mediterranean and "a horizontal line extending from the Don River through the Aegean and continuing along the Red Sea-Nile River corridor,"[4] and the O, the circular band that surrounds everything is Ocean. Generally speaking, these maps are intended to demonstrate both geographic reality and religious truth. In the Hereford and the Psalter world maps Christ is depicted at the top presiding over the world, and in one particular version— the Ebstorf world map—the head of Christ appears at the top with His hands to either side and His feet at the bottom, suggesting both that His body is metaphorically the same as the world and, thus, that those individuals who reside within that space enjoy the benefits and protection provided by Christ and His Church. In a related fashion, the Hereford map "has protruding labels bearing the letters M, O, R, S, death"—which serve as "a reminder of the limits of the material world" and the consequences for those who transgress these boundaries.[5] Geography then was at the service of religion and reflected its ideas and dogma. Dante the Poet's description (*Inf.* 26.90-142) of Ulysses's last voyage beyond the pillars of Hercules and into the uncharted waters of

Ocean has both religious significance and eternal consequences: Not only has Ulysses defied his gods by transgressing the limits, he has gone beyond the boundaries of the body of Christ, and thus his journey is destined to conclude badly. More on this later.

The Mediterranean was the common ground, as it were, for the territories and the peoples on its rim; it was, from the earliest times, the locus of martial action and piracy, of trade and commerce, of Crusades and pilgrimages, and of the migrations of peoples. The sea was often associated with romantic deeds and heroic adventures, but it was seen above all as a dangerous place. In addition to the constant menace of pirates, sudden storms could surprise and harm unsuspecting travelers; hidden reefs and rocky shorelines could damage vessels with unwary pilots. Horrible monsters (Scylla for one), treacherous natural phenomena (the whirlpool Charybdis, for example), and alluring enchantresses such as the Sirens lurked everywhere and posed formidable dangers to those who plied the waters. Today we often forget the perils of the sea, as for example when we read the romantically-inspired lines by John Masefield: "I must go down to the seas again, to the lonely sea and the sky, / and all I ask is a tall ship and a star to steer her by ...".[6] But even with all this high-minded individualistic spirit, we have sobering memories of the indestructible Titanic on its fateful maiden voyage and the mighty ore freighter, the Edmund Fitzgerald, trying to cross Lake Superior in the winter of 1975 ... .

The special relationship–past and present–of Italy, and the Mediterranean

According to one encyclopedia account, "Italy's location and shape have not only given it easy access to the sea but make it a transit land between Europe and Africa and the Levant. It looks to both the western and the eastern Mediterranean and is a link between that sea and the Germanic and Slav lands to the north".[7] Italy's coastline measures some 4,660 miles, and the peninsula is bordered on three sides by those areas of the Mediterranean known as the Ligurian, Tyrrenian, Ionic, and Adriatic seas. Given its natural geographic situation, Italy has always been very conscious of its relationship with Neptune, and in recent years this symbiotic relationship has shown signs of severe stress: pollution levels in certain areas have increased dramatically, as for example at Genoa and Naples and along the Adriatic coastline near the mouth of the Po river. In similar ways, Venice, the Queen of the Adriatic, suffers from the severe damage that periodic inundations, *acqua alta* (high water), cause. For centuries, the sea has been the pathway for prosperity and disaster for Italy.

Prosperity came through commerce and the opening of new trade routes; the shipbuilding industry (e.g., the Arsenal in Venice) would rival General Motors and Ford for the speed of its production line, and would probably win hands down over them in terms of quality. Certain towns that once were major naval and economic powers have declined in prestige and importance, and often survive today only as tourist attractions (e.g., Amalfi). Disaster could and did come because of the relative ease with which pirates could stage surprise raids on coastal towns and cities, and because of the equally great facility with which large armies could stage major invasions of countries, either to subjugate or to liberate them, as, for example, the landings of the Allied troops at Anzio, Salerno, and in Sicily during the Second World War.

Because of its position in the Mediterranean world, Italy is a cultural crossroads of many and various peoples; some come only to visit and then return home, while others settle in to stay, and still others move on to other destinations. Italy is the link between all of the countries and peoples located in Europe, the Middle East and North Africa. Proof of this rich and diverse cultural heritage can be seen in the art and architecture, in the language and customs found in Italian cities on the coast or near the sea. In Palermo, for example, we find much evidence of this blending of cultural traditions: the Church of St. John of the Hermits with its moorish domes and the Palatine Chapel in the Norman Palace with its resplendent mosaics and oriental geometrical patterns. More evidence of Italy as the link and crossroads of cultures is given millions of times over every summer when the tourists come in droves to visit the museums, churches, art galleries, archeological sites, mountains, small fishing villages, scenic coastlines, and beaches of "la bella Italia".

The familiarity that the Romans and, subsequently, the Italians enjoyed with the Mediterranean is aptly characterized by the appellative *Mare Nostrum, Nostro Mare*, "our sea," and this familiarity, together with the introduction of the magnetic compass, led to the making of extensive and elaborately detailed navigation maps, which are vastly different from the schematic T-O variety. The "portolan maps," as they are called, charted the variegated coastlines and innumerable ports and, as such, were indispensable to those commercial tradesmen who navigated the waters.[8] Despite their seeming familiarity with the Mediterranean, sailors were well aware of the ever present dangers associated with sea travel. And, of course, they were especially wary of the great unknown and uncharted expanse of Ocean, that lay beyond the straits of Gibraltar. Cautionary tales circulated, as for example concerning the unknown end that the Vivaldi brothers met after they sailed from Genoa in 1291, passed the pillars of Hercules, and disappeared into the Atlantic, attempting to circumnavigate Africa and, by thus finding a direct sea route to India, cornering the market on spices from the Orient. It has been suggested that their story served in part to inspire Dante's tale of the last voyage of Ulysses.[9]

To return for a moment to the images evoked at the beginning of this essay, I would suggest that our relationship and experience today with the solar system and, more generally, with the universe, is the modern counterpart to that which obtained in the Middle Ages with the Mediterranean and the unknown reaches of Ocean. On the one hand, there is the comfort of familiar sights and places, and, on the other hand, the discomfort, the *disagio* provoked by our ignorance of these vast, largely unknown and uncharted areas. The Argonauts of yesteryear have become today's Astronauts, and the etymological descriptor—*nauta*, "sailor, mariner"—remains the same in both and provides the association with the sea and ships. At the same time, we recognize that unpredictable things can occur in our familiar little world, that all may not be as safe and sound as we think, just as the Mediterranean was a source of constant wonder and surprises in the Middle Ages, despite the seemingly easy familiarity that those who lived along its shores had with it.

It is precisely this ambiguous relationship with the Mediterranean Sea that stirred the imagination of medieval Italian writers. The sea represented all that was exotic; the arrival from afar of strange peoples with strange customs bearing strange objects and speaking in strange tongues instilled wonder in the residents of *terra firma*—the land lubbers. The sea was also viewed as an exotic refuge, a place apart from the ordinary haunts of a land-locked, essentially urban society. The dangers of the sea journey became metaphoric for those encountered in the course of our earthly existence—we are born, proceed through life's storms, and arrive—hopefully—at a safe port at the end of our journey, if—a big "if"—we are able to avoid shipwreck on the reefs, rocks, and other difficulties en route. In the medieval imagination the uncertainties of life were associated with the operation of Fortune and her wheel, and her presentation relied in large part on sea imagery. The abode of Fortune was often thought to be located near the sea or on an island.[10] Good Fortune was depicted as a vessel plying the seas with full sails; adverse Fortune was seen as a sinking ship with broken mast and crumpled sails.[11]

The sea, and the Mediterranean in particular, was vital in various ways to all the peoples on its rim, and exerted a powerful shaping influence on the medieval imagination.[12] In the remainder of this essay, I would like to focus on three distinct and diverse ways in which medieval Italian writers—especially Dante, Petrarch and Boccaccio—incorporate the Mediterranean in their works and to examine the potential significance of these varying uses.

Reality

As a "real" place the Mediterranean serves at least three roles in the medieval imagination. (1) Its physical characteristics are the object of disinterested study and description. (2) Its harshness and inhospitable nature occasions complaints of various sorts. (3) Its role as the scene for historical events provides writers with a powerful natural backdrop for their narratives.

In his incomplete encyclopedic poem, *Il Dittamondo* (composed 1345-67), Fazio degli Uberti gives an overview of world geography and history, describing countries, rivers, mountains, and bodies of water, discussing the historical/mythological/legendary events that took place in these various places, and presenting the stories of their numerous inhabitants and protagonists. In the *Dittamondo* the Mediterranean serves as the realistic backdrop for certain parts of the erudite geographical disquisition with no attempt at allegorical interpretation.[13]

In several letters Petrarch comments on the very real dangers inherent in the Mediterranean and refers to his own extreme distaste for sea voyages, a dislike he acquired early on in life when he traveled with his family from Genoa to Marseilles on a small vessel and suffered horribly from seasickness.[14] In a letter to Cardinal Giovanni Colonna (*Fam.* V. 5; November 26, 1343) Petrarch describes a terrific storm in Naples and the damage it caused, namely the destruction of numerous ships in the harbor and the loss of many lives:[15]

> Then suddenly a new clamor arose. Undermined by the waters, the very spot on which we stood began to sink. We fled to higher land. One could not look out to open sea; mortal sight could not bear the angry visages of Jove and Neptune. Mountainous waves rolled in from Capri to Naples. The sea was not blue, not black with storm, but all horribly white with foam. ... We on land barely saved ourselves; at sea and in the port no ship escaped. Three long ships, called galleys, of Marseilles, had just arrived from Cyprus; they lay at anchor after their long voyage, ready to depart on the morrow. With a universal cry of horror, we watched them sink; but no one could bring them any aid. Not one of the sailors or pilots was saved. Other ships of all sorts, some of them bigger, had taken refuge in the harbor, and these met the same fate. ... I won't have tired out my fingers and your ears in vain if this one important point is clear. I ask you never again to bid me confide my life to wind and waves, for in this I should not be willing to obey either you or the Pope of Rome or my own father, if he should return to

life. I'll leave the air to the birds and the sea to the fish; I am a land animal, and I prefer roads. I won't refuse to visit the bequivered Sarmates or the perfidious Moors, as long as my feet can touch the ground. Send me where you will, even to the Indies; but if by water, I refuse. ... How can you persuade me, with what blandishments, to sail again? Will you tell me to choose a stout ship, with skilled sailors? But that was the case with the lost vessels. Will you say to enter harbor at sundown, cast anchor at night, guard against an enemy, coast along the shore? But those ships were wrecked by day, in harbor, with anchors firmly grounded on the bottom, hardly more than an oar's length from the shore, under the eyes of thousands of pitying friends. I know what learned men may reply, that danger is everywhere the same, that it is merely more evident at sea. All right; so be it; but I was born on land, and you will do me a great favor if you will allow me to die there. There is hardly any sea between us in which I haven't been shipwrecked. To be sure, one of the most admired Sentences of Publilius Syrus runs: "You can't blame Neptune if you're shipwrecked a second time." Farewell.

At various points in the *Divine Comedy* Dante refers to historical events that have occurred at sea, some of which have had a decisive effect on the course of history—although obviously not as significant as the battles of Actium or Lepanto. In *Inferno* 28 Pier di Medicina prophesies the drowning of two noblemen from Fano at the hands of the one-eyed tyrant of Rimini, Malatestino. According to this prophecy—and in the *Divine Comedy* all prophecies of historical events are 100% accurate—, this foul deed will occur in the Adriatic near the coastal town of La Cattolica:

> E fa sapere a' due miglior da Fano,
> a messer Guido e anco ad Angiolello,
> che, se l'antiveder qui non è vano,
>   gittati saran fuor di lor vasello
> e mazzerati presso a la Cattolica
> per tradimento d' un tiranno fello (vv. 76-81).

[And let the two best men of Fano know—/ I mean both Messer Guido and Angiolello—/ that, if the foresight we have here's not vain, / they will be cast out of their ship and drowned, / weighted down with stones, near La Cattolica, / because of a foul tyrant's treachery.]

This act is described as one of the most treacherous to have ever been witnessed by Neptune in the whole of the Mediterranean:

Tra l'isola di Cipri e di Maiolica
non vide mai sì gran fallo Nettuno,
non da pirate, non da gente argolica.
    Quel traditor che vede pur con l'uno,
e tien la terra che tale qui meco
vorrebbe di vedere esser digiuno,
    farà venirli a parlamento seco;
poi farà sì, ch'al vento di Focara
non sarà lor mestier voto nè preco (vv. 82-90).

[Between the isles of Cyprus and Majorca, / Neptune has never seen so cruel
a crime / committed by the pirates or the Argives. / That traitor who sees only
with one eye / and rules the land which one who's here with me / would wish
his sight had never seen, will call / Guido and Angiolello to a parley, / and then
will so arrange it that they'll need / no vow or prayer to Focara's wind!]

Fantasy

More powerful for the literary imagination than these real and/or realistic
evocations of the perils of the sea is the use of the sea as an exotic place and as
a bearer of exotic things. In an early sonnet, composed probably in the 1280s,
Dante expresses his desire to be cast adrift on a little boat together with two
male friends (Guido and Lapo) and their three female companions:[16]

Guido, i' vorrei che tu e Lapo ed io
fossimo presi per incantamento,
e messi in un vasel ch'ad ogni vento
per mare andasse al voler vostro e mio,
sì che fortuna od altro tempo rio
non ci potesse d   are impedimento,
anzi, vivendo sempre in un talento,
di stare insieme crescesse 'l disio.
E monna Vanna e monna Lagia poi
con quella ch'è sul numer de le trenta
con noi ponesse il buono incantatore:
e quivi ragionar sempre d'amore,
e ciascuna di lor fosse contenta,
sì come i' credo che saremmo noi.

[Guido, I wish that Lapo, you and I, / in one enchantment bound, right now could be / inside a vessel faring on the sea, / braving the wind, to your content and mine. / Not only would no gale or stormy sky / impediment or menace ever be, / but living there in constant harmony, / we would forever for more closeness sigh. / And Mona Vanna and Mona Lagia, then, / with the one numbered in the thirty best, / I wish the good enchanter there would place, / where we would ever about love converse, / and each of them would be of joy possessed, / just as I reckon we would also be.]

This fantasy cruise on the "love boat" reflects, in part, the marvelous atmosphere of the Arthurian romances (the "buono incantatore" is undoubtedly Merlin) and, in part, the desire to escape the frenetic pace of urban life in the late thirteenth-century Italian communes, Florence in particular. It is an idyll, a day dream that captures the romantic allure of the sea, and the wild freedom that it symbolizes. This desire to be isolated with congenial companions is also reflected by Giovanni Boccaccio in his creation of the *lieta brigata*, the happy group of ten young people—seven women and three men—who leave plague-ridden Florence and establish their own harmonious society in the hills outside the city.[17] Petrarch, too, conceives his happy state of solitude as existing outside the hub-bub of the city, in a pleasant rustic setting and in the company of like-minded individuals.[18]

In several sonnets written during his extended stay in Naples, Boccaccio uses the sea as the scene of action. In one of these he transforms the traditional topos of the meeting between lover and lady on a city street into an even more highly charged event. He imagines the arrival of his beloved on board a small craft, accompanied by her gracious companions:[19]

Su la poppa sedea d'una barchetta,
che 'l mar segando presta era tirata,
la donna mia con altre accompagnata,
cantando or una or altra canzonetta.
Or questo lito e or quest'isoletta,
e ora questa e or quella brigata
di donne visitando, era mirata
qual discesa dal cielo una angioletta.
Io, che seguendo lei vedeva farsi
da tutte parti incontro a rimirarla
gente, vedea come miracol nuovo.
Ogni spirito mio in me destarsi
sentiva, e con amor di commendarla
sazio non vedea mai il ben ch'io provo.

[On the bridge of a small ship that was rapidly moving through the sea my lady and her companions sat and sang now one song now another. As she went now to this shore and now to this island, and to visit now this and now that group of women, my lady was gazed at as though she were an angel descended from heaven. As I followed her, I saw people come from all around to gaze at her and I saw her to be a wondrous miracle. I felt every spirit in me awaken and recognized that I would never tire of praising her with loving words because of the happiness I feel. (Translation mine.)]

As they sing, the women progress from shore to shore, island to island in the Bay of Naples paying visits to other companies of equally gracious ladies. The poet's beloved is honored by all as a heavenly creature, very much in the *dolce stil novo* tradition, but because of the change in venue—from the urban cityscape to the natural seascape—we note a decidedly more eroticized atmosphere that draws its power from the inherently mysterious and exotic nature of the sea itself. Of course, the association between love and the sea goes back to ancient myth, with the birth of Venus from the sea, and in the early Italian poetic tradition, we find a certain amount of lexical/phonic play on the similarities of the words for "sea" (*mare*), "love" (*amore*) and "to love" (*amare*), "bitter" (*amaro*; the bitterness of love's torment), and "death" (*morte*).[20] In Italian literature love has repeatedly been described with sea imagery (e.g., in the verses of Giacomo da Lentini, Cielo d'Alcamo, and others),[21] and a late thirteenth-century narrative poem known as the *Mare Amoroso*—the "amorous sea"—contains a virtually complete repertoire of the standard descriptive modes that poets use when speaking of the beloved woman and of love in general.[22] Toward the end of the composition the poet states that the following verses will appear on his tomb: "Chi vuole amare, li convien tremare, / bramare, chiamare, sì come 'l marinaio in mare amaro; / e chi no me crede, mi deggia mirare per maraviglia, / ché per amor son morto in amarore" ["Whoever wishes to love must necessarily tremble, ardently desire, and cry out, just as the sailor in the bitter sea; and let the one who does not believe me look at me with wonder, for because of love I have died in a state of bitterness." (Translation mine.)].

In another sonnet Boccaccio presents a more rarified picture of his lady who is conveyed to him across the sea enveloped in a cloud:

Toccami 'l viso zefiro tal volta
più che l'usato alquanto impetuoso,
quasi se stesso allora avesse schiuso
dal cuoi' d'Ulisse, e la catena sciolta.
E poi ch'è l'alma tutta in sé raccolta,
par ch'e' mi dica: "Leva il volto suso;

mira la gioia ch'io, da Baia effuso,
ti porto in questa nuvola rinvolta".
Io lievo gli occhi, e parmi tanto bella
veder madonna entr' a quell'aura starse,
che 'l cor vien men sol nel maravigliarse.
E, com'io veggio lei più presso farse,
lievomi per pigliarla e per tenella:
e 'l vento fugge, ed essa spare in quella.

[Zephyr sometimes touches my face with more than the usual force almost as though he had released himself from the leather bag of Ulysses and loosed the seal. And when he has my complete attention, it seems he says to me: 'Lift up your head, look at the joy that I, direct from Baia, bring you wrapped in this cloud'. I raise my eyes and it seems to me such a beautiful sight to see my lady motionless within that cloud that my heart is faint from sheer wonder. And as I see her come closer and closer, I rise up to catch her and to hold on to her, and the wind flees and she disappears at the same moment. (Translation mine.)]

The entire sonnet is unified by the play on the double principle of inclusion/exclusion, captivity/freedom, corporeality/insubstantiality: the unusual force of the breeze from Baia is likened to the winds that Ulysses released from the leather container he had received from Aeolus, god of the winds; the west wind zephyr both captures the soul of the poet and bears the image of the beloved enclosed in the cloud. The lover raises himself toward the sublime image, but his attempts to embrace the ephemeral and elusive object of his desire come to naught, for the gap between the material and the divine, between the real and the ideal is too great to bridge. In this instance the sea is the bringer of wondrous, yet unattainable joy.

In numerous tales in the *Decameron* Boccaccio employs the Mediterranean to excellent effect, for example, the various maritime adventures of Landolfo Rufolo (II, 4), Madonna Beritola (II, 6), Madonna Zinevra (II, 9), the pirate Paganino da Monaco (II, 10), and Gian di Procida (V, 6). However, it is perhaps the story of Alatiel (II, 7) that best exemplifies the exotic and erotic connotations of the sea. Boccaccio's synopsis that precedes the story reads as follows:[23]

Il soldano di Babilonia ne manda una sua figliuola a marito al re di Garbo, la quale per diversi accidenti in ispazio di quatro anni alle mani di nove uomini perviene in diversi luoghi: ultimamente, restituita al padre per pulcella, ne va al re del Garbo, come prima faceva, per moglie.

[The Sultan of Babylon sends one of his daughters as a wife for the King of Algarve; in a series of misadventures, she passes through the hands of nine men in different lands in the space of four years; finally, she is returned to her father, who believes she is still a virgin, and then continues on her way, as she had before, to the King of Algarve to marry him.]

Most of the action of this *novella* takes place on the Mediterranean; indeed, Alatiel makes numerous sea journeys, each with a different man and each directed toward a different port. The constant criss-crossing of the sea delays the final resolution of her situation and seems to parody the voyages of single-minded travelers who are en route for a particular purpose toward a particular goal: merchants and pilgrims—to precise ports/markets for the one, and to holy shrines for the other. Alatiel's voyage is circular, however, in that through the strange operation of Fortune, she returns finally to her father who is then able to deliver her to her intended husband—still a virgin! The power of the sea in matters of love is clear in this tale. Moreover, the inextricable relationship of the sea and Fortune is underlined by Boccaccio who sets seven of the ten stories on the Second Day on or near the sea, and this particular day is dedicated to the theme of Fortune and how those "who having gone through a series of misfortunes come to an unexpected happy end" ("chi, da diverse cose infestato, sia oltre alla speranza riuscito a lieto fine," I, conclusione).

Metaphor/Allegory

We shall conclude our investigation of the shaping influence of the Mediterranean—and the sea in general—on the medieval imagination with some considerations on its role in the metaphorical and allegorical structure of literary works. In the *Divine Comedy* Dante's geography, both received and constructed, assumes symbolic significance: Jerusalem, as is customary, is located at the center of the land mass in the northern hemisphere, and the Mountain of Purgatory with the Garden of Eden at its summit is described as an island in the middle of the southern hemisphere of water. From this arrangement comes the marvelous symmetry, whereby the place where humankind fell—Eden—is exactly at the antipodes of the place where humankind was redeemed through Christ's sacrifice on the Cross–Jerusalem. We learn further that souls are transported to the island/mountain of Purgatory on a special boat that, piloted by an angel, leaves from Ostia, the ancient seaport of Rome. Thus, the Mediterranean and geography in general assumes an important role in Dante's literary and theological imagination.

On numerous instances poets employ nautical images and the sea journey in particular as metaphors for human existence, as for example in the following sonnet by Boccaccio:

> Assai sem raggirati in alto mare,
> et quanto possan gli empiti de' venti,
> l'onde commosse e i fier accidenti,
> provat'abbiamo; né già il navicare
> alcun segno, con vela o con vogare,
> scampati ci ha dai perigli eminenti
> fra' duri scogli e le secche latenti,
> ma sol Colui che, ciò che vuol, può fare.
> Tempo è omai da reducersi in porto
> e l'ancore fermare a quella pietra
> che del tempio congiunse e dua parieti;
> quivi aspettar el fin del viver corto
> nell'amor di Colui, da cui s'impetra
> con umiltà la vita de' quieti.

[For a long time we have traveled on the high seas and have experienced the challenges posed by the winds and waves and other elements. No indication has kept our navigation—with either sails or oars—safe from the dangers that crop up amidst the harsh rocks and the hidden shoals, except for the One who has the power to do whatever He wills. Now it is time to return to port and to fix our anchor on that rock that joined the two walls of the temple; there we shall await the end of our short life in the love of the One from whom we humbly pray for the life of the blessed. (Translation mine.)]

Faith in God is the only sure thing in this life, and we must ultimately put our trust in Him in the hope that our brief earthly existence will have a happy conclusion.

In a well-known and widely-imitated sonnet Petrarch compares himself and his desperate state to a ship piloted by love:[24]

> Passa la nave mia colma d'oblio
> per aspro mare a mezza notte il verno,
> enfra Scilla e Caribdi, et al governo
> siede 'l signore, anzi 'l nimico mio.
> A ciascun remo un penser pronto e rio
> che la tempesta e 'l fin par ch'abbi a scherno;
> la vela rompe un vento humido eterno
> di sospir', di speranze et di desio.
> Pioggia di lagrimar, nebbia di sdegni

bagna e rallenta le già stanche sarte,
che son d'error con ignorantia attorto.
Celansi i duo mei dolci usati segni;
morta fra l'onde è la ragion et l'arte,
tal ch'incomincio a desperar del porto (*Canzoniere*, 189).

[My ship laden with forgetfulness passes through a harsh sea, at midnight, in winter, between Scylla and Charybdis, and at the tiller sits my lord, rather my enemy; each oar is manned by a ready, cruel thought that seems to scorn the tempest and the end; a wet, changeless wind of sighs, hopes, and desires breaks the sail; a rain of weeping, a mist of disdain wet and loosen the already weary ropes, made of error twisted up with ignorance. My two usual sweet stars are hidden; dead among the waves are reason and skill; so that I begin to despair of the port.]

Petrarch is completely overcome with passion. Such is the power of love that he cannot think of anything else. It is midnight and the light of reason is absent, just as the once valuable ropes of reason are now slack and twisted with errors. Even Laura's eyes, his "two usual sweet stars," once trusted and true guides to a better way of life, are hidden, and he fears that he will perish amid the treacherous waves without ever arriving at his safe haven.

In his treatise on philosophy, the *Convivio*, Dante describes the course of human life using nautical imagery:[25]

... lo testo intende mostrare quello che fa la nobile anima ne l'ultima etade, cioè nel senio. E dice ch'ella fa due cose: l'una, che ella ritorna a Dio, sì come a quello porto onde ella si partio quando venne ad intrare nel mare di questa vita; l'altra si è, che ella benedice lo cammino che ha fatto, però che è stato diritto e buono, e sanza amaritudine di tempesta. E qui è da sapere, che, sì come dice Tullio in quello De Senectute, la naturale morte è quasi a noi porto di lunga navigazione e riposo. Ed è così: [ché], come lo buono marinaio, come esso appropinqua al porto, cala le sue vele, e soavemente, con debile conducimento, entra in quello; così noi dovemo calare le vele de le nostre mondane operazioni e tornare a Dio con tutto nostro intendimento e cuore, sì che a quello porto si vegna con tutta soavitade e con tutta pace (IV, xxviii, 1-3).

[... the text proposes to describe how the noble soul acts in the last age of life (that is, in senility). It says that the noble soul does two things: first, that it returns to God as to that port from which it departed when it came to enter into the sea of this life; second, that it blesses the journey that it has made, because it has been straight and good and without bitterness of storm. Here it should be observed that a natural death, as Tully says in his book *On Old Age*, is, as it were, a port and site of repose after our long journey. This is quite true, for just as a good sailor lowers his sails as he approaches port and, pressing forward lightly, enters it gently, so we must lower the sails of our worldly preoccupations and return to God with all our mind and heart, so that we may reach that port with perfect gentleness and perfect peace.]

Speaking of this movement of the soul to God at the end of its earthly life, Dante inveighs against those who would not take the proper precautions, who would not prepare themselves properly for death, and cites the examples of Lancelot and Guido da Montefeltro:

> Rendesi dunque a Dio la nobile anima in questa etade, e attende lo fine di questa vita con molto desiderio e uscir le pare de l'albergo e ritornare ne la propria mansione, uscir le pare di cammino e tornare in cittade, uscir le pare di mare e tornare a porto. O miseri e vili che con le vele alte correte a questo porto, e là ove dovereste riposare, per lo impeto del vento rompete, e perdete voi medesimi là dove tanto camminato avete! Certo lo cavaliere Lancelotto non volse entrare con le vele alte, né lo nobilissimo nostro latino Guido montefeltrano. Bene questi nobili calaro le vele de le mondane operazioni, che ne la loro lunga etade a religione si rendero, ogni mondano diletto e opera disponendo (*Convivio* IV, xxviii, 7-8).

[The noble soul, then, surrenders itself to God in this age of life and awaits the end of this life with great desire, and seems to be leaving an inn and returning to its proper dwelling, seems to be coming back from a journey and returning to the city, seems to be coming in from the sea and returning to port. O you miserable and debased beings who speed into this port with sails raised high! Where you should take your rest, you shipwreck yourselves against the force of the wind and perish at the very place to which you have so long been journeying! Certainly the knight Lancelot did not wish to enter with his sails raised high, nor the most noble of the Italians, Guido of Montefeltro. These noble men did indeed lower the sails of their worldly preoccupations and late in life gave themselves to religious orders, forsaking all worldly delights and affairs.]

Here in *Convivio* Lancelot is presented in a positive light as a model of the proper way a person should conclude his life, in clear reference to his self-imposed seclusion in the monastery as related in at least one of the Old French prose romances. Similarly, Guido da Montefeltro is depicted as one who, towards the end of his life, retires from his profession as military strategist and becomes a Franciscan friar. Readers of the *Divine Comedy* will remember that

Dante's view of these two individuals undergoes a radical transformation—Lancelot becomes a negative *exemplum* (in *Inferno* 5), and Guido's conversion was discovered to be insincere, and he is relegated to one of the lowest regions of Hell for evil counselling (*Inferno* 27).

More interesting in my view is the variety of ways—some traditional and some innovative—in which Dante incorporates nautical imagery and its complex set of associations. Dante's knowledge of the configuration of the Mediterranean and the location of particular cities and islands plays a crucial part in his metaphorical account of the decline of human civilization over time. The figure he invents to represent the various historical ages—Gold, Silver, Bronze, Iron—and, moreover, to serve as the source of the infernal rivers is the Old Man of Crete, the *Veglio di Creta*, whom Virgil describes in *Inferno* 14 as follows:

> In mezzo mar siede un paese guasto,
>   ... che s'appella Creta,
> sotto 'l cui rege fu già 'l mondo casto.
>   Una montagna v'è che già fu lieta
> d'acqua e di fronde, che si chiamò Ida;
> or è diserta come cosa vieta.
>   Rëa la scelse già per cuna fida
> del suo figliuolo, e per celarlo meglio,
> quando piangea, vi facea far le grida.
>   Dentro dal monte sta dritto un gran veglio,
> che tien volte le spalle inver' Dammiata
> e Roma guarda come süo speglio.
>   La sua testa è di fin oro formata,
> e puro argento son le braccia e 'l petto,
> poi è di rame infino a la forcata;
>   da indi in giuso è tutto ferro eletto,
> salvo che 'l destro piede è terra cotta;
> e sta 'n su quel, più che 'n su l'altro, eretto.
>   Ciascuna parte, fuor che l'oro, è rotta
> d'una fessura che lagrime goccia,
> le quali, accolte, fóran quella grotta.
>   Lor corso in questa valle si diroccia;
> fanno Acheronte, Stige e Flegetonta;
> poi sen van giù per questa stretta doccia,
>   infin, là dove più non si dismonta,
> fanno Cocito; e qual sia quello stagno
> tu lo vedrai, però qui non si conta (vv. 94-120).

[A devastated land lies in midsea, / a land called Crete ... . / Under its king the world once lived chastely. / Within that land there was a mountain blessed / with leaves and waters, and they called it Ida; / but it is withered now like some old thing. / It once was chosen as a trusted cradle / by Rhea for her son; to hide him better, / when he cried out, she had her servants clamor. / Within the mountain is a huge Old Man, / who stands erect—his back turned toward Damietta— / and looks at Rome as if it were his mirror. / The Old Man's head is fashioned of fine gold, / the purest silver forms his arms and chest, / but he is made of brass down to the cleft; / below that point he is of choicest iron / except for his right foot, made of baked clay; / and he rests more on this than on the left. / Each part of him, except the gold, is cracked; / and down that fissure there are tears that drip; / when gathered, they pierce through that cavern's floor / and, crossing rocks into this valley, form / the Acheron and Styx and Phlegethon; / and then they make their way down this tight channel, / and at the point past which there's no descent, / they form Cocytus; since you are to see / what that pool is, I'll not describe it here.]

While obviously drawing upon Ovid's *Metamorphoses* (I, 89ff) and the description of the great image in Nebuchadnezzar's dream in the book of Daniel (2.31-35), Dante is clearly making this figure his and his alone, especially because of the distinction between the two feet, one of iron and one of clay, that would represent the two powers of Empire and the Papacy. The fact that the weight is placed primarily on the clay foot, on the Church, indicates the assumption—or perhaps better the usurpation—of temporal power by the Papacy. The weeping statue undoubtedly represents the vulnerability of fallen humankind, and its position in the midst of the sea—*in mezzo mar*—with its back to the East (to Damietta in Egypt) and with its gaze toward the West (to Rome) "as if it were his mirror" (*come süo speglio*) suggests the movement of civilization westward. We recall that Aeneas and Paul both stopped in Crete on their journeys to Rome, from Troy and from Jerusalem respectively. The movement of civilization, the respective *translatio* of Empire and Church from East to West is signaled by these two voyages. As a place half-way between East and West, Crete is a most appropriate place to locate the statue of humankind, fallen but looking toward the future redemption that will come from Rome. There Empire and Church should eventually be united in the shared mission of leading humankind to earthly and spiritual happiness, to the *beatitudinem huius vite* and to the *beatitudinem vite ecterne*, as Dante phrases it in his treatise on world government, *De Monarchia*.[26] Dante's precise geographical knowledge of the Mediterranean serves and supports his allegorical purpose, such that the progression of history is seen within its exact topographical parameters.

We had occasion earlier to refer to Dante's account of Ulysses's last voyage and the geographical-religious reasons for its ultimate failure. Within the economy of the poem Dante the Poet-Pilgrim recognizes the association between himself and Ulysses. Indeed, in the verses preceding the encounter with the Ithacan hero Dante makes special note of the dangers of unbridled "talent" (*ingegno*):

> Allor mi dolsi, e ora mi ridoglio
> quando drizzo la mente a ciò ch'io vidi,
> e più lo 'ngegno affreno ch'i' non soglio,
>   perchè non corra che virtù nol guidi;
> sì che, se stella bona o miglior cosa
> m'ha dato 'l ben, ch'io stessi nol m'invidi (*Inf.* 26.19-24).

[It grieved me then and now grieves me again / when I direct my mind to what I saw; / and more than usual, I curb my talent, / that it not run where virtue does not guide; / so that, if my kind star or something better / has given me that gift, I not abuse it.]

Ulysses was the bold adventurer who, in Dante's imagination, embarked on one last, great voyage, and let us turn our attention to that stirring account:

> Quando
>   mi diparti' da Circe, che sottrasse
> me più d'un anno là presso a Gaeta,
> prima che sì Enëa la nomasse,
>   né dolcezza di figlio, né la pieta
> del vecchio padre, né 'l debito amore
> lo qual dovea Penelopè far lieta,
>   vincer potero dentro a me l'ardore
> ch'i' ebbi a divenir del mondo esperto
> e de li vizi umani e del valore;
>   ma misi me per l'alto mare aperto
> sol con un legno e con quella compagna
> picciola da la qual non fui diserto.
>   L'un lito e l'altro vidi infin la Spagna,
> fin nel Morrocco, e l'isola d'i Sardi,
> e l'altre che quel mare intorno bagna.
>   Io e' compagni eravam vecchi e tardi
> quando venimmo a quella foce stretta
> dov' Ercule segnò li suoi riguardi
>   acciò che l'uom più oltre non si metta;

da la man destra mi lasciai Sibilia,
da l'altra già m'avea lasciata Setta.
   "O frati," dissi, "che per cento milia
perigli siete giunti a l'occidente,
a questa tanto picciola vigilia
   d'i nostri sensi ch'è del rimanente
non vogliate negar l'esperïenza,
di retro al sol, del mondo sanza gente.
   Considerate la vostra semenza:
fatti non foste a viver come bruti,
ma per seguir virtute e canoscenza."
   Li miei compagni fec' io sì aguti,
con questa orazion picciola, al cammino,
che a pena poscia li avrei ritenuti;
   e volta nostra poppa nel mattino,
de' remi facemmo ali al folle volo,
sempre acquistando dal lato mancino.
   Tutte le stelle già de l'altro polo
vedea la notte, e 'l nostro tanto basso,
che non surgëa fuor del marin suolo.
   Cinque volte racceso e tante casso
lo lume era di sotto da la luna,
poi che 'ntrati eravam ne l'alto passo,
   quando n'apparve una montagna, bruna
per la distanza, e parvemi alta tanto
quanto veduta non avëa alcuna.
   Noi ci allegrammo, e tosto tornò in pianto;
ché de la nova terra un turbo nacque
e percosse del legno il primo canto.
   Tre volte il fé girar con tutte l'acque;
a la quarta levar la poppa in suso
e la prora ire in giù, com' altrui piacque,
   infin che 'l mar fu sovra noi richiuso (*Inf.* 26.90-142).

[When / I sailed away from Circe, who'd beguiled me / to stay more than a year there, near Gaeta— / before Aeneas gave that place a name— / neither my fondness for my son nor pity / for my old father nor the love I owed / Penelope, which would have gladdened her, / was able to defeat in me the longing / I had to gain experience of the world / and of the vices and the worth of men. / Therefore, I set out on the open sea / with but one ship and that small company / of those who never had deserted me. / I saw as far as Spain, far as Morocco, /

along both shores; I saw Sardinia / and saw the other islands that sea bathes. / And I and my companions were already / old and slow, when we approached the narrows / where Hercules set up his boundary stones / that men might heed and never reach beyond: / upon my right, I had gone past Seville, / and on the left, already passed Ceüta. / "Brothers," I said, "o you, who having crossed / a hundred thousand dangers, reach the west, / to this brief waking-time that still is left / unto your senses, you must not deny / experience of that which lies beyond / the sun, and of the world that is unpeopled. / Consider well the seed that gave you birth: / you were not made to live your lives as brutes, / but to be followers of worth and knowledge". / I spurred my comrades with this brief address / to meet the journey with such eagerness / that I could hardly, then, have held them back; / and having turned our stern toward morning, we / made wings out of our oars in a wild flight / and always gained upon our left-hand side. / At night I now could see the other pole / and all its stars; the star of ours had fallen / and never rose above the plain of the ocean. / Five times the light beneath the moon had been / rekindled, and, as many times, was spent, / since that hard passage faced our first attempt, / when there before us rose a mountain, dark / because of distance, and it seemed to me / the highest mountain I had ever seen. / And we were glad, but this soon turned to sorrow, / for out of that new land a whirlwind rose / and hammered at our ship, against her bow. / Three times it turned her round with all the waters; / and at the fourth, it lifted up the stern / so that our prow plunged deep, as pleased an Other, / until the sea again closed—over us.]

The moral lesson, of course, is to practice moderation, to obey divine commands and limits, not to seek forbidden knowledge, to remember one's place in the universe, and to avoid the mad and proud pursuit of earthly knowledge. In the Christian universe all such activities can lead only to defeat and damnation. Whereas Ulysses's voyage through the Mediterranean and out into the uncharted waters of Ocean serves as a sort of counter-type, a negative exemplum for Dante in his real-allegorical pilgrimage, two other travelers/seafarers within the limits of the Mediterranean—Aeneas and Paul— serve as positive *exempla*. These figures are presented as paradigmatic in *Inferno* 2 when the Pilgrim declares that he is "not Aeneas, not Paul" ("Io non Enëa, io non Paulo sono," v. 32). However, despite this initial disclaimer, Dante will, in the course of the *Divine Comedy*, become both a new Aeneas and a new Paul, for the Pilgrim's mission is just as necessary in fourteenth-century Italy as were those of his forebears in their own historical moments. Dante's poem will become the agent for change in society, for the moral and spiritual betterment of humankind, for the reestablishment of order and justice in institutions both secular and sacred, and for a better balancing of power between Church and Empire. The Poet's vision of the perfectly ordered afterlife, his presentation of the operation of Divine Justice, and his blueprint for the regeneration of human society stand as a powerful witness both to his faith and to his literary talents. At the beginning of *Purgatorio* Dante, using the time honored metaphor of the literary work as a ship, refers to his own metaphorical seafaring on the "little vessel of [his] talent":[27]

> Per correr miglior acque alza le vele
> ormai la navicella del mio ingegno,
> che lascia dietro a sé mar sì crudele;
>   e canterò di quel secondo regno
> dove l'umano spirito si purga
> e di salire al ciel diventa degno (*Purg.* 1.1-6).

[To course across more kindly waters now / my talent's little vessel lifts her sails, / leaving behind herself a sea so cruel; / and what I sing will be that second kingdom, / in which the human soul is cleansed of sin, / becoming worthy of ascent to Heaven.]

And it is precisely through his use of this "poetic ship" that Dante demonstrates the great power the (Mediterranean) sea had in shaping his literary imagination. At the beginning of *Paradiso* Dante once again uses this metaphor, but with an even greater insistence:

> O Voi che siete in piccioletta barca,
> desiderosi d'ascoltar, seguiti
> dietro al mio legno che cantando varca,
>   tornate a riveder li vostri liti:
> non vi mettete in pelago, ché forse,
> perdendo me, rimarreste smarriti.
>   L'acqua ch'io prendo già mai non si corse;
> Minerva spira, e conducemi Appollo,
> e nove Muse mi dimostran l'Orse.
>   Voialtri pochi che drizzaste il collo
> per tempo al pan de li angeli, del quale
> vivesi qui ma non sen vien satollo,
>   metter potete ben per l'alto sale
> vostro navigio, servando mio solco
> dinanzi a l'acqua che ritorna equale (*Par.* 2.1-15).

[O you who are within your little bark, / eager to listen, following behind / my ship that, singing, crosses to deep seas, / turn back to see your shores again: do not / attempt to sail the seas I sail; you may, / by losing sight of me, be left astray. / The waves I take were never sailed before; / Minerva breathes, Apollo pilots me, / and the nine Muses show to me the Bears. / You other few who turned your minds in time / unto the bread of angels, which provides / men here with life—but hungering for more— / you may indeed commit your vessel to / the deep salt-sea, keeping your course within / my wake, ahead of where waves smooth again.]

Dante is indeed the new voyager, the one who, although moving through uncharted waters, is doubly sure, both of his destination and of his ability to lead others to it. Although similar to Ulysses in the daring and unprecedented nature of his deeds, Dante has embarked upon his sea journey under much different conditions than the foolhardy and proud Ithacan. Indeed, the Florentine poet has the guarantee of Divine Grace for his mission which, unlike Ulysses's, is not for individual glory or earthly fame, but rather for the salvation and well-being of all the world ("in pro del mondo che mal vive," *Purg.* 32.103). That Dante successfully arrives at his goal after having crossed such troubled waters is a tribute both to his knowledge of the sea and to the seaworthiness of his poetic craft. Dante, perhaps best of all medieval authors, incorporated the Mediterranean in all of its manifestations and made it one of the most powerful and enduring images that we find in literature.

Notes:

[1]   "Et eunt homines mirari alta montium, et ingentes fluctus maris, et latissimos
lapsus fluminum, et Oceani ambitum, et gyros siderum, et relinquunt se ipsos ... "
(*Conf.* 10.8). In *St. Augustine's Confessions*, trans. William Watts, 2 vols.
(Cambridge, MA, 1979), II: 99, 100.

[2]   Francesco Petrarca, *Rerum familiarium libri* IV. 1. For English versions of this
letter, see the translations by Aldo S. Bernardo, Francesco Petrarca, *Rerum
familiarium libri: I-VIII* (Albany, NY, 1975); and Morris Bishop, *Letters from
Petrarca* (Bloomington, IN, 1966).

[3]   The text of the *Comedy* follows that established by Giorgio Petrocchi for the
Edizione Nazionale of the Società Dantesca Italiana, *La Commedia secondo
l'antica vulgata* (Milano, 1966-67). The English translation is that of Allen
Mandelbaum, *The Divine Comedy of Dante Alighieri: Paradiso* (New York, NY,
1986).

[4]   Arthur H. Robinson, *Early Thematic Mapping in the History of Cartography*
(Chicago, IL, 1982), p. 10. The magisterial study of medieval maps and
mapmaking is that of David Woodward, "Medieval *Mappae mundi*," chapter 18 in
Vol. 1 of *The History of Cartography*, ed. J. B. Harley and David Woodward
(Chicago, IL, 1987), pp. 286-370. For photographic reproductions of the maps
mentioned in this section, in addition to Robinson and Woodward, see P. D. A.
Harvey, *Medieval Maps* (Toronto, 1991). For other pertinent discussions of
medieval maps and mapmaking, especially for their relationship to literary texts,
see, among others, the following studies: Scott D. Westrem, ed., *Discovering New
Worlds: Essays on Medieval Exploration and Imagination* (New York, NY, 1991)
and especially his "Introduction: 'From Worlde into Worlde'" (pp. ix-xxxiii), and
John B. Friedman, *The Monstrous Races in Medieval Art and Thought*
(Cambridge, MA, 1981) and especially Chapter 3 "At the Round Earth's Imagined
Corners" (pp. 37-58).

[5]   Harvey, *Medieval Maps*, p. 32.

[6]   John Masefield, "Sea-Fever," in his collection *Salt-Water Ballads* (1902; repr.
London, 1903), p. 59.

[7]   *Encyclopedia Brittanica* (1968), 12:737.

[8]   For information about and photographic reproductions of the portolan maps
mentioned in this section, see, among others, Harvey, *Medieval Maps*, and the
extensive treatment given the subject by Tony Campbell, "Portolan Charts from the
Late Thirteenth Century to 1500," chapter 19 in Vol. 1 of *The History of
Cartography*, (pp. 371-463).

[9]   This notion is often repeated by commentators on Dante's poem (e.g., the
commentary by Umberto Bosco and Giovanni Reggio, Dante Alighieri, *La Divina
Commedia: Inferno* [Firenze, 1979], p. 378). See, among others, the study by Peter
S. Hawkins, "'Out upon Circumference': Discovery in Dante," in *Discovering New
Worlds*, pp. 193-220. For the opposing view that Dante's tale of Ulysses's last
voyage may have in fact influenced the subsequent historical interpretation

concerning the voyage of the Vivaldi brothers, see Francis M. Rogers, "The Vivaldi Expedition," *Annual Report of the Dante Society* 73 (1955), 31-45. Rogers provides an accurate historical accounting of what little is known about the ill-fated voyage.

[10] See the fundamental study by Howard R. Patch, *The Goddess Fortuna in Medieval Literature* (Cambridge, MA, 1927), and Chapter IV ("The Dwelling-Place of Fortune") in particular.

[11] These images are present in the mid-sixteenth-century book by Jean Cousin, *Le Livre de Fortune*, With Introduction and Notes by Ludovic Lalanne, trans. H. Mainwaring Dunstan, (Paris, 1883).

[12] For an overview of the importance of the Mediterranean in the ancient world, see Michael Grant, *The Ancient Mediterranean* (New York, NY, 1969). In *Mediterranean: Portrait of a Sea* (New York, NY, 1971), Ernle Bradford provides a wide-ranging study that surveys the history of the sea from antiquity to the modern era.

[13] Fazio degli Uberti, *Il Dittamondo e le rime*, ed. Giuseppe Corsi, 2 Vols. (Bari, 1952). References to the Mediterranean Sea and the various lands that lies on its shores are numerous in the *Dittamondo*, as, for example, in the following passages: I. ix-x; III. i-iii, vi, xi-xv; V. i-ix.

[14] For accounts of Petrarch's life, see Morris Bishop, *Petrarch and His World* (Bloomington, IN, 1963), and Ernest Hatch Wilkins, *Life of Petrarch* (Chicago, 1961).

[15] Bishop's translation in *Letters from Petrarch*.

[16] The text of the poem follows the edition of Gianfranco Contini, Dante Alighieri, *Rime* (Torino, 1965). The translation is that of Joseph Tusiani, *Dante's Lyric Poems* (Brooklyn, NY, 1992).

[17] In the *Decameron* Boccaccio uses this adjective (*lieta*: "Introduzione," p. 103) and other descriptors (e.g., *onesta*: "Proemio," p. 13) to refer to his group of ten young people (*Decameron*, ed. Vittore Branca, 2 Vols. [Torino, 1980]).

[18] Petrarch's views on the benefits of solitude are presented in his treatise, *De vita solitaria*.

[19] The text follows the edition of Vittore Branca: Giovanni Boccaccio, *Rime*, in Vol. V of *Tutte le opere* (Milano, 1992).

[20] The Italian poets were perhaps following the Old French pun on *la mer* ("ocean") / *l'amer* ("love") / *l'amer[tume]* ("bitterness"), which Chrétien de Troyes employs in *Cligés* (vv. 533-549); see Michelle A. Freeman, "*Cligés*," in *The Romances of Chrétien de Troyes: A Symposium*, ed. Douglas Kelly (Lexington, KY, 1985), pp. 89-131, esp. 103-104. Among the early Italian poets we have, for example, the verses (13-14) in Pier della Vigna's *canzone* "Amando con fin core e co speranza": "La morte m'este amara, che l'amore / mutaomi in amarore" ["Death is bitter to me, for it changed my love to bitterness"]; see the edition of Bruno Panvini, *Le rime della scuola siciliana* (Firenze, 1962), pp. 128-30. Similarly, in a sonnet by the Pistoian poet Meo Abbracciavacca, we find the initial verse: "Amore amaro, a morte m'hai feruto" ["bitter love, you have wounded me to the point of death"];

see the edition of Guido Zaccagnini and Amos Parducci, *Rimatori siculo-toscani del Dugento, serie prima: Pistoiesi-lucchesi-pisani* (Bari, 1915), p.17.

[21] In Giacomo's *canzone* "Madonna, dir vo voglio," we find that love of the woman has the poet in a sort of the stormy sea: "Lo vostr'amor che m'ave / in mare tempestoso ... " (vv. 49-50; see the edition of Gianfranco Contini, *Poeti del Duecento*, 2 Vols. [Milano & Napoli, 1960], I:51-54). The sea also appears in several crucial passages in Cielo d'Alcamo's *contrasto* "Rosa fresca aulentissima" (for the text of the poem see Contini, *Poeti del Duecento*, I: 173-85).

[22] For the text of the poem see Contini, *Poeti del Duecento*, I: 483-500.

[23] The translation is that of Mark Musa and Peter Bondanella, Giovanni Boccaccio: *The Decameron* (New York, NY, 1982).

[24] The text follows the edition of Gianfranco Contini: Francesco Petrarca, *Canzoniere* (Torino, 1968). The translation is that of Robert M. Durling, *Petrarch's Lyric Poems: The "Rime Sparse" and Other Lyrics* (Cambridge, MA, 1976).

[25] The text follows the edition of Cesare Vasoli, in Dante Alighieri, *Opere minori*, Tomo I, Parte II (Milano & Napoli, 1988). The translation is that of Richard H. Lansing, *Dante's "Il Convivio" ("The Banquet")* (New York, NY, 1990).

[26] The complete passage in *De Monarchia* is as follows:

"Duos igitur fines providentia illa inenarrabilis homini proposuit intendendos: beatitudinem scilicet huius vite, que in operatione proprie virtutis consistit et per terrestrem paradisum figuratur; et beatitudinem vite ecterne, que consistit in fruitione divini aspectus ad quam propria virtus ascendere non potest, nisi lumine divino adiuta, que per paradisum celestem intelligi datur" (III, xv, 7).

[Twofold, therefore, are the ends which unerring Providence has ordained for man: the bliss of this life, which consists in the functioning of his own powers, and which is typified by the earthly Paradise; and the bliss of eternal life, which consists in the enjoyment of that divine vision to which he cannot attain by his own powers, except they be aided by the divine light, and this state is made intelligible by the celestial Paradise.]

The text of *De Monarchia* follows the edition of Bruno Nardi, in Dante Alighieri, *Opere minori*, Tomo II (Milano & Napoli, 1979). The translation is that of Herbert W. Schneider: Dante Alighieri, *On World-Government or De Monarchia* (New York, NY, 1957).

[27] For this metaphor see Ernst Robert Curtius, *European Literature and the Latin Middle Ages*, trans. Willard R. Trask (New York, NY, 1963), pp. 128-30.

Brenda Deen Schildgen

ISLAM IN BOCCACCIO'S *DECAMERON* AND CHAUCER'S *CANTERBURY TALES*

Introduction

Scholars have described a number of features of the Christian response to contact with Islam. In addition to narrow-minded prejudice that exhibits little knowledge of Islam found in many medieval *Chansons de geste*,[1] medieval intellectuals, led by Peter the Venerable, abbot of Cluny, developed an intense interest in the Moslem religion which led not only to a translation of the Koran into Latin by the Cluniac order under Peter the Venerable's patronage, but to the eventual translation of Averroes, Avicenna, and Aristotle.[2] In fact, as R. W. Southern put it, by the late Middle Ages, Islamic learning had become "classical" learning.[3] Third, trade was not only an essential feature of the relationship between Christian Europe and Islam, but the marketing relationships between the two were often equitable.[4] Fourth, Islam was perceived by those in power as a political-ideological threat because it appeared to be a movement in which religion and political aspirations were combined.[5] Finally, there is the issue of what Maxime Rodinson refers to as "les musulmans fictifs," the hermeneutic of exoticism and difference conferred on the Moslems.[6]

This paper, while showing the workings of these aspects of medieval Latin-Islamic relationships, compares and contrasts the treatment of Islam in Chaucer's "Man of Law's Tale" and two of Boccaccio's tales in the *Decameron*.[7]

Particularly in 1.3 and 10.9, Boccaccio shows a broad-minded and tolerant attitude towards religious conviction and cultural exchange in contrast to Chaucer's exposure of Islam as a dangerous and perfidious opposition to the Christian world. A comparison of the treatment of Islam in Boccaccio's *Decameron* and Chaucer's *Canterbury Tales* also draws attention to a radical difference between the cultures of the Mediterranean and those of northern Europe at the close of the medieval period. Though both Chaucer and Boccaccio show respect for Islam as a source of learning, and both reflect the established trading relationships between the two worlds, Chaucer's tale vehemently condemns fraternizing with Islam, while Boccaccio, in contrast, argues for the confraternity of the three Middle-Eastern religions and for mutually beneficial relationships. However, Chaucer's tale does not promote crusade politics; on the contrary, he draws a sharp line between the unconverted (both western pagans and eastern Moslems), pointing to the west as the site for evangelism and political reform. This emphasizes a radical difference between the two writers, suggesting not just a deviation in temperament and ideological conviction, but more importantly a difference in aesthetic purpose, at least in the tales that deal with the non-Christian world. Furthermore, and more importantly, the contrast dramatizes the diversity of Latin Christian literary attitudes towards Islam in the fourteenth century, particularly between the North and the Mediterranean regions.

Boccaccio's Character of Saladin

Both tales from the *Decameron* have Saladin as a main character. As has been known for some time, Saladin, the Islamic ruler who successfully retook Jerusalem in 1187, perhaps because of the enlightened approach he took to religious difference, was romanticized in many late medieval texts.[8] Boccaccio treats him as a model of chivalry, sharp intelligence, and magnanimity. But Boccaccio goes further than this romanticizing. He uses Saladin to probe what constitutes the cultural difference between these so-called enemies of Christianity and his own cultural sphere. Indeed Story 3, day 1, contributes to setting the tone for the entire collection, for it argues for a kind of secular humanism aligned with mutually satisfying business dealings that will characterize many of the tales. Filomena, one of the older young women, tells the tale, and she remarks to her companions that her tale is a reaction to the previous in which "di Dio e della verità della nostra fede è assai bene stato detto" (I.3.3) ("we have heard such fine things concerning God and the truth of our religion" [42]), for it showed Abraham, a Jew, choosing to convert to Christianity.

Filomena says that her tale, also about a Jew, named Melchizedek, on the other hand, will "discendere oggimai agli avvenimenti a agli atti degli uomini" (I.3.3) ("descend at this juncture to the deeds and adventures of men" [42]). In keeping with its secular humanism, she insists that the moral of the story is that "il senno di grandissimi pericoli trae il savio e ponlo in grande e sicuro riposo" (I.3.4) ("prudence extricates the wise from dreadful perils and guides them firmly to safety" [42]). Saladin is a hero to match the Florentine ideal of one who had succeeded in life because of worth and not birth,—"Il Saladino, il valore del quale fu tanto, che non solamente di piccolo uomo il fé di Babillonia soldano" (I.3.6) ("Saladin, whose worth was so great that it raised him from humble beginnings to the sultanate of Egypt" [*sic*] [42]). As Filomena points out, finding himself in need of money, because of excessive munificence as well as warfare, Saladin attempts to trick Melchizedek by asking him which of the three laws is the true one. Melchizedek, conscious that this is a trick question resorts to the parable of the three rings, in which all rings are exact copies of the one original, proving that the three laws are indistinguishable one from the other and they were made thus by their original owner in order to prevent squabbling and enmity among his sons. When Saladin realizes that Melchizedek has cleverly avoided his trap, he asks directly for what he wanted in the first place. They become fast friends and find much mutual profit in their relationship.

Where can this story be placed in the context of medieval religious conviction, merchant values,[9] crusades, or attitudes towards Islam, for example? First, the story supports cross-cultural, cross-religious merchant values and honest dealings that will result in profit and even friendship. Second, "force" disguised as "verbal" reason in Saladin's initial foray proves ineffective in achieving financial advantage. Third, the parable itself puts religious difference in abeyance on behalf of financial transactions and friendship. The *Novellino*[10] version of the three rings lacks the framing that Boccaccio has adopted here, and by itself, it argues for the successfully counterfeited equality of the rings and of the religions they represent. In Boccaccio's context, the story and the counterfeit it uses as its ruse become a rhetorical stratagem to avoid a business defeat. That does not mean that Boccaccio dismisses the religious meaning of the parable; rather, in Boccaccio's story, business transactions and relationships based on mutual benefit take precedence over all other interests, and thus the three-ring parable applies successfully in the world of commerce, to argue for mutual profit and exchange among the followers of the three indistinguishable laws.

Saladin is once more a central character on the tenth day, story 9. As in the earlier story, we see him as both bellicose and generous. He has come to Italy in disguise to appraise his opponents in an upcoming crusade confrontation. Told by the king for the day, Panfilo claims the story is to use Saladin as an exemplar of friendship, and the story manages to draw a sharp contrast between Christian/Islamic politics and military aspirations and friendship that crosses ethnic, religious, and cultural boundaries. Disguised as a Cypriot merchant, Saladin leads his Italian benefactor to remark, "Piacesse a Dio che questa nostra contrada producesse così fatti gentili uomini, chenti io veggio che Cipri fa mercatanti (X.9.18) ("Would to God that this country of ours produced gentlemen of a kind to compare with what I see of the merchants of Cyprus" [767]). Saladin, on the other hand, as recipient of his Italian friend's generosity concludes that, "se li re cristiani son così fatti re verso di sè chente costui è cavaliere, al soldano di Babilonia non ha luogo l'aspettarne pure un ..." (X.9.35) ("if the kings of Christendom are such excellent princes as this man is a knight, the Sultan of Babylon will be powerless to resist a single one of them" [771]). One friend outdoes the other in generosity and munificence, making friendship and generosity the subject of the relationship between Islam and Christianity and consigning the crusade to the background.

However, this is the only tale in the collection that depends on magic for its happy denouement. After Torello's capture by Saladin's forces in the crusade, it is Saladin's magicians that arrange for Ser Torello to be transported back to his wife who has been pressured to remarry when her husband has failed to return from Egypt. While magic is the "exotic" property of Islamic culture, here it becomes the means to return generosity between men who are equals in generosity. But the magic element that is so rare in the collection tampers with the optimistic tone of the tale, for it reminds us of the unlikelihood that such happy endings or that such reciprocity might happen. Nonetheless, in Boccaccio's treatment of Saladin and the Islamic world he represents, we see that though he recognizes that crusades exist, he deliberately obscures the religious differences that justified them and dramatizes instead what profit and pleasure can result from encountering the Arab world. He demonstrates too that true worth (that which is earned and shown by actions, not that with which one is born) is evident even though disguises and that friendship and mutual benefit can overcome cultural and religious difference.

Chaucer's Man of Law's Tale

Chaucer's *Man of Law's Tale*, on the other hand, as the only *Canterbury Tale* that deals directly with Islam, makes use of medieval *allegoresis* to unfold a political argument that exposes Islam as a dangerous and perfidious enemy. In *The Treatise on the Astrolabe*, Chaucer showed that he respected Islamic learning, but in this story he distinguishes intellectual concerns from religious-political policy and actions and unnegotiable Christian truth.

Until recently critical studies overlooked the Chaucerian contrast between Islam and Christianity or between "hethenesse" and Christianity that structurally underlies the tale.[11] That a central feature of the story is one of Christian evangelism is emphasized by the teller's insistence on informing us of the religious status of the people Constance encounters at every point in her forced journey. Constance is an allegorical figure, just as the two opposed sides, Syria and Britain are allegorized to represent "heathen" and "Christian," with Rome made to represent the center of Christendom.[12] But Chaucer does not advance a politically and ideologically inspired crusade program in contrast to Philippe de Mézières, a rabid fourteenth-century French supporter of a renewed crusade, who used political allegory in his crusade propaganda. Both Philippe's *Songe du*

Vieil Pélerin[13] and his *Epistre au Roi Richart*[14] were known at John of Gaunt's and King Richard's respective courts. Chaucer's knowledge of Philippe's work is further supported by his narrative in the *Monk's Tale* of the tragic history of Peter, king of Cyprus (VII. 2388-2398), under whom Philippe de Mézières was chancellor (1359-1369).

In Part I of the tale, stories of Constance's nobility have been relayed to the Sultan by wealthy Syrian merchants who have traded in Rome. Representing the commercial relationship between Islam and Christianity, their mercantile connection to Rome appears to work for mutual advantage:

> Now fil it that the maistres of that sort
> Han shapen hem to Rome for to wende;
> Were it for chapmanhod or for disport … (II.141-143).

The Sultan, his desires stirred by their reports of the child of the Roman emperor, wants to marry her:

> To han hir figure in his remembrance,
> That al his lust and al his bisy cure
> Was for to love hire while his lyf may dure (II.187-189).

Such marriages between Christian and "Saracen" were not uncommon in the Middle Ages,[15] and they were used, as indeed most marriages amongst the wealthy and privileged, for economic or political advantage. Chaucer emphasizes the commercial element, while eliminating any individualistic conversion prior to the Sultan's desire for her.

The Sultan's interest in Constance, like the trading activities of his fellow Syrians, stems from a relationship of parity between the two realms. However, the Christian insistence that he convert to Christianity before the marriage can take place establishes a power relationship in which Christianity is held as unnegotiable, a fact that the Sultan's advisors are quick to note. Suggesting a commercial element in the center of Islamic religious practice, the Sultan's abandonment of his own Law and his conversion emerge as features in his bartering negotiations for his bride. This spurious conversion is in direct contrast with the later conversions of Hermengyld and Alla in England because it is not the result of grace but a condition for the marriage:

> Rather than I lese
> Custance, I wol be cristned, douteleess.
> I moot been hires; I may noon oother chese (II. 225-227).

The Sultan's transacted conversion distinguishes it from King Alla's of Britain who chooses Constance and her religion because of direct experience with divine agency. It points to a moral corruption at the core of Islamic cultural practice, for the Sultan abandons an absolute "faith" for a personal desire. Because he wants to possess her, the Sultan is even willing to set aside the advice of his counselors who remind him, "... there was swich diversitee/Bitwene hir bothe lawes" (II.220-224).

Focussing on Law as the main criterion for concern, their advice recognizes authentic differences in laws, and they argue that no Christian would wed into "oure lawe sweete/That us was taught by Mahoun" (II.224). On the other hand, the Sultan's conspiracy in his own seduction shows that for a reward he is willing to accept Christianity's aversion to difference and assertion of it sown intrinsic superiority. His unremitting desire overcomes him, taking his commitment to his "sweete lawe" with it. On the Roman side, the marriage is viewed as a benefit for the Church for it will aid "in destruccioun of mawmettrie" ("destruction of idolatry"). The conversion project, the political-ideological program in action, supported by the "popes mediacioun, and al the churche" overrides geographical spaces, and cultural differences are made disposable if the religious tokens are observed. Reluctantly, "The day is comen of hir departynge;/I seye, the woful day fatal is come" (260-261), and Constance leaves Rome, the center of Christian life and power for Syria, the "strange nacioun" (268).

In addition to reciting Constance's own hesitations about her impending marriage, the narrator, in a twenty-eight line hyperbolic address to the audience, makes the event epic in its implications by comparing the misery at Constance's leaving for Syria with the tears at Troy when Pyrrus broke the wall, when Thebes fell, and when Hannibal harassed Rome (II.288-294). The collapse of the differences between history and literature in these examples brings together paradigmatic examples of treachery and irrational brutality associated with Thebes, Carthage, and the Greeks. Pyrrus and Hannibal are the traditional mythologized enemies of Rome,—one literary and one historical example of the brutality of the Greeks and the rapaciousness of the Carthaginians. Both represent cultures conquered by the ancient Romans, but in this fourteenth-century tale these cultural domains spatially outside the world of Roman Christianity become parallel to Syrian Islam. In the ideology of the tale, like the Carthaginians and the Greeks, Syrian Islam threatens the Latin world.

The Man of Law's Tale dramatizes how and why the hopes of such an allegorical political-religious marriage are doomed, for resentments against this alliance exist even before Constance arrives. In fact, the narrator spends an unremitting sixty lines on the fears and animosities felt against this alliance on the Moslem side, which the Sultan's mother expresses and nurtures in others.

Furthermore, the narrator informs us of the treacherous plot the Sultan's mother has masterminded to undo her son's plan to abandon his "olde sacrifices" (II. 235) and accept "Cristen mariage" (II. 369). Aware of their cultural difference and recognizing a betrayal of their religious integrity in her son's willing abandonment of his "law" for his marriage, the Sultana lays out a geographical-political space that this marriage threatens to dissolve. Chaucer assigns a defense to the Sultana's position, for she argues against the intended marriage and conversion on religious grounds. The objections Chaucer assigns her show that he knew that Islam was a monotheistic religion in contrast to the popular opinions expressed in widely disseminated *chansons de geste* (*Chanson de Roland* and *Aliscans*, for example),[16] which made Moslems idolaters with numerous gods, or found in the medieval encyclopedias (Vincent of Beauvai's *Speculum historiale* or Brunetto Latini, *Livres dou Trésor*), where Mohammed is portrayed as "seducer of Arabs," or a failed monk.[17] Unlike many of his contemporaries in England, Chaucer shows that he knows that Islam was a religion of the "Law," as revealed in its center text, the Koran, and the Mohammed was that religion's prophet:

> "Lordes," quod she, ye knowen everichon,
> How that my sone in point is for to lete
> The hooly lawes of our Alkaron,
> Yeven by Goddes message Makomete,
> But oon avow to grete God I heete,
> The lyf shal rather out of my body sterte
> Or Makometes lawe out of myn herte!
>
> What sholde us tyden of this newe lawe
> But thraldom to oure bodies and penance,
> And afterward in helle to be drawe,
> For we reneyed Mahoun oure creance?
> But, lordes, wol ye maken assurance,
> And I shal seyn, assentynge to my loore,
> And I shall make us sauf for everemoore? (II. 330-343).

The Sultana's professed pious commitment to "the hooly lawes of Alkaron," which she uses to promote her rhetorical appeal for treason against her son, parallels the fervor found in martyrs who have died rather than be converted from Christianity. (The Second Nun's story of St. Cecelia is just such a story within the Canterbury collection). But the difference between St. Cecelia's response to the assault on her faith is that she accepts martyrdom, whereas, the Sultana, like Judas, seeing that she cannot stop the marriage, chooses treachery and conspiracy in a fatal effort to catapult her son's plans perhaps indeed because she wants to rule alone: "For she hirself wolde al the contree lede"(II. 434). She elects murder and treachery rather than martyrdom. She will feign accepting the religion (II. 351), allow baptism (II. 352), and say that she will deny her old religion (II. 376), while planning to murder her son and all those who have willingly accepted Christianity. Having laid the groundwork for her murderous plot, this second Semiramis (II. 359), in an act typologically parallel to Judas's betrayal of Jesus, "kiste hir sone" (II. 385). Here the hermeneutics of exoticism triumph as the fictive "saracen," treacherous, barbarous, and most of all, unchanging from ancient Babylon to modern Syria, takes possession of the narrative. The comparison of the Sultana with Semiramis is an important detail, for Semiramis was the Assyrian Empress, who according to legend, was infamous for making it legal in her kingdom to practice incest. According to Orosius's historiographical theory, the Assyrian Empire that Semiramis led declined providentially, its degeneracy making way for the eventual triumph of Christian Rome. He writes that she had an incestuous relationship with her son, wore men's clothing and a male heart, and tried to conquer all Asia and bring it under her rule of law.[18]

By eliding the differences between the Sultana and Semiramis, Chaucer aligns Assyria and Syria, history and myth, and religion and politics as he connects ancient Babylon, the emblematic decadent city in the Judaeo-Christian imagination, to contemporary Islam, a connection designed to recall an unregenerate history of interconnected sexual-political conspiracy and betrayal and to support it with biblical authority. Dante specifically remarks that she ruled where now the Sultan rules (*Inferno* V), while Chaucer calls the mother of the Sultan a second Semiramis. The confraternity between Semiramis and the Sultana argues that there is no difference between the Islam of contemporary politics and the mythological Babylon, of which Semiramis was queen. Her history is important to *The Man of Law's Tale* because like Semiramis, the sultana, a "feyned womman" (II. 362), would choose to rule without her son (II. 434). The Sultana, as second Semiramis, is the "unchanging abstraction of oriental treachery".[19] Her actions, the murder of her son and all his converted allies and the expulsion of Constance (II. 428-441), eventually lead to a further bloody clash between her people and the Romans. Ominous signs at Constance's initial crossing over the boundaries into the alien territory warned that the journey was spatially transgressive. In contrast, the narrator's perfunctory, almost mechanical recitation of the Roman vengeance visited on the Syrians to punish them for their treatment of Constance, like the punishment allotted the Jews in the *Prioress's Tale*, denies their humanity:

For which this Emperour hath sent anon
His senatour, with roial ordinance,
And othere lordes, God woot, many oon,
On Syrryens to taken heigh vengeance.
They brennen, sleen, and brynge hem to meschance
Ful many a day; but shortly—this is th'ende— (II. 960-966).

Together, the Sultan's naïve wish to override differences, his mother's desperate and violent plot to return the spatial-cultural boundary *status quo*, and the Roman "heigh vengeance" succeed in building an impenetrable wall between the Christian and Islamic world. Showcasing the violence and treachery of the Syrians succeeds in reenforcing religious-cultural suspicions and fears; thus the *Man of Law's Tale*, reenforces the boundaries that define, underlie, and organize culture.[20]

Though likewise rife with internal turmoil (the plot of the knight to slander and ruin Constance and the parallel to the Syrian mother-in-law plot which sends her back to Rome), the events in Britain contrast with the utter failure of Constance's earlier marriage to Syria. Converting many, she marries King Alla and gives birth to the Christian child who will rule a unified Christian world as emperor (II. 1121-1123). The folk-tale doubling between the Syrian and British sections of the tale (arrival by boat, conversions, mother-in-laws who falsify their words and actions, murder plots, and exile on a boat) are specific and purposeful, for they emphasize the differences between the world of Islamic Syria and converted Christian Britain. They set up the geographical space of Christianity in contrast to the Syrian space, the "barbre nacioun". King Alla's conversion, despite the earlier intermittent success and failure of conversion efforts in Britain, and unlike the Sultan's, is profound and results in Alla's penitential pilgrimage to Rome to expiate his regret for his ruthless murder of his mother who had masterminded the vicious plot against Constance.

Charting the irremediable conflict between Islam and Christianity, Chaucer's tale also condemns the controversial border crossing from the start. Though Constance and the Christian humility she represents survive the "eastern" experience, her own initial fears about the enterprise, and her role as the vulnerable and powerless means for negotiation between the two cultural spheres, dramatize the story's concerns about social-political dealings with the Islamic world, no matter how much their religious goals are proclaimed. The last words Constance utters in the story after her return to Rome and reunion with her father, "Sende me namoore unto noon hethenesse/But thonketh my lord heere of his kyndenesse" (II. 1112-1113) is a plea to end forays into "hethenesse," which here are equated with Islam.

Conclusion

Because both Chaucer and Boccaccio stage these stories by having other characters tell them, it is difficult to ascribe the attitudes expressed to their authors. Nonetheless, the completely different views of Islam represented by each author raise some intriguing questions. Boccaccio makes the religious laws indistinguishable and recommends friendship based on equality and mutual benefit. Chaucer draws a line between the two worlds. What might explain these differences? Briefly, the last Christian stronghold in the Middle East had fallen in 1298. Though advocates of crusading remained, crusade politics no longer inspired much support from kings or from the divided Church.[21] Boccaccio's collection was completed in 1353, at a time when the plague had severely undermined all existing social structures. This was not a time for contemplating crusades even though Turkish power was beginning to assert itself.[22] Second, by including cross-social, economic, and religious friendships, marriages, and affairs, the merchant atmosphere of Boccaccio's masterpiece debates these challenges to erstwhile social practices; third, Boccaccio's collection includes both a local[23] and cross-cultural Mediterranean environment of merchants, pirates, lovers, and unstable political realms. Fourth, Boccaccio's work emphasizes that secular merchant values support mutually beneficial commerce between the disparate worlds.

Similarly, in the *Man of Law's Tale*, merchant actions bring Islam and Christianity together, but Chaucer shows this as potentially dangerous and destructive to the Christian world. Crusades were again in the air in the late fourteenth century, but Chaucer, or his narrator, does not seem to support them, at least in this tale. Nonetheless, the unmediated conversion features of the tale (Alla's conversion; his reconciliation with Constance in Rome), suggest that the tale is intended to support Christian conversion, to establish a heroic past for "Englissh" Christianity, and to emphasize the necessity of future conversion.

What if Chaucer did know the *Decameron*? Then the *Man of Law's Tale* would become a comment on that tolerant attitude upheld in Boccaccio's tale. It would become the expression of the concerns of a man who saw the Roman church in crisis and the efficacy of its Law under siege. It would highlight the serious note struck by the second fragment's theme of Christian conversion that punctuates if not dominates the *Canterbury Tales*, a theme that radically distinguishes Chaucer's literary purposes from Boccaccio's. In the late fourteenth century, it reveals the difference between an "Englissh" writer's fear of Islam and a mid-century Florentine's broad-minded secular humanism.

Notes:

[1] Norman Daniel, *The Arabs and Medieval Europe* (London & New York, NY, 1975); Y. and Ch. Pellat, "L'idée de Dieu chez les 'Sarasins' des Chansons de Geste," *Studia Islamica* 22 (1965), 5-42; C. Meredith Jones, "The Conventional Saracen in the Songs of Geste," *Speculum* 17 (1942), 201-25; Norman Daniel, *Heroes and Saracens: An Interpretation of the Chansons de Geste* (Edinburgh, 1984).

[2] James Kritzeck, *Peter the Venerable and Islam* (Princeton, NJ, 1964); Ugo Monneret de Villard, *Lo studio dell' Islam in Europa nel XII e nel XIII secolo* (Città del Vaticano, 1944); Archibald Lewis, ed., *The Islamic World and the West A.D. 622-1492* (New York, NY, 1970); R. W. Southern, *Western Views of Islam in the Middle Ages* (Cambridge, MA, 1962).

[3] *Western Views of Islam*, p. 77.

[4] Maxime Rodinson, *Europe and the Mystique of Islam* (Seattle, WA, 1987); R. S. Lopez, "L'importanza del mondo islamico nella vita economica europea," in *L' occidente e l' Islam nell' alto medioevo* (Spoleto, 1965); Eliyahu Ashtor, *East-West Trade in the Medieval Mediterranean*, ed. Benjamin Z. Kedar (London, 1986); Eliyahu Ashtor, *The Medieval Near East: Social and Economic History*, Collected Studies (London, 1978).

[5] Carl Erdman, *The Origin of the Idea of Crusade*, tr. Marshall W. Baldwin and Walter Goffart (Princeton, NJ, 1977).

[6] Maxime Rodinson, *Europe and the Mystique of Islam*; see also Thierry Hentsch, *L' Orient imaginaire. La vision politique occidenttale de l' Est méditerranéen* (Paris, 1988).

[7] All references to the *Canterbury Tales* are to the Riverside edition, *The Riverside Chaucer*, 3rd ed., general editor, Larry D. Benson (Boston, MA, 1997); references to the *Decameron* are from Giovanni Boccaccio, *Decameron*, in *Tutte le Opere di Giovanni*, ed. Vittore Branca, Vol. 4 (Milan, 1976). Translations are from Giovanni Boccaccio, *The Decameron*, tr. G. H. McWilliam (London, 1995).

[8] See Dorothy Metliski, *Matter of Araby in Medieval England* (New Haven, CT, 1977); Américo Castro, "Présence du Sultan Saladin dans les littératures romaines," *Diogènes* 8 (1954) [also in English translation, "The Presence of the Sultan Saladin in the Romance Literatures," in *An Idea of History: Selected Essays of Americo Castro 1954*, tr. and ed. Stephen Gilman and Edmund L. King (Columbus, OH, 1977)]; see also Gaston Paris, *Leggenda di Saladino*, tr. Mario Menghini (Firenze, 1896).

[9] Vittore Branca emphasized this element in the *Decameron*, calling it a mercantile epic. See Vittore Branca, *Boccaccio Medievale* (Firenze, 1956).

[10] *Le cento novelle antiche o libro di novelle e di bel parlar gentile detto anche Novellino*, ed. Letterario di Francia (Torino, 1945).

[11] Critics have sustained the long-standing tradition of Chaucerian scholarship which divides between those who choose to make the story and its teller the object of Chaucerian irony and those who wish to make it conform to a presumed

medieval Christian ideology. More recent criticism, using methodologies ranging from deconstruction to feminism has dwelt on social, economic, and political implications in the tale and its telling. See Paul Olson, *The Canterbury Tales and the Good Society* (Princeton, NJ, 1986); Sheila Delany, *Writing Woman* (New York, NY, 1983); Alfred Shoaf, "'Unwemmed Custance': Circulation, Property, and Incest in the *Man of Law's Tale*," *Exemplaria* 2/1 (March, 1990), 287-302; Carolyn Dinshaw, "The Law of Man and Its 'Abhomynacions,'" *Exemplaria* 1/1 (March, 1989), 117-48; Laurel L. Hendrix, "'Pennance profytable': The Currency of Custance in Chaucer's *Man of Law's Tale*," *Exemplaria* 6/1 (1994), 141-66; David Wallace, "'Deyntee to Chaffare': Men of Law, Merchants and the Constance Story," Chapter 7, *Chaucerian Polity* (Palo Alto, CA, 1997), pp. 182-211.

[12]   V. A. Kolve, *Chaucer and the Imagery of Narrative: The First Five Canterbury Tales* (Stanford, CA, 1984) argues that Constance, the heroine in the tale is the ship of the church.

[13]   G. W. Coopland, ed., *Le Songe due Vieil Pèlerin of Philippe de Mézières I and II* (Liverpool, 1969).

[14]   G. W. Coopland, tr. and original text ed., *Letter to King Richard. A Plea Made in 1395 for Peace between England and France* (Liverpool, 1975).

[15]   Norman Daniel, *Islam and the West. The Making of an Image* (Edinburgh, 1960), pp. 115, 116, 132, and 201; Maxime Rodinson, *Europe and the Mystique of Islam*, p. 8.

[16]   Pierre Le Gentil, *La Chanson de Roland*, 2nd ed. (Paris, 1967); *Aliscans*, Tome I and II, ed. Claude Régnier (Paris, 1990).

[17]   Brunetto Latini adopting a position somewhat like the Nestorian Christian explanation of Vincent, says Mohammed was a monk who fell into error. See Brunetto Latini, *Li Livres dou Tresor de Brunetto Latini*, ed. Francis J. Carmody (Berkeley, CA, 1948), I:88 ["Comment Sainte Eglise Essaucha," p. 69].

[18]   Pauli Orosii, *Historiarum adversum paganos, Libri VII, Corpus scriptorum ecclesiasticorum latinorum*, ed. and comm. Carolus Zangermeister (Vindobonae, 1882), I:4, 43. Dante, too, condemns Semiramis to the circle of the lustful. See *Inferno* V.52-60 from the Petrocchi text in *The Divine Comedy*, 3 Vols., tr. with comm. Charles S. Singleton (Princeton, NJ, 1970-1975).

[19]   Edward W. Said, *Orientalism* (New York, NY, 1979), p. 8.

[20]   Michel de Certeau, "Montaigne's 'Of Cannibals'," in *Heterologies: Discourse on the Other*, tr. Brian Massumi (Minneapolis, MN & London, 1986), pp. 68-69.

[21]   For the crusades in the later Middle Ages, see Sylvia Schein, *Fideles Crucis. The Papacy, the West, and the Recovery of the Holy Land 1274-1314* (Oxford, 1991); Aziz Suryal Atiya, *The Crusade and the Later Middle Ages* (London, 1938).

[22]   Norman Housley, T*he Avignon Papacy and the Crusades, 1305-1378* (Oxford, 1986). J. J. N. Palmer, *England, France and Christendom 1377-99* (London, 1972), p. 14, writes, "After breaking into Europe in mid-century, the Ottoman Turks had expanded at the expense of their Christian neighbors with astonishing rapidity. The battle of Marrica (September 1371) established their hegemony in

the Balkans, and in the course of the next few years the king of Bulgaria, the princes of Serbia, and even the emperor of Byzantium became tributaries to the sultan. In the 1380s vassaldom began to give way to complete subjection".

23   See Nigel Thompson, *Chaucer, Boccaccio and the Debate of Love* (Oxford, 1996) for a discussion of "local" cultures in the *Decameron*.

Vincent Corrigan

INTERNATIONAL ELEMENTS
IN THE CODEX CALIXTINUS:
MAPPA MUNDI AND THE ALLELUIA GROUP

The *Mappa mundi*

From the perspective of its inhabitants, Compostela lay very near, if not at, the center of the world. Its cathedral was reputed to house the remains of St. James the Greater, brother of John and supposed missionary to Spain. After James' martyrdom in Jerusalem, so the legend goes, his body was miraculously returned to Galicia by his disciples, who buried it on the site later known as Compostela. Because of this, Compostela became a pilgrimage center equal in importance to Rome and Jerusalem, attracting peoples from all corners of the earth.

The most important testament to the cult of James at Compostela is the Codex Calixtinus.[1] This manuscript, attributed to Pope Calixtus II (1119-24) and now housed in the Cathedral of Santiago, consists of five books: Liturgies; Miracles; Translation of James to Spain; an account of Charlemagne's Spanish campaigns (Pseudo-Turpin); and the Pilgrims' Guide, including the appendix of polyphonic music. By far the most important is the first book, which contains all of the texts—readings, sermons, blessings, and so forth— and all of the music for the celebration of the various feasts of the Saint, an enormous amount of material. Among the texts is the sermon *Veneranda dies*, a treatise on pilgrimage again attributed to Calixtus, which lists 74 nations and peoples who visit Compostela and the Cathedral.

Illuc populi barbari et domestici cunctorum cosmi climatum adveniunt, scilicet Franci, Normanni, Scotti, Hiri, Galli, Theutonici, Yberi, Wasconi, Baleari, Navarri impii, Bascli, Gotti, Provinciales, Garasqui, Lotharingi, Gauti, Angli, Britones, Cornubienses, Flandri, Frisi, Allobroges, Itali, Apuli, Pictavi, Aquitani, Greci, Armeni, Daci, Noroequi, Russi, Iorianti, Nubiani, Parthi, Romani, Galate, Ephesi, Medi, Tuscani, Kalabriani, Saxones, Siciliani, Asiani, Ponti, Bitiniani, Indiani, Creti, Hierosolimitani, Antiocheni, Galilei, Sardani, Cipriani,

Ungari, Bulgari, Ysclavoni, Africani, Perse, Alexandrini, Egiptii, Suriani, Arabes, Colosenses, Mauri, Ethiopes, Philipenses, Capadoci, Corinti, Elamite, Mesopotamiani, Libiani, Cirenenses, Pamphiliani, Ciliciani, Iudei et cetere gentes innumerabiles cunctae linguae tribus et naciones ad eum tendunt per catervas et phalanges, cum gratiarum actione vota sua domino persolventes, premia laudum deferentes.[2]

[To that place come peoples foreign and native of all parts of the world,[3] namely: Franks, Normans, Scots, Irish,[4] Gauls, Teutons, Iberians, Vascones, *Baioari*,[5] wicked Navarres, Basques, Goths, Provincals, *Garasques*,[6] Lotharingians, Gotlanders,[7] Angles, *Britons* (Bretons?), Cornwallians, Flemish, Frisians, Allobrogues, Italians, Apulians, Picts (Poitevins?), Aquitanians, Greeks, Armenians, Dacians, Norwegians, Russians, *Iorianti*,[8] Nubians, Parthians, Romans, Galatians, Ephesians, Medes, Tuscans, Calabrians, Saxons, Sicilians, Asians, Pontians, Bythinians, Indians, Cretans, Jerusalemites, Antiochans, Galileans, Sardinians, Cypriots, Hungarians, Bulgars, Slavs, Africans, Persians, Alexandrinians, Egyptians, Syrians, Arabians, Colossians, Moors, Ethiopians, Philippians, Capadocians, Corinthians, Elamites, Mesopotamians, Lybians, Cyrenians, Pamphilians, Cilicians, Judeans—and the remaining innumerable peoples of all languages, tribes, and nations reach out to him in crowds and battalions with thanksgiving, rendering their offerings to the Lord, bringing away the rewards of (their) praises.]

This is an onomasticon of places and peoples, representing the whole of the known world.[9] Some of the geography of this world is determined as much by history and scripture as it is by national and linguistic boundaries. It includes all of the recipients of Paul's epistles except Thessalonians, and they fall into two closely placed groups: Romans, Galatians, and Ephesians; Colossians, Philippians, Corinthians. In addition, almost all of the peoples listed in Acts 2.7-12 as witnessing the apostles' Pentecost sermons are recorded: Parthians, Medes, Elamites, Mesopotamians, Judeans, Cappadocians, inhabitants of Pontus, Asia, Pamphilia, Egypt, Lybia/Cyrenia, and Romans (again), Cretans, and Arabians. Only the Phrygians are missing. Together these groups account for 20 of the 74 peoples mentioned.

Most of the Mediterranean island groups are recognized: the Balearic Islands (possibly), Sicily, Crete, Sardinia, and Cyprus. Furthermore, major cities get special recognition: Rome, Jerusalem, Antioch, and Alexandria.[10] But most of the entries concern national and ethnic boundaries. Of course the European countries and the British Isles figure prominently. Quite detailed ethnic and linguistic subdivisions are given for France (eight entries),

Germany (three entries), Spain (four entries), the Low Countries (two entries), Italy (five entries), and the British Isles (six entries), at least 28 items, including historical as well as contemporaneous peoples. Eastern Europe (six entries), Asia Minor (three entries), the Near East (ten entries) and the entirety of North Africa are also represented (six entries). Finally, there are some that surprised me: Sweden (Gotland), Norway, Russia, and India.

It may be that the various nationalities would gravitate to one or the other of the Cathedral's nine chapels surrounding the main altar, for further on in the same sermon we read:

> Nimio gaudio miratur, qui peregrinantum chorus circa beati Iacobi altare venerandum vigilantes videt: Theutonici enim in alia parte, Franci in alia, Itali in alia catervatim commorantur, cereos ardentes manibus tenentes, unde tota ecclesia ut sol vel dies clarissima illuminantur. Unusquisque cum patriotis suis per se vigilias sapienter agit. ... Ibi audiuntur diversa genera linguarum, diversi clamores barbarorum loquele et cantilene Theutonicorum, Anglorum, Grecorem, ceterarumque tribuum et gentium diversarum omnium mundi climatum. Non sunt loquele neque sermones, quorum non resonent voces illorum.[11]

> [One marvels with exceeding joy, who sees the chorus of pilgrims keeping watch around the venerable altar of St. James: Germans on one side, French on another, Italians on another standing in groups, holding burning tapers in their hands, which illuminate the whole church as the sun or rather the brightest day. Each one with his compatriots by themselves wisely performs the vigils. ... There are heard diverse genera of tongues, diverse shouts of barbarous languages and the prattle of Germans, Angles, Greeks, and of all the other tribes and diverse races of all climes of the world. There are neither languages nor tongues whose voices do not resound.]

In any event, the intent of these passages is clear. Compostela is a city of international importance, because it attracts not only its European neighbors, but people from the entire Mediterranean rim to the south and east, and from the Scandanavian countries to the north. This is a *mappa mundi*, one in which all roads lead to Compostela.

The Alleluia group

Given the emphasis on the international appeal of the Cult of St. James in the pilgrimage sermon, it would be surprising if the music did not make some gesture in the same direction.[12] It does so here and there throughout the liturgies, but nowhere more clearly than in the group of Alleluias used in the mass for the feast day. There are four pieces in this cluster: *Sanctissime apostole Iacobe*, *Hic Iacobus*, *Vocavit Ihesus*, and the prosa *Gratulemur et letemur*, assigned to the various feasts of the the Saint. Of course the main feast day, July 25, contains all of them, as is shown in Table 1. An additional prosa *Clemens servulorum* first appears in the mass for July 26. What appears to be a new prosa, *Boanerges qui numcuparis* on July 27, is actually the conclusion of *Gratulemur et letemur*.

Table 1

Alleluias for the Feasts of St. James

July 25:	Alleluia. Sanctissime apostole Iacobe
	Alleluia. Hic Iacobus
	Alleluia. Vocavit Ihesus
	Prosa. Gratulemur et letemur
July 26:	Alleluia. Vocavit Ihesus
	Prosa. Clemens servulorum
July 27:	Alleluia. Sanctissime apostole Iacobe
	Prosa. Boanerges qui numcuparis
July 28:	Alleluia. Hic Iacobus
	Prosa. Clemens servulorum
July 29:	Alleluia. Vocavit Ihesus
	Prosa. Boanerges qui numcuparis
July 30:	Alleluia. Sanctissime apostole Iacobe
	Prosa. Clemens servulorum
July 31:	Alleluia. Vocavit Ihesus
	Prosa. Gratulemur et letemur
Aug. 1:	Alleluia. Hic Iacobus
	Prosa. Clemens servulorum
Oct. 3:	Alleluia. Vocavit Ihesus
	Prosa. Clemens servulorum
Dec. 30:	Alleluia. Vocavit Ihesus
	Prosa. Gratulemur et letemur

A.   *Alleluia. Sanctissime apostole Iacobe*
The CC attributes *Alleluia/Sanctissime apostole Iacobe* to Calixtus himself.

This attribution refers only to the text, which is non-biblical, for in 1935 Peter Wagner pointed out that its melody was identical to another Alleluia, *Levita Laurentius*.[13] In fact, this is only part of the story, for both of these alleluias are members of a large family of texts, all of which use the same melody.[14] This family is shown in Table 2.

Table 2

Alleluia 1—Family of Texts

Title	Feast	Number of Sources
Apparuerunt apostolis		1
Beatus servus		2
Concussum est	St. Michael, Sept. 29	46
Confirma hoc deus		1
Diffusa est gratia		11
Dominus in sina		
In omnem terram		1
Iterum autem videbo		7
Laetabitur iustus	Common of Saints	70
Laetamini in Domino		
Levavi oculos meos		1
Levita Laurentius	St. Lawrence, Aug. 10	18
Nativitas gloriosae	Nativity BVM	25
O Martine presul	St. Martin of Tours	2
Optimam partem	St. Mary Magdalen	4
Repleti sunt omnes		2
Sanctissime apostole	St. James, July 25	3
Veni electa mea	Common of Virgins	1
Video caelos	St. Stephen, Dec. 26	1

The melody is most often associated with the text *Laetabitur iustus* for Common of Saints or of Martyrs. After that, most manuscripts assign it to the feast of St. Michael (*Concussum est mare*). With the text *Nativitas, Solemnitas*, or *Presentio gloriose virginis*, it is also used at feasts of Mary, most commonly the Nativity on Sept. 8. In England it carried the text *Optimam partem* for the feast of Mary Magdalene. In two French sources it has the text *O Martine presul* for use on the feast of St. Martin of Tours. *Sanctissime apostole* itself was also sung in the church of St. Jacques de la Boucherie in Paris for the dedication feast on Oct. 6.[15]

Polyphonic settings abound. The late 13th-century theorist Anon. IV attributes the three-part organum *Alleluia/Nativitas* to Perotin.[16] In W1 the scribe has written the alternate text *Optimam partem* below the syllables of both the two- and three-part versions of *Nativitas*.[17] An organal setting of *Sanctissime*

Iacobe apostole itself appears in W2 along with two other works, *Nativitas*, and *Iudicabunt sancti*, all three of which have the same music and appear as a group between ff. 16 and 21.

Example 1 shows a comparison of *Sanctissime apostole* with three of its related chants.

Example 1
Alleluia. Sanctissime apostole Iacobe

The value of this comparison rests in what it says about the final melisma. In all settings, the melody to the Alleluia serves as a melisma for the last part of the verse, prior to the repetition of the Alleluia itself. Only two of them, *Nativitas* and the Sarum version of *Letabitur*, include the *jubilus* in this melisma. In the CC, the last syllable of *Sanctissime apostole* occurs at the end of a line and is followed by a custos on *c*. This pitch refers neither to the repetition of the Alleluia after the verse, nor to the up-coming second Alleluia. Instead, it refers to the first note of the *jubilus*. Thus, for a proper performance of the piece, the *jubilus* should be added at this point, either before the repetition of the Alleluia, or perhaps as a substitute for it.

B.   *Alleluia. Hic Iacobus*
The text to *Hic Iacobus* is also attributed to Calixtus. It was thought by Wagner that *Hic Iacobus* was newly composed,[18] but in fact, it is nearly identical to the *Alleluia/Iste sanctus digne*, used for the Common of Saints, and readily available in the St. Yrieix and Sarum Graduals.[19] In Example 2 the three versions are compared. At St. Yrieix *Iste santus digne* was used on the feast of St. Martin of Tours, as the first of the Alleluias for the feast day mass.[20]

Example 2
Alleluia. Hic Iacobus

The CC parallels the St. Yrieix version more closely than it does the Sarum version, but it differs from both in many passages. The most significant differences are the interpolated words in the verse (*primatum tenet*) and the modest final melisma, which is completely absent in St. Yrieix and quite extended in Sarum.

C.   *Alleluia. Vocavit Ihesus*
The text to the third alleluia, *Vocavit Ihesus*, is drawn from the new Testament,

Mark 3.17. In many ways this is the most interesting piece in the group. It appears to be newly composed, or rather its melodic structure, so clearly based on the pentachord and tetrachord, is quite different from the style of the previous two Alleluias. There is also a series of *binariae* over the last syllable of *Boanerges*, a feature noted by Peter Wagner and Hendryk van der Werf, a thoroughly un-Gregorian melodic gesture.[21]

Example 3
Alleluia. Vocavit Ihesus

Perhaps because it was newly composed and not a member of the canon of Alleluias, *Vocavit Ihesus* could be subject to considerable reworking. It is entered at the end of the manuscript on f. 192', this time with its text translated into Greek (See Ex. 3).[22] It thus relates to the oldest of international traditions, the *Missa Graeca*, popular in France and elsewhere from the middle of the ninth century onward. Although Alleluias were not regular features of the *Missa Graeca*, they can be found in manuscript collections from northern France and England.[23] The performance cues in the CC are quite detailed. Apparently the soloists sing the entire verse in Greek, after which the chorus enters where it normally would (*Quod est filii*). A cue is even given for the repetition of the Alleluia after the verse, something almost never found.

Vocavit Ihesus also appears in the manuscript's collection of polyphonic works (f. 189') as a two-part composition, in which the portions of the chant sung by the soloists were set polyphonically. *Vocavit Ihesus* is thus associated with the newest musical development of the twelfth century, melismatic organum. At this point we should recall the series of *binariae* mentioned earlier, very much unlike chant, but similar to passages in Aquitanian polyphony. Perhaps we have here, as van der Werf speculated, a newly composed Alleluia, conceived polyphonically from the outset, then stripped of its duplum and served up in Gregorian guise early in the manuscript, and in a Hellenized version at the end.

Example 4
Alleluia. Vocavit Ihesus (Organum)

D.   *Alleluia. Gratulemur et letemur*

The last member of the Alleluia group is the prosa *Gratulemur et letemur*, a sequence dedicated to St. James and found in many sources from the 12th century.[24] Its most distinctive feature is the use of 33 non-Latin words, each of which bears a Latin gloss in the manuscript to show the word replaced. A list of these words and their glosses is given in Table 3.

Table 3

Gratulemur et letemur—Word List

H 1.b	cemeha	=	iocunda	H 5.b	rama	=	alta
H 2.a	nizaha	=	victoria	H 6.a	omer	=	dicit
H 2.b	hole	=	scandens	H 6.b	magiz	=	nunciat
H	haiom	=	hodie	H 7.a	guezoloz	=	magna
H	nichtar	=	coronatur	H	sezim	=	demonia
H 3.a	ahiu	=	frater	H	rahim	=	mala
H	meuorah	=	benedicti	H	rozef	=	eiciebat
H	iamah	=	mare	H	zarha	=	splendens
H	nicra	=	vocatur	H 7.b	nazan	=	dedit
H 3.b	mezaper	=	predicator	G	athanato	=	inmortali
H	emuna	=	veritatis		(αθανατο)		
H	bihuza	=	Iudea	F 8.b	vunt	=	vadunt
G 4.	ysquirros	=	fortis		sus	=	sursum
	(ισχυρος)				eia	=	perge
G	cosmi	=	mundi		ultreia	=	vade ante
	(κοσμι)						
G	climata	=	partes	H 10.b	leholam	=	eterna
	(κλιματα)						
H 5.a	devar	=	sermo	H	amaha	=	plebi tue
H	quezossa	=	sanctus				

H = Hebrew; G = Greek; F = Old French; Numbers show versicle

Twenty-five of them are Hebrew words, four are Greek, one (*vunt*) is Old French, and the last three form a phrase of encouragement for the pilgrims to Compostela found interspersed throughout the manuscript (*sus eia, ultreia*).[25]

Example 5

Gratulemur et letemur

According to the inscription in the CC, the work was abbreviated by Calixtus. The nature of this abbreviation becomes clear when the Calixtine version is compared to the setting in Paris BN lat. 778 from Narbonne.[26] The Narbonne version consists of 19 double versicles. Portions of its text (versicles 4, 5, 7, and 11-16) are devoted to the apochryphal story of James, Ermogenes, and

Philetus recounted in the Apostolic History of Pseudo-Abdias.[27] All references to this story, and all of the melodic lines to those versicles, are deleted in the CC.[28] Furthermore, a new versicle 10, *Boanerges qui numcuparis*, replaces the text of the standard 17th versicle, but retains its melody. It seems that this versicle took on a life of its own. The rubrics for the prosa on July 27 and 29 indicate only *Boanerges qui numcuparis*, not the whole of *Gratulemur*.

Summary and Conclusions

Internationalism shown in *Veneranda dies* and elsewhere in the literary portions of the CC manifests itself in lists of peoples and places, which are incorporated into the familiar framework of a sermon, a hymn text, and so forth. This may strike us as a somewhat naive or shallow technique, nothing more than name dropping. However we should not judge the compiler of the manuscript by current standards. Pseudo-Calixtus had a passion for lists, and his lists of nationalities show the author of *Veneranda dies* to be aware of the world at large and the role of the Iacobean pilgrimage in it. To the extent that the CC represents civic notions, this holds true for the inhabitants of Compostela as well.

The four works comprising the Alleluia group form the familiar framework for the same sort of international gesture. The first two Alleluias are part of the large canon of Alleluia melodies, but with new texts. The third is apparently newly-composed, but is based on a biblical text. The prosa is the widely recorded one for the feast of St. James, but with major emendations in both text and music. Thus, three of the four works represent the European tradition of Alleluias and sequences, while the fourth is patterned on that tradition.

Hebrew and Greek words replace standard Latin texts and are incorporated into the familiar chants. The languages chosen are those of Christendom and its heritage; there is no attempt to embrace Arabic. Of course the music is European throughout. As far as I know, the services do not use Eastern chant, and there is neither musical borrowing from other cultures, nor assimilation of foreign concepts or techniques into a Western framework. Yet within the limitations of the day, the spirit of internationalism is here as well, a tradition, firmly rooted in the culture of France and Aquitaine, reaching out as much as possible to embrace the world at large.

Appendix

Ex. 1. Alleluia. Sanctissime apostole Iacobe

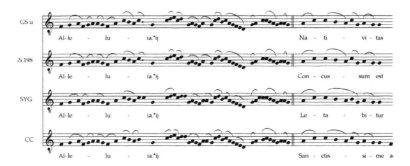

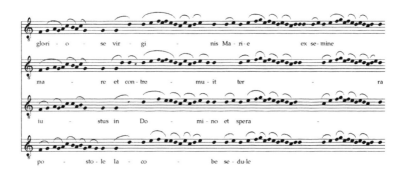

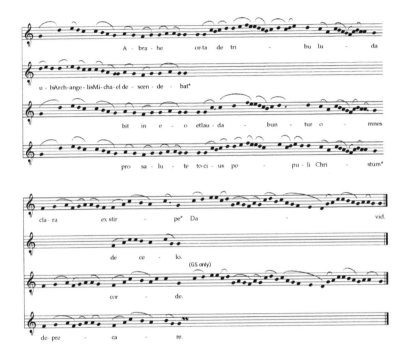

Ex. 2. Alleluia. Hic Iacobus

Ex. 3. Alleluia. Vocavit Ihesus

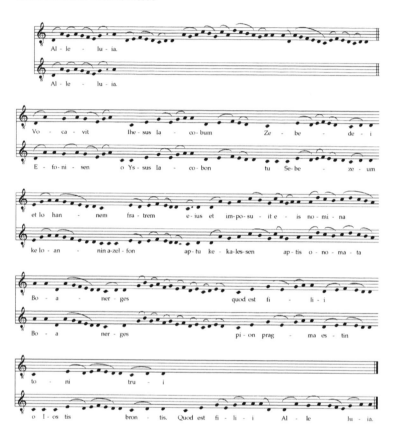

236

Ex. 4. **Alleluia. Vocavit Ihesus (Organum)**

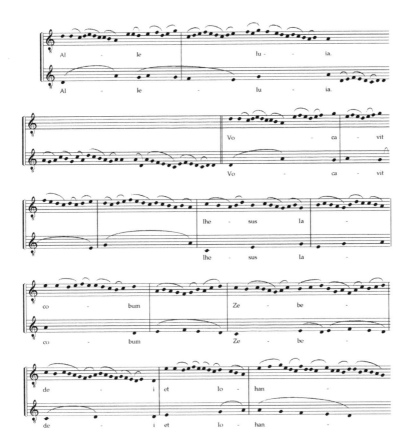

Ex. 5. Gratulemur et letemur

Notes:

[1] The following sigla are used for manuscripts mentioned in this study:

CC   *Liber Sancti Iacobi. Codex Calixtinus de la Catedral de Santiago de Compostela* (Madrid, 1993).

GS   Walter Howard Frere, ed. *Graduale Sarisburiense: A Reproduction in Facsimile of a Manuscript of the Thirteenth Century* (1894; repr. London, 1966).

SYG   *Le Codex 903 de la Bibliothèque Nationale de Paris (XIe siècle): Graduel de Saint-Yrieix,* Paléographie musicale XIII (Tournai, 1925).

W1   James H. Baxter, ed. *An Old St. Andrews Music Book: Cod. Helmst. 628* (1931; repr. New York, NY, 1973).

W2   Luther Dittmer, ed. *Wolfenbüttel 1099 (1206),* Publications of Medieval Musical Manuscripts 2 (Brooklyn, NY, 1960).

[2] Walter Muir Whitehill, Germán Prado, and Jesús Carro García, *Liber Sancti Iacobi. Codex Calixtinus* (Santiago de Compostela, 1944), pp. 148-49. Shorter lists occur in at least two other pieces in the liturgical section. *Psallat chorus,* the hymn for Matins on the vigil, refers in its fifth stanza to the "Armenians, Greeks, Apulians, Angles, Gauls, Dacians, Frisians, and all other peoples, tongues and tribes" who hasten to Compostela. The conductus *Salve festa dies* on f. 131' (NOT the processional song on 116') urges:

Qui velut alta Pharus lumen protendit ad Indos, Gaudeamus.

Quem Yspanus, Maurus, Persa, Brittanus amat, Gaudeamus.

[Let us praise the one who, like the lighthouse of Pharus, extends to India.

Let us praise the one whom the Spaniard, the Moor, the Persian, the Brittain loves.]

[3] 'Cosmi climati' is glossed in *Gratulemur et letemur* as 'mundi partes'.

[4] Or perhaps Welsh?

[5] Balearians? Bavarians? *Baioari* was read by Whitehill et al., *Codex Calix*tinus, (p. 148) as *Baleari,* the inhabitants of the Balearic Islands, a reasonable assumption since it falls among Iberian place names. However, it may also refer to Bavaria. See A. Moralejo, C. Torres, and J. Feo, *Liber Sancti Jacobi: "Codex Calixtinus"* (Santiago de Compostela, 1951), pp. 198-99.

[6] *Garasques,* since it is grouped with other western European locales, probably refers to Gascony, not to the Germanic peoples living between Weser and Elbe, or the inhabitants of a city in ancient Macedonia. See Moralejo et al., *Liber,* p. 198, note to line 25.

[7] The island province of Sweden.

[8] *Iorianti,* since it comes after Russia and Norway, probably refers to the inhabitants of Jory, in Poland, or to Jutland, not the Jordanians or the inhabitants of the Jura mountains.

[9] For the artistic analogue of this passage, see Peter Barber, "Visual Encyclopaedias: The Hereford and other Mappae Mundi," *The Map Collector* 48 (Autumn 1989), 2-8. See also A. L. Moir, *The World Map in Hereford Cathedral* (Leominster, Herefordshire, England, 1979). Plate VII gives a detailed version of the world map

showing the British Isles, France and Spain, on which is found both Compostela and the Cathedral of St. James (Templum Sancti Iacobi).

[10] Some of these are ambiguous. There were, for instance, three Antiochs, the important one in Syria, one in Phrygia and a third in Judea. Similarly there were three Alexandrias: the important one in Egypt, and two others in Asia Minor and Syria. I assume the reference in the sermon to be to the major city.

[11] Whitehill et al., *Codex Calixtinus*, p. 149.

[12] The parade of nations is followed by a similar but shorter catalogue of instruments: "Alii citharis psallant, alii liris, alii timphanis, alii tibiis, alii fistulis, alii tubis, alii sambucis, alii violis, alii rotis Brittannicis vel Gallicis, alii psalteriis, alii diversis generibus musicorum cantando vigilant, alii peccata plorant, alii psalmos legunt, alii elemosinas cecis tribuunt" (Whitehill et al., *Codex Calixtinus*, p. 149).

["They keep awake, some by playing citharas, others lyres, others timpanis, others pipes, others trumpets, others harps, others viols, others Breton or Gallican rotas, others psalteries, others by singing various kinds of music, some lament their sins, others recite psalms, others give alms to the blind".]

The same internationalism inspiring the list of nations is not so clearly present here. The terms used are of only the most general sort. Most of them refer to string instruments, either plucked (the psaltery) or bowed (viols). In addition, there are at least three wind instruments and one drum. However, some of the names are so ambiguous that the very nature of the instrument is in doubt. A sambuca, for instance, was either a type of harp, a triangular psaltery, or a double-pipe woodwind instrument. 'Lira' could refer to a bowed string instrument, a hurdy-gurdy, a Maghribi recorder, or a Morrocan reed pipe. It is even difficult to determine the number of instruments listed. Is the author referring to two instruments when he speaks of the 'Breton or Gallican rotas,' or is he describing a single instrument which carried two names?

[13] Peter Wagner, *Die Gesänge der Jakobsliturgie zu Santiago de Compostela* (Freiburg, 1931), p. 145.

[14] Karl-Heinz Schlager, *Thematischer Katalog der ältesten Alleluia-Melodien aus Handschriften des 10. und 11. Jahrhunderts* (München, 1965), p. 196, No. 274.

[15] See Alejandro Planchart, "Guillaume Dufay's Masses: A View of the Manuscript Traditions," in *Dufay Quincentenary Conference*, Papers Read at the Dufay Quincentenary Conference, Brooklyn College, Dec. 6-7, 1974, ed. Alan W. Atlas (Brooklyn, NY, 1976), pp. 28-29.

[16] Fritz Reckow, ed., *Der Musiktraktat des Anonymus 4*, Beihefte zum Archiv für Musikwissenschaft, Vol. 4 (Wiesbaden, 1967), p. 82.

[17] W1, ff. 6v-7, 36-36v (new foliation).

[18] Wagner, *Gesänge*, p. 145

[19] Schlager, *Thematischer Katalog*, p. 206, No. 294. Schlager does not list the CC or this text.

[20] Robert Plötz has shown the close association between the developing cult of St. James in Spain and the cult of St. Martin centered in Tours. See "Peregrinatio ad Limina Sancti Jacobi," in *The Codex Calixtinus and the Shrine of St. James*, ed.

John Williams and Alison Stones (Tübingen, 1992), pp. 37-49, esp. p. 45.

[21] Wagner, *Gesänge*, p. 145. See also Hendrik van der Werf, "The Composition Alleluya Vocavit Jesus in the Book Named 'Jacobus'," in *De Music Hispana et Aliis. Miscelánea en honor al Prof. Dr. José López-Calo, S.J.*, ed. Emilio Casares and Carlos Villanueva, Vol. 1 (Compostela, 1990), pp. 197-207. Van derWerf reviews the notational features of the CC and compares the monophonic setting of *Alleluia Vocavit Ihesus* with its polyphonic version given later in the manuscript to determine the proper alignment of the added voice. The article concludes that the chant differs significantly from Gregorian plainchant, that the work was conceived polyphonically from the outset, and that both versions may have been among the first examples of music composed with the aid of writing tools.

[22] This is not the text from the Greek Bible, but a translation of the Latin version into Greek. See Wagner, *Gesänge*, p. 170. Greek source material seems to have fascinated the compiler of the Codex Calixtinus. Christopher Hohler mentions the Passion of St. Eutropius (Pilgrim's Guide, Ch. VIII), which 'Calixtus' says was written in Greek by Dionysius, Bishop of Paris and sent by Pope Clement to Greece. 'Calixtus' found it in a Greek school in Constantinople and translated it into Latin. An English translation of the Guide has recently been issued, William Melczer, *The Pilgrim's Guide to Santiago de Compostela* (New York, NY, 1993). The coverage of St. Eutropius begins on p. 110. See "A Note on Jacobus," *Journal of the Warburg and Courtauld Institutes* 35 (1972), 50. Hohler also mentions another translation from Greek by 'Calixtus,' James dying prayer in the *Magna Passio* (Whitehill et al., *Codex Calixtinus*, p. 94: "Precem apostolicam que in fine huius passionis habetur ex libris Grecorum in Latinum translatavi". [I have translated the apostolic prayer which is found in the end of this passion from books of the Greeks into Latin.] The prayer itself is on p. 101).

[23] See Charles Atkinson, "Zur Entstehung und Überlieferung der 'Missa Graeca'," *Archiv für Musikwissenschaft* 39 (1982), 113-45, and "The *Doxa*, the *Pisteuo*, and the *Ellinici Fratres*: Some Anomalies in the Transmission of the Chants of the 'Missa Graeca'," *Journal of Musicology* 7 (1989), 81-106. See also Louis Brou, "Les Chants en langue grecque dans les liturgies latines," *Sacri eruditi* 1 (1948), 165-80; 4 (1952), 226-38, and "L'Alleluia gréco-latin 'Dies Sanctificatus' de la messe du jour de Noël: Origine et évolution d'un chant bilingue et protéiforme," *Revue grégorienne* 23 (1938), 170-75; 24 (1939), 1-8, 81-89, 202-13.

[24] See Guido Dreves, *Analecta Hymnica*, Vol. 17, *Hymnodia Hiberica: Carmina Compostellana* (Leipzig, 1894), pp. 195-96 for the macaronic version. A lengthy note on p. 196 gives the Hebrew words and their Latin equivalents, and the music is given on pp. 222-24. The standard version of the text can be found in *Analecta Hymnica* 8, p. 146.

[25] According to Christopher Hohler (p. 76), the inclusion of apparently genuine Greek and Hebrew words has a 'ridiculous effect'. I am not at all sure that this was the intent, although it might have that effect now. It is just as likely that the redactor wished to convey the international appeal of the saint, or to demonstrate his

knowledge of languages, and in the sequence chose this way to do it.

[26] See Margot Fassler, *Gothic Song: Victorine Sequences and Augustinian Reform in Twelfth-Century Paris*, Cambridge Studies in Medieval and Renaissance Music (Cambridge, 1993). Appendix 2 (pp. 351-67) gives an inventory of three sequence sources from Nevers ca. 1175, one of which, Paris, BN 3126, contains *Gratulemur et letemur*. Appendix 4 (pp. 375-88) is an inventory of two late 12th- or early 13th-century sequence manuscripts, Paris, BN lat. 1086 and Paris, BN lat. 778 from Narbonne. Wagner, *Gesänge*, (p. 87) gives the Narbonne version immediately following his edition of the CC version and discusses the relationship between the two (p. 138). Prado (Whitehill et al., *Codex Calixtinus*, pp. 90-92) gives the text from the Prosario of Huesca from the late 11th or early 12th century.

[27] See Montague Rhodes James, *The Apocryphal New Testament* (Oxford, 1960), pp. 462-69, esp. p. 463.

[28] This may reflect the author's intent to rid the services of St. James of all apocryphal material. However, the CC itself contains (Chapter IX) this passage from Pseudo-Abdias, which it calls the Great Passion (*Apostolus Christi Iacobus per sinagogas ingrediens*), and which it says could be read on both the feast of St. James, July 25, and the feast of St. Josias, July 26. Furthermore the Prologue to the Great Passion attests to the authenticity of this passage. See Whitehill et al., *Codex Calixtinus*, pp. 93ff.

INDEX OF ANCIENT AND MEDIEVAL AUTHORS